How to Write Tales of Horror, Fantasy & Science Fiction

EDITED BY J.N. WILLIAMSON

Writer's Digest Books

Cincinnati, Ohio

99 98 97 96 95   7 6 5 4 3

Library of Congress Cataloging-in-Publication Data

How to write tales of horror, fantasy, and science fiction.
  Bibliography: p.
  Includes index.
  1. Fantastic fiction—Authorship. 2. Horror tales—Authorship. 3. Science fiction—Authorship.
  I. Williamson, J.N. (Jerry N.)
PN3377.5.F34H68 1987   808.3'876   87-6068
ISBN 0-89879-483-8

Design by Joan Ann Jacobus

What we call fiction is the ancient way of knowing, the total discourse that ante-dates all the special vocabularies. . . . Fiction is democratic, it reasserts the authority of the single mind to make and remake the world.

—E. L. Doctorow,
Esquire August 1986

If you go too far in fantasy and break the string of logic, and become nonsensical, someone will surely remind you of your dereliction. . . . Pound for pound, fantasy makes a tougher opponent for the creative person.

—Richard Matheson,
Interview, *Masques* 1984

Acknowledgments

With gratitude for my wife Mary and to her and to my students of Writer's Digest School, all of whom have advanced my own education; to Mort Castle particularly and to Robert Bloch, Ray Bradbury, John Maclay, and David Taylor; to Horror Writers of America, Science Fiction Writers of America, Small Press Writers and Artists Organization, and the Fantasy & Science Fiction Workshop; to Nan Dibble, Jean M. Fredette, Howard Wells, David Lewis, and Kirk Polking, as well as to the gifted women and men who chose generously to support their talented peers.

About the Editor

Ask J.N. Williamson for his credits and stand back. A list of the 35 books he has written or edited would fill this space and leave no room for his awards (many), his professional credentials (impressive and somewhat offbeat), and the variation of his other published work (such as more than 75 short stories and four nonfiction books.

Partial lists will have to do. Williamson is the author of *Ghost*, *The Longest Night*, and *Noonspell*; editor of both the Balrog Award-winning *Masques* and *Masques II*, popular anthologies of horror fiction; and editorial consultant for Cloverdale Press.

He maintains contact with hundreds of writers through his association with clubs and conventions, and is currently secretary/treasurer of the Horror Writers of America.

Before becoming a full-time writer and editor, he was a Fuller Brush man, an editor-in-chief, a professional drummer, a self-employed astrologer, an insurance investigator, a singer and recorded vocalist—the list goes on. He has been married for 26 years to Mary T. Williamson, a literary agent and a contributor to this book.

Contents

The Editor's Foreword:

"Certain of What We Do Not See"   *1*

Introduction:

How to Write Horribly for Fun and Profit

by Robert Bloch   *7*

Chapter 1

Run Fast, Stand Still, *or,* The Thing at the Top of
the Stairs, *or,* New Ghosts from Old Minds

by Ray Bradbury   *11*

Chapter 2

Plotting as Your Power Source

by J. N. Williamson   *20*

Chapter 3

Reality and the Waking Nightmare: Setting and
Character in Horror Fiction

by Mort Castle   *28*

Chapter 4

One View: Creating Character in Fantasy and
Horror Fiction

by Steve Rasnic Tem   *35*

Chapter 5

"Oh, Just Call Me Cuthbert": The Naming Game

by Thomas Millstead   *42*

Chapter 6

Involving *Your* Reader from the Start

by William F. Nolan   *46*

Chapter 7

Freedom of Originality in Fantastic Fiction—and
How to Use It

by James Kisner   *51*

Chapter 8

Creating Fantasy Folk

by Ardath Mayhar   *56*

Chapter 9

Keeping the Reader on the Edge of His Seat

by Dean R. Koontz   *59*

Chapter 10

Stepping Into the Shadows

by Charles L. Grant   *64*

Chapter 11

Innocence and Terror—The Heart of Horror

by Robert R. McCammon   *67*

Chapter 12

World Building in Horror, Occult, and Fantasy
Writing

by Marion Zimmer Bradley   *71*

Chapter 13

Sword and Sorcery, Dragon and Princess

by Darrell Schweitzer   *77*

Chapter 14

Science Fiction: Hard Science and Hard Conflict

by Michael A. Banks   *82*

Chapter 15

Researching Science Fantasy

by Sharon Baker   *88*

Chapter 16

Avoiding What's Been Done to Death

by Ramsey Campbell   *96*

Chapter 17

Why Novels of Fear Must Do More than Frighten

by Dean R. Koontz   *101*

Chapter 18

The Supernatural? Naturally!

by J. N. Williamson   *106*

Chapter 19

Sexist Stereotypes and Archetypes: What to Do
with Them/What the Writing Woman Can Hope
For

by Jeannette M. Hopper   *112*

Chapter 20

"They Laughed When I Howled at the Moon"

by Richard Christian Matheson   *120*

Chapter 21

The Psychology of Horror and Fantasy Fiction
by Katherine Ramsland, Ph.D.   *124*

Chapter 22

Fantasy and Faculty X
by Colin Wilson   *131*

Chapter 23

A "Do" List for Getting Your Literary Agent
by Mary T. Williamson   *140*

Chapter 24

Putting It on the Editor's Desk
by Alan Rodgers   *147*

Chapter 25

The Mechanics and Mystique of Submitting Your
Novel
by Patrick LoBrutto   *151*

Chapter 26

Darkness Absolute: The Standards of Excellence
in Horror Fiction
by Douglas E. Winter   *156*

Chapter 27

Overview of Horror, SF and Fantasy:
A Long-range Market Study
by Janet Fox   *165*

Contributors to This Book   *177*

The Top Ten "Favorites" List—in Horror,
Fantasy, & SF—(Novels and Short Stories)   *186*

Recommended Reading Library of Horror,
Fantasy, and Science Fiction   *206*

Index   *233*

The Editor's Foreword

"Certain of What We Do Not See"

For the past two years (at this writing), according to figures supplied *Publishers Weekly* by nationwide bookstore chains, science fiction has accounted for approximately 10 percent of all the novels sold in America.

Encouraging enough. Even better was what was not specifically stated: that all forms of fantasy fiction, not SF alone, constituted that 10 percent. In the same issue of *PW* (May 23, 1986), it's reported that "within fantasy the horror field is expanding more rapidly today."

Charles N. Brown, Editor/Publisher of *Locus,* was quoted as saying, "New writers can get published and be paid for their work (in fantasy) more easily than in other fields."

This book exists to enlighten you about the various ways you may take full advantage of such a golden opportunity. It offers you newly written advice, insights, and asides, apt examples and sometimes far-ranging information meant to help you write publishable novels or stories for the three genres coexisting beneath that umbrella term, *fantasy:* horror, or dark fantasy; science fiction; and fantasy itself.

Suitably enough, given the mind set and creative liberty suggested by the word itself, fantasy is many things to many people and this book has been assembled in a fashion that recognizes that fact. Consider the social organizations that exist: Science Fiction Writers of America stresses SF but welcomes writers of horror and fantasy; Horror Writers of America seeks horror authors but admits other fantasists; Small Press Writers and Artists Organization (SPWAO) primarily admits horror and fantasy creators; while SF and Fantasy Workshop seeks fantasy and SF craftsmen and has few authors of horror in its company.

Citing this diverse situation enables a significant point to be made about the stylish chapters you're about to read: Many—possibly most—of the gifted professionals generously providing their expertise have written successfully in all the wonderful realms of fantasy. Robert Bloch and Ray Bradbury have also written mystery/detective fiction.

Should you doubt their versatility, glance back at the end of this book, where you'll discover the Messrs. Bradbury and Bloch joined by Theodore Sturgeon, Stephen King, Richard Matheson, Harlan Ellison, and certain others have garnered "favorites" votes in *more than one* genre, often with the *same* work of fiction. Daniel Keyes' emotion-touching "Flowers for Algernon," which became the empathetic film *Charly,* drew votes in both science fiction and horror. Ellison's "Jefty Is Five" drew nods in all three categories, as did Bradbury's worldwide favorite, *The Martian Chronicles,* Jerome Bixby's "It's a *Good* Life!,'" and others.

Yet while these facts attest to the protean imaginations of many beloved writers and fly in the face of editors of the recent past who knee-jerked a "no" when a yarn did not fit a single category, they are especially useful in demonstrating why *all* the chapters awaiting you contain valuable kernels of information—*and* in indicating to you that what you write may have a wider market than you've believed. That, in addition, your easiest route to publication may very well be found in one or more of the intriguing genres examined in this volume.

Fantasy contains a "wish fulfillment motif, or a horror motif," said Professor Robert A. Collins, Florida Atlantic University, Editor of *Fantasy Review.*[1] Fantasy puts these motifs "into a [written] world so that the reader can enjoy indulging in that wish fulfillment or fear." Or, as Anatole France expressed it, "To know is nothing at all; to imagine is everything." That's a fantasist's pure credo, excepting certain science fiction writers.

Those fantasy yarns with spiritual vision or insight "have a pattern of significance behind them," according to Colin N. Manlove, University of Edinburgh (Scotland). "It's got a great zest for being and a very poignant sense of how things can so easily be lost. This adds a flavor and strength to the sense of beauty there is in [many varieties of] fantasy."

Fantasy is, of course, the stuff of dream and nightmare, and because all of us have different dreams and nightmares, fantasy provides the freedom to sidestep the no-longer fertile fields explored by earlier authors. Dr. Abraham H. Maslow wrote[2] that a creative person "must be courageous," a "gambler who comes to tentative conclusions in the absence of facts . . ." To invent or create, Maslow observed, "you must have the arrogance of creativity."

When faced by creative people with the "fear of one's own greatness,"

---

1. Most of the quotes utilized in this foreword appeared originally in the issue cited of *Publishers Weekly* or have appeared in books of well-known quotations.

2. Abraham H. Maslow, *The Farther Reaches of Human Nature* (New York: The Viking Press, 1971).

Maslow liked asking them, "If not you, then who else?" He said that a prerequisite of creativeness was the ability "to become timeless, selfless, outside of space, of society, of history." Hence, particularly gifted writers of speculative fiction are viewed as quite healthy; creating becomes "the act of a whole man . . . most organized, integrated, unified . . . in the service of the fascinating matter-in-hand."

Besides, as *Locus*'s Brown suggests, "There's always room for fresh voices" in the fantasy field.

Nancy Varian Berberick's explanation of why she writes fantasy appeared first in the useful *Scavenger's Newsletter* (March '86):

> Fantasy is the language we first learn. Christian, Jew, Buddhist, whatever, it is the language of our religions. What is faith but the ability to imagine the fantastic and choose to believe in it? ('Now faith is being sure of what we hope for and certain of what we do not see.' —Hebrews 11:1).
>
> Fairy tales are also the stuff of childhood. But while there is much that is grim about the Grimms' tales, there's also a freedom that teaches there are places children may visit which do not appear on any map. Here a child learns that he will encounter the unexpected. In this "country," witches hold sway, dragons fly, and trolls live under bridges. And a child learns life will not tie itself up in tidy endings after four TV commercial breaks.
>
> Life, these tales tell the child, deals out its own form of justice.
>
> And while he is learning these lessons, his imagination is *soaring*. He believes not with the faith an adult brings to *his* chosen realities, but . . . for the *time it takes to read the tale*. That is the heart of *all* fantasy.
>
> Fantasy readers and writers make the leap beyond time. Travel to unmapped countries. Treat with princes and deal with dragons.
>
> One learns best in one's native tongue, and fantasy is the language I learned in childhood. Life's lessons, hard and adult, are still, for me, most easily learned in that language.

Science fiction is "not about reality, it's about sharpening our *understanding* of reality," observed British author Brian W. Aldiss. It is "fiction about that which is not but might be," added Jim Baen, publisher of Baen Books, "or what might have been but never was—as far as we know."

TOR Books' Beth Meacham added that science fiction is "a subset of fantasy," yes, with "a suspension of disbelief brought about by scientific or pseudoscientific language."

In these quotations, a penetrating laser beam shines upon the distinction between SF and other forms of fantasy. Where readers may require no explanation for the sudden appearance of an elf, unicorn, grotesque monster—or entire novels that are set upon worlds that no one at all *usually* believes in—the invention of science fiction depends to a surprising extent upon *substantiation;* however unlikely, improbable, even impossible. Increasingly, in recent years, it also depends upon science or the extrapolation of science that is up-to-the-minute and generally accepted (at the very least) as workable scientific theory.

Beyond that, however, contemporary SF demands *far more* than a grasp of modern technology or high-tech. At possibly its most illuminating, it adheres to the conviction expressed by the late John Erskine: "We have not really budged a step until we take up residence in someone else's point of view."

Which is a lovely way of broaching the point that much of the science fiction that wins awards and endures is *viewpoint fiction.* Sometimes it is strongly, strangely, or individualistically *moralistic* fiction. On other planets, in other periods of time, SF frequently views life "as we know it" on Earth today through mirrors of both keenly satirical distortion and piercingly detached clarity. If SF is no more the fiction of ideas today than horror or specialized fantasy at its finest, it definitely retains its reputation of gallant, new, ideological service to those views, aspirations, and transcendent changes with which good people of good will are always, albeit mutely, perhaps, concerned for the future course of humankind.

Jack Williamson, a gifted and affable patriarch of SF, expressed it this way for *Publishers Weekly:* "Reading SF requires a certain flexibility. I don't know whether members of the SF audience are any brighter than the average run of people but they're more open-minded." More searching, caring, disposed to question the status quo politically, theologically, sociologically, and in numerous other ways.

In Sam J. Lundwall's perceptive *Science Fiction: What's it All About* (Ace Books, 1971), he projected that SF "will go farther out—but in a speculative rather than a distant sense." So it has, and presumably, will continue to advance.

Ahead of you will be found chapters of fresh information closely concerned with the involvements and demands of today's science-fiction marketplace and audience. Yet in a broader way, SF here is inspected and discussed in the greater context of its vibrant existence as but one long-respected, influential aspect of the mammoth fantastic umbrella. Knowing how to engage your readers' attention quickly, plotting, and freedom of originality are no more important to good SF writing than they are to horror—or for that matter, crime and mystery fiction. The book you're reading now examines their *specific* and *essential uses* in the creation of publishable (raise the umbrella, please!) fantasy. Creating effective, page-turning suspense, knowing about the risks of sexist stereotyping, and the element of humor in genre fiction are just as necessary to horror, fantasy, and science fiction as they are to mainstream fiction.

Or should be.

Horror is "the most popular and the most creative aspect of the business today," Charles Brown of *Locus* has stated. *Why* is that?

Short-story writer Dennis Hamilton points out that horror "has endured effectively longer than any other form." There was, clearly, no science fiction before there was science. "The ancient Egyptians," Hamilton asserts, "concocted tales of spiritual revenge to discourage tomb scavengers. And a million years *prior* to the Egyptian refinement, the caveman painted real-life horrors on the walls of his house. . . . The first monsters."

Yet authors of horror are not only asked constantly why they "do" it—nobody asks SF writers why they invent alternate universes, then place multimillions of "persons" in peril; or why they create androids that are clear improvements over people—but obliged as well to question the very label under which they write. *Supernatural* or *occult fiction, weird tales, dark fantasy,* and *tales of terror* are but a few of the euphemisms behind which the dreaded word *horror* is sometimes concealed—and lurking.

Currently, the genre fills the niche once occupied by nineteenth-century fantasy, by detective yarns, westerns, and then science fiction: No one wants to admit they read it, but sooner or later, everybody *does*.

It had not been my plan to discuss that aspect of the matter, but a letter from a fast-rising writer of horror and SF, James Kisner—whose chapter is an important part of this volume—seems worth quoting: "I find that many critics do not enjoy reading. They go at it as adversaries of the author, not as friends of the reading public who want simply to know what is or is not a good read." Cogently, Kisner adds, "Fiction is notably infected with critics who can't enjoy something on an *entertainment level*."

But the truth is that when it is written especially well, modern horror fiction—whatever the claims of the given publisher or even the pretensions of a given author—is quite frequently more entertaining than it is anything else! And so, gentle published-writer-to-be, was the majority of classics in literature, art being (in my view) both accidental and incidental.

Writer-teacher Mort Castle, who's also a contributor to this book, put it effectively in his introduction to a small collection of my stories[3]: "Edgar Allan Poe wrote formula fiction. He figured out the formula! There's this story about a nutty captain looking for an albino whale and that's *Moby Dick* and you can say that Melville wrote formula stuff because it's an *adventure* story, huh? . . . And Charles Dickens and Mark Twain and Steve Crane! Formulas, right?

Twain, the prototypical American author, said, "You can't depend on your judgment when your imagination is out of focus." The fiction of fright triggers a reader's imagination by *alarming* it, cleanses the capacity for judgment and discernment by reminding the reader there may well be things beyond the workaday world that are even more frightening and imposing than what

3. NEVERMORE!, Maclay & Associates, Inc., 1983.

they've experienced that day. By contrast, most of the decision making that readers are obliged to render seems simpler, more logical, solvable. Statistics have been offered which argue that horror in books and motion pictures sells better at times of national crisis. It seems to make sense that horror also sells well when individuals face individual crises, which develop more frequently.

"Our conscious intellect is too exclusively analytic . . . and so it misses a great deal of reality, especially within ourselves," Maslow wrote. Since creativeness is "the opposite of dissociation," he remarked, the "whole man" becomes possible through "the recovery of aspects of the unconscious and preconscious"—the "poetic, metaphoric, mystic, primitive, archaic, childlike."

Horror—often, other kinds of fantasy—contains all that.

Indeed, "writing in this genre is more important than meets the eye, partly because horror is *all around us*," comments David W. Taylor, professor of English at Moravian College, Bethlehem, Pennsylvania. "There's real horror in loneliness and rage, in twisted love and jealousy. The writer need look no further than the next street corner to find his subject matter: the constant degradation of women, the shame of the street people, the unspeakable isolation of a nursing home, the underground missile silo overflowing with pent-up doom.

"Some readers *don't know* they would appreciate horror fiction," Professor Taylor proceeds, "because such frights are so closely woven into the fabric of our lives and have become so *acceptable* that we give them no more thought than a fish does to the water it swims in. This genre of writing offers us a way to make horror a throbbing, black thing behind the bed, a thing that will not be loved, but *cannot be ignored*—if we are to be enlightened by it. All of the vast potential of literature is stored here, waiting to be tapped and channeled into fresh, exciting stories."

If, for the time it takes you to write your story or your novel, you are able, as well as you can, to be "certain of what we do not see," the many worlds of horror, fantasy, and science fiction may welcome you. Each author represented in this book intends to point the way.

J. N. Williamson
Indianapolis: June 1986

Introduction

How to Write Horribly for Fun and Profit

Robert Bloch

They told me I could extend this introduction to a length of three thousand words.

But cheer up—it's going to be shorter.

During the lifetime I've misspent writing fantasy, horror, mystery-suspense, and science fiction in books, magazines, radio, television, films, and the insides of matchbook covers, I never learned enough that would take that many words to explain the requirements.

In fact, what I did learn was very little. Since I lacked the privilege of attending college, and was always too busy writing to take any writing courses, all that I know or think I know comes from personal experience. As such, it's totally subjective, a matter of opinion, and my only excuse for passing it along to you is because it seems to have worked for me.

Let's start with a brief—and biased—overview of the field today.

According to the latest available statistics (as of 9:28 a.m., Pacific Standard time), there are approximately one hundred science-fiction titles published each and every month. And according to my own criteria, about 80 percent of these novels are hackwork. In many cases, these efforts aren't really novels at all, but merely short stories or novelettes padded and blown up to novel lengths to satisfy the demands of the publishers and the greed of the writers. Since the current market for short fiction is limited, the Procrustean bed of publishing has been arbitrarily lengthened, and story ideas are stretched accordingly. The results, however, are pretty thin.

Did I mention a Procrustean bed? Permit me to correct myself; I should have used the plural form. Not only are many of these efforts elongated to novels, but the present fashion dictates that they be further expanded into trilogies.

From a commercial standpoint, this seems like a good idea for all concerned, including readers who are hooked on serial sagas and the continued adventures of familiar characters.

But in terms of solid, substantial craftsmanship, it's increasingly obvious that most of us aren't up to the demands made by such unbridled verbosity. Much of the output acclaimed in advertising as epics can be at merciful best described as a *"fast read"*—a term, by the way, which I detest, along with its terminological twin, the *"easy read."*

Worthwhile work, whatever its category or length, deserves better than dismissal as a "read" of any sort. If its theme, inherent ideas, and manner of execution are up to the proper literary standards, it should qualify as at least a *reread*—something to be savored and resurrected in reprint for the edification and enjoyment of generations yet unborn. Wells, Huxley, and Orwell can still enthrall today, despite dated references and failed prophecies, because their concepts and characters are endowed with timeless truths that endure.

The bottom line is that these writers had something to say and knew how to say it. They didn't choose the science-fiction *genre* because it was a "good market"—indeed, at the time they wrote their classics it was a very poor market. They wrote science fiction because it was the best vehicle for the story they wanted to tell and the ideas they wanted to express. The same considerations dictated the length of their efforts. Some of Wells's finest work was in the field of short stories. Given the self-conscious commercialism of many of today's science fictioneers, he could have easily taken a number of such notions and pumped them up to novel length. But if he had, the virtues would be lost in verbiage, and it's doubtful that these tales would be remembered, let alone reprinted, today.

As you surely must have guessed, my primary advice to science fiction writers and would-be writers is to evaluate story ideas objectively and write them up in whatever length is most effective.

The same dictum holds true, in my opinion, for writers of what is termed *high fantasy*—a category which embraces such categorical imperatives as the presence of wicked wizards, noble heroes, talking animals, and a background of legendary worlds, mythical kingdoms, and perilous quests. There is no rule which says that a story about unicorns, virgins, and other mythical figures must succumb to a token Tolkienism and stretch out into an interminable number of volumes. There are exceptions: Andre Norton, Robert Adams, Stephen Donaldson, Marion Zimmer Bradley, and a few others come readily to mind—writers who have created a realm so rich that it becomes a fitting background for many tales. But there are also instances in which the author's fantasy soars so high for only a single journey and further flights of fancy should be grounded. Again, it's a matter of intellectual honesty: when an extended itinerary into an imaginary world is contemplated, it's best to ask oneself, "Is this trip necessary?"

In *"dark fantasy"*—a polite euphemism for horror—the same holds true with a vengeance. And this vengeance, in the form of a short life span succeeded by eternal oblivion, is visited upon writers who insist on dragging out a story beyond its proper length. Much of Poe's work is effective because of brevity, and it is questionable if he'd be remembered had he chosen to embody M. Valdemar or the narrator of *The Black Cat* or *The Pit and the Pendulum* in novel form. M. R. James found the short length ideal for his ghost stories; no-relative namesake Henry James didn't need more than a novelette to do justice to *The Turn of the Screw*. And he never found it necessary to write a sequel, *The Return of the Screw*. Arthur Machen and H. P. Lovecraft accomplished the same thing in both short stories and novelettes, without the necessity of introducing sex scenes, sociological commentary, and other extraneous but length-extending impediments.

But the temptation exists today. A Chelsea Quinn Yarbro can give us the continuing story of her vampirical Count Saint-Germain over a span of many centuries, and a Stephen King can write the commercially-demanded "big book" with the requisite skill to capture his large audience. But there aren't that many Yarbros or Kings around with such tales and the talent to tell them. The result is that countless imitators turn out series and fat novels based on the flimsiest of notions. Soaked with sex and marinated in meaningless violence, some of this work succeeds on the fast-read level, but I strongly doubt if it will endure, or even be endurable, to the sensibilities of readers in the decades ahead.

A sidebar here about content. Today's films have set the standards—or the substandards—for both science fiction and horror, apparently acting on the precept that one good picture deserves five bad sequels. Science-fiction films increasingly depend upon elaborate special effects as a substitute for genuine story content. So-called horror films are even worse: they depend not only on special effects but on heavy-handed sex and violence that have little to do with story lines. Graphic gore and nauseating cruelty are substituted for true terror, and the basic audience appeal is to the legions of louts who revel in roller derbies. Taking their cues from this, many writers of horror fiction have sought to duplicate visual excesses with the written word; again, it's doubtful if they've managed to achieve anything except raise the speed level of a fast read.

Another problem pertaining to writing horror and/or supernatural fiction is the matter of interior logic. Nightmares can be and usually are inconsistent and episodic. But in order to scare the daylights out of a wide-awake reader, it's vitally necessary that the premise—myth, legend, common superstition, or uncommon invention of the author—be based on a seemingly logical belief, operating within its own rules and limitations. Killing off a monster and giving him mouth-to-mouth or tongue-in-cheek resuscitation until at last he meets Abbott and Costello may have worked well in the old Universal horror movies, but it's not a sure-fire formula for the printed page. The *best* horror films, like the best fiction, depend on inspiring the truly chilling notion that "This *could* happen in real life—and worse than that, it could happen to *me*." Evoking that response isn't easy, but it brings lasting rewards far beyond the reach of the drive-in gross-out movie or the fast read of the local newsstand.

Mystery fiction is another matter. Here, the series hero or heroine is a writer's guide to potential fame and fortune, for most mystery fans want the mixture as before. These are the viewers who seem to prefer television series in which the detective or amateur solves a murder each and every week, and they seek out similar fare in fiction. My advice to writers in this *genre* is "Go for it," because it seems to be the only game in town—a game which has been afoot since the days of Sherlock Holmes.

But in my personal opinion, I am a firm believer that in order for a writer to do his or her best, he must incorporate originality, a prime ingredient for success. If the theme is old, the twist or payoff should be new. The story should be written in the length that is most effective. When the primary consideration is to tailor it for the market, all too often one ends up with the sorry realization that the emperor has no clothes.

Of course, all these admittedly anachronistic notions can and should be dismissed if you're only looking for a fast buck. In such a case, just do the exact *opposite* of what I've advised here: Get a premise, any kind of a premise you can beg, borrow, or steal; blow it up into the biggest book or the longest series you can manage. Substitute sex for substance and violence for vitality, and God bless.

But there's just one more thing I've learned during my years as a writer and as a friend and observer of writers. Most of them, no matter how fast a "read" they turn out, have a secret ambition to do something that will be remembered as worthwhile in their chosen field.

If that happens to apply to you, then perhaps the simplistic suggestions I've made here may be of some use in your endeavors.

In any case, I hope I have at least given you . . . an easy read.

Robert Bloch
Los Angeles: May 1986

Chapter 1

Run Fast, Stand Still,
or,
The Thing at the
Top of the Stairs,
or,
New Ghosts from
Old Minds

Ray Bradbury

Run fast, stand still. This, the lesson from lizards. For all writers. Observe almost any survival creature, you see the same. Jump, run, freeze. In the ability to flick like an eyelash, crack like a whip, vanish like steam, here this instant, gone the next—life teems the earth. And when that life is not rushing to escape, it is playing statues to do the same. See the hummingbird, there, not there. As thought arises and blinks off, so this thing of summer vapor; the clearing of a cosmic throat, the fall of a leaf. And where it was—a whisper.

What can we writers learn from lizards, lift from birds? In quickness is truth. The faster you blurt, the more swiftly you write, the more honest you are.

In hesitation is thought. In delay comes the effort for a style, instead of leaping upon truth which is the *only* style worth deadfalling or tiger-trapping.

In between the scurries and flights, what? Be a chameleon, ink-blend, chromosome change with the landscape. Be a pet rock, lie with the dust, rest in the rain-water in the filled-barrel by the drainspout outside your grandparents' window long ago. Be dandelion wine in the ketchup bottle capped and placed with an inked inscription: June morn, first day of Summer, 1923. Summer 1926, Fireworks Night. 1927: Last Day of Summer. LAST OF THE DANDE-LIONS, Oct. 1st.

And out of all this, wind up with your first success as a writer, at $20 a story, in *Weird Tales*.

How *do* you commence to start to begin an almost new kind of writing, to terrify and scare?

You stumble into it, mostly. You don't know what you're doing, and suddenly, it's done. You don't set out to reform a certain kind of writing. It evolves out of your own life and night scares. Suddenly you look around and see that you have done something almost fresh.

The problem for any writer in any field is being circumscribed by what has gone before or what is being printed that very day in books and magazines.

I grew up reading and loving the traditional ghost stories of Dickens, Lovecraft, Poe, and later, Kuttner, Bloch, and Clark Ashton Smith. I tried to write stories heavily influenced by various of these writers, and succeeded in making quadruple-layered mudpies, all language and style, that would not float, and sank without a trace. I was too young to identify my problem, I was so busy imitating.

I almost blundered into my creative self in my last year in high school, when I wrote a kind of long remembrance of the deep ravine in my home town, and my fear of it at night. But I had no story to go with the ravine, so my discovering the true source of my future writing was put off for some few years.

I wrote at least a thousand words a day every day from the age of twelve on. For years Poe was looking over one shoulder, while Wells, Burroughs, and just about every writer in *Astounding* and *Weird Tales* looked over the other.

I loved them, and they smothered me. I hadn't learned how to look away and in the process look not at myself but at what went on behind my face.

It was only when I began to discover the treats and tricks that came with word association that I began to find some true way through the minefields of imitation. I finally figured out that if you are going to step on a live mine, make it your own. Be blown up, as it were, by your *own* delights and despairs.

I began to put down brief notes and descriptions of loves and hates. All during my twentieth and twenty-first years I circled around summer noons and October midnights, sensing that there somewhere in the bright and dark seasons must be something that was really me.

I finally found it one afternoon when I was twenty-two years old. I wrote the title "The Lake" on the first page of a story that finished itself two hours later. Two hours after that I was sitting at my typewriter out on a porch in the sun, with tears running off the tip of my nose, and the hair on my neck standing up.

Why the arousal of hair and the dripping nose?

I realized I had at last written a really fine story. The first, in ten years of writing. And not only was it a fine story, but it was some sort of hybrid, something verging on the new. Not a traditional ghost story at all, but a story about love, time, remembrance, and drowning.

I sent it off to Julie Schwartz, my pulp agent, who liked it, but said it was not a traditional tale and might be hard to sell. *Weird Tales* walked around it, touched it with a ten-foot pole, and finally decided, what the hey, to publish it, even though it didn't fit their magazine. But I must promise, next time, to write a good old-fashioned ghost story! I promised. They gave me twenty dollars, and everyone was happy.

Well, some of you know the rest. "The Lake" has been reprinted dozens of times in the 44 years since. And it was the story that first got various editors of other magazines to sit up and notice the guy with the aroused hair and the wet nose.

Did I learn a hard, fast, or even an easy lesson from "The Lake"? I did not. I went back to writing the old-fashioned ghost story. For I was far too young to understand much about writing at all, and my discoveries went unnoticed by me for years. I was wandering all over the place and writing poorly much of the time.

During my early twenties, if my weird fiction was imitative, with an occasional surprise of a concept and a further surprise in execution, my science fiction writing was abysmal, and my detective fiction verged on the ludicrous. I was deeply under the influence of my loving friend, Leigh Brackett, whom I used to meet every Sunday at Muscle Beach in Santa Monica, California, there to read her superior Stark on Mars tales, or to envy and try to emulate her *Flynn's Detective* stories.

But along through those years I began to make lists of titles, to put down long lines of *nouns*. These lists were the provocations, finally, that caused my better stuff to surface. I was feeling my way toward something honest, hidden under the trap door on the top of my skull.

The lists ran something like this:

THE LAKE. THE NIGHT. THE CRICKETS. THE RAVINE. THE ATTIC. THE BASEMENT. THE TRAP DOOR. THE BABY. THE CROWD. THE NIGHT TRAIN. THE FOG HORN. THE SCYTHE. THE CARNIVAL. THE CAROUSEL. THE DWARF. THE MIRROR MAZE. THE SKELETON.

I was beginning to see a pattern in the list, in these words that I had simply flung forth on paper, trusting my subconscious to give bread, as it were, to the birds.

Glancing over the list, I discovered my old love and fright having to do with circuses and carnivals. I remembered, and then forgot, and then remembered again, how terrified I had been when my mother took me for my first ride on a merry-go-round. With the calliope screaming and the world spinning and the terrible horses leaping, I added my shrieks to the din. I did not go near the carousel again for years. When I really did, decades later, it rode me into the midst of *Something Wicked This Way Comes.*

But long before that, I went on making the lists. THE MEADOW. THE TOY CHEST. THE MONSTER. TYRANNOSAURUS REX. THE TOWN CLOCK. THE OLD MAN. THE OLD WOMAN. THE TELEPHONE. THE SIDEWALKS. THE COFFIN. THE ELECTRIC CHAIR. THE MAGICIAN.

Out on the margin of these nouns, I blundered into a science-fiction story that was not a science-fiction story. My title was "R is For Rocket." The published title was "King of the Grey Spaces," the story of two boys, great friends, one elected to go off to the Space Academy, the other staying home. The tale was rejected by every science-fiction magazine because, after all, it was only a story about friendship being tested by circumstance, even though the circumstance was space travel. Mary Gnaedinger, at *Famous Fantastic Mysteries,* took one look at my story and published it. But, again, I was too young to see that "R is For Rocket" would be the kind of story that would make me as a science-fiction writer, admired by some, and criticized by many who observed that I was no writer of science fictions, I was a "people" writer, and to hell with that!

I went on making lists, having to do not only with night, nightmares, darkness, and objects in attics, but the toys that men play with in space, and the ideas I found in detective magazines. Most of the detective material I published in my twenty-fourth year in *Detective Tales* and *Dime Detective* is not worth rereading. Here and there, I fell over my own shoelaces and did a nearly good job of remembering Mexico, which scared me, or downtown Los Angeles during the Pachucho riots. But it would take me the better part of forty years to assimilate the detective/mystery/suspense genre and make it work for me in my latest novel, *Death Is a Lonely Business.*

But back to my lists. And *why* go back to them? Where am I leading you? Well, if you are a writer, or would hope to be one, similar lists, dredged out of the lopside of your brain, might well help you discover *you,* even as I flopped around and finally found me.

I began to run through those lists, pick a noun, and then sit down to write a long prose-poem-essay on it.

Somewhere along about the middle of the page, or perhaps on the second page, the prose poem would turn into a story. Which is to say that a character suddenly appeared and said, "That's *me*"; or, "That's an idea *I like*!" And the character would then finish the tale for me.

It began to be obvious that I was learning from my lists of nouns, and that I was further learning that my *characters* would do my work *for* me, if I let them alone, if I gave them their heads, which is to say, their fantasies, their frights.

I looked at my list, saw SKELETON, and remembered the first artworks of my childhood. I drew skeletons to scare my girl cousins. I was fascinated with those unclothed medical displays of skulls and ribs and pelvic sculptures. My favorite tune was " 'Tain't No Sin, To Take Off Your Skin, and Dance Around in Your Bones."

Remembering my early artwork and my favorite tune, I ambled into my doctor's office one day with a sore throat. I touched my Adam's apple, and the tendons on each side of my neck, and asked for his medical advice.

"Know what you're suffering from?" asked the doc.

"What?"

"*Discovery* of the larynx!" he crowed. "Take some aspirin. Two dollars, please!"

Discovery of the larynx! My God, how *beautiful*! I trotted home, feeling my throat, and then my ribs, and then my medulla oblongata, and my kneecaps. Holy Moses! Why not write a story about a man who is terrified to discover that under his skin, inside his flesh, *hidden*, is a symbol of all the Gothic horrors in history—a skeleton!

The story wrote itself in a few hours.

A perfectly obvious concept, yet no one else in the history of writing weird tales had ever scribbled it down. I fell into my typewriter with it and came up with a brand-new, absolutely original tale, which had been lurking under my skin since I first drew a skull and crossbones, aged six.

I began to gain steam. The ideas came faster now, and all of them from my lists. I prowled up in my grandparents' attics and down in their basements. I listened to the middle-of-the-night locomotives wailing across the northern Illinois landscape, and that was death, a funeral train, taking my loved ones away to some far graveyard. I remembered five o'clock in the morning, pre-dawn arrivals of Ringling Brothers, Barnum and Bailey, and all the animals parading by before sunrise, heading for the empty meadows where the great tents would rise like incredible mushrooms. I remembered Mr. Electrico and his traveling electric chair. I remembered Blackstone the Magician dancing magical handkerchiefs and vanishing elephants on my hometown stage. I remembered my grandfather, my sister, and various aunts and cousins, in their coffins and gone forever in the tombyards where the butterflies settled like flowers on the graves and where the flowers blew away like butterflies over the stones. I remembered my dog, lost for days, coming home late on a winter night with snow and mud and leaves in his pelt. And the stories began to burst, to explode from those memories, hidden in the nouns, lost in the lists.

My remembrance of my dog, and his winter pelt, became "The Emissary," the story of a boy, sick in bed, who sends his dog out to gather the seasons in his fur, and report back. And then, one night, the dog comes back from a journey to the graveyard, and brings "company" with him.

My listed title THE OLD WOMAN became two stories, one "There Was an Old Woman," about a lady who refuses to die and demands her body back from the undertakers, defying Death, and a second tale, "Season of Disbelief," about some children who refuse to believe that a very old woman was ever young, was ever a girl, a child. The first story appeared in my first collection, *Dark Carnival*. The second became part of a further word-association test I gave myself, called *Dandelion Wine*.

We can surely see now, can't we, that it is the personal observation, the odd fancy, the strange conceit, that pays off. I was fascinated by old people. I tried to solve their mystery with my eyes and young mind but was continually astounded to realize that once upon a time they had been me, and some day up ahead I would be them. Absolutely impossible! Yet there the boys and girls were, locked in old bodies, a dreadful situation, a terrible trick, right before my gaze.

Pilfering from my list, again, I seized out the title THE JAR, the result of my being stunned at an encounter with a series of embryos on display in a carnival when I was twelve and again when I was fourteen. In those long-gone days of 1932 and 1934, we children knew nothing, of course, absolutely nothing about sex and procreation. So you can imagine how astounded I was when I prowled through a free carnival exhibit and saw all those fetuses of humans and cats and dogs, displayed in labeled jars. I was shocked by the look of the unborn dead, and the new mysteries of life they caused to rise up in my head later that night and all through the years. I never mentioned the jars and the formaldehyde fetuses to my parents. I knew I had stumbled on some truths which were better not discussed.

All of this surfaced, of course, when I wrote *"The Jar,"* and the carnival and the fetal displays and all the old terrors poured out of my fingertips into my typewriter. The old mystery had finally found a resting place, in a story.

I found another title in my list, THE CROWD. And, typing furiously, I recalled a terrible concussion when I was fifteen and ran from a friend's house at the sound, to be confronted by a car that had hit an obstruction in the street and rocketed into a telephone pole. The car was split in half. Two people lay dead on the pavement, another woman died just as I reached her, her face ruined. Another man died a minute later. Still another died the next day.

I had never seen anything like it. I walked home, bumping into trees, in shock. It took me months to get over the horror of that scene.

Years later, with my list before me, I remembered a number of peculiar things about that night. The accident had occurred at an intersection surrounded on one side by empty factories and a deserted schoolyard, and on the opposite side, by a graveyard. I had come running from the nearest house, a hundred yards away, Yet, within moments, it seemed, a crowd had gathered. Where had they all come from? Later on in time, I could only imagine that some came, in some strange fashion, out of the empty factories, or even more strangely, out of the graveyard. After typing for only a few minutes, it came to me that, yes, this crowd was *always* the same crowd, that it gathered at *all* accidents. These were victims from accidents years ago, doomed to come back and haunt the scene of new accidents as they occurred.

Once I hit on this idea, the story finished itself in a single afternoon.

Meanwhile, the carnival artifacts were gathering closer, their great bones starting to thrust up through my skin. I was making longer and longer prose poem excursions about circuses that arrived long after midnight. During those years, in my early twenties, prowling a Mirror Maze on the old Venice Pier with my friends Leigh Brackett and Edmond Hamilton, Ed suddenly cried, "Let's get out of here, before Ray writes a story about a dwarf who pays his way in here every night so he can stand and make himself tall in the big stretch mirror!" "That's it!" I shouted, and ran home to write "The Dwarf." "That'll teach me to shoot off my mouth," said Ed, when he read the story the next week.

THE BABY on that list was, of course, me.

I remembered an old nightmare. It was about being born. I remembered lying in my crib, three days old, wailing with the knowledge of being thrust out into the world; the pressure, the cold, the shrieking into life. I remembered my mother's breast. I remembered the doctor, on the fourth day of my life, bending over me with a scalpel to perform circumcision. I remembered, I remembered.

I changed the title from THE BABY to *"The Small Assassin."* That story has been anthologized dozens of times. And I had lived the story, or part of it, from my first hour of life onward, and only truly remembered and nailed it down in my twenties.

Did I write stories based on every single noun in my pages and pages of lists?

Not all. But most. THE TRAPDOOR, listed way back in 1942 or '43, didn't surface until three years ago, as a story in *Omni*.

Another story about me and my dog took more than fifty years to surface. In "Bless Me, Father, For I Have Sinned," I went back in time to relive a beating I had given my dog when I was twelve, and for which I had never forgiven myself. I wrote the story to at last examine that cruel, sad boy and put his ghost, and the ghost of my much-loved dog, to rest forever. It was the same dog, incidentally, who brought "company" back from the graveyard in *The Emissary*.

During these years, Henry Kuttner, along with Leigh, was my teacher. He suggested authors—Katherine Anne Porter, John Collier, Eudora Welty—and books—*The Lost Weekend, One Man's Meat, Rain in the Doorway*—to be read and learned from. Along the way, he gave me a copy of *Winesburg, Ohio,* by Sherwood Anderson. Finishing the book, I said to myself, "Someday I would like to write a novel laid on the planet Mars, with somewhat similar people." I immediately jotted down a list of the sorts of folks I would want to plant on Mars, to see what would happen.

I forgot *Winesburg, Ohio* and my list. Over the years, I wrote a series of stories about the Red Planet. One day, I looked up and the book was finished, the list complete, *The Martian Chronicles* on its way to publication.

So there you have it. In sum, a series of nouns, some with rare adjectives, which described a territory unknown, an undiscovered country, part of it Death, the rest Life. If I had not made up these prescriptions for Discovery I would never have become the jackdaw archaeologist or anthropologist that I am. That jackdaw who seeks bright objects, odd carapaces and misshapen femurs from the boneheaps of junk inside my head, where lay strewn the remnants of collisions with life as well as Buck Rogers, Tarzan, John Carter, Quasimodo, and all the other creatures who made me want to live forever.

In the words of the old Mikado song, I had a little list, save it was a long one, which led me into Dandelion Wine country and helped me move the Dandelion Wine country up to Mars, and ricocheted me back into dark wine territory as Mr. Dark's night train arrived long before dawn. But the first and most important pileup of nouns was the one filled with leaves whispering along the sidewalks at three a.m. and funerals wheeling by on empty railtracks, following, and crickets that suddenly, for no reason, shut up, so you could hear your own heart, and wish you couldn't.

Which leads us to a final revelation—

One of the nouns on my list in high school was The Thing, or, better yet, The Thing at The Top of The Stairs.

When I was growing up in Waukegan, Illinois, there was only one bathroom; upstairs. You had to climb an unlit hall halfway before you could find and turn on a light. I tried to get my dad to keep the light on all night. But that was expensive stuff. The light stayed off.

Around two or three in the morning, I would have to go to the bathroom. I would lie in bed for half an hour or so, torn between the agonized need for relief, and what I knew was waiting for me in the dark hall leading up to the attic. At last, driven by pain, I would edge out of our dining room into that hall, thinking: run fast, leap up, turn on the light, but whatever you do, don't look up. If you look up before you get the light on, *It* will be there. The Thing. The terrible Thing waiting at the top of the stairs. So run, blind; don't look.

I ran, I leaped. But always, I couldn't help it, at the last moment, I blinked and stared into the awful darkness. And it was always there. And I screamed and fell back downstairs, waking my parents. My dad would groan and turn over in bed, wondering where this son of his had come from. My mother would get up, find me in a scrambled heap in the hall, and go up to turn on the light. She would wait for me to climb up to the bathroom and come back-down to have my tearstained face kissed and my terrified body tucked in bed.

The next night and the next night and the night after that, the same thing happened. Driven mad by my hysteria, Dad got out the old chamber pot and shoved it under my bed.

But I was never cured. The Thing remained there forever. Only moving West when I was thirteen got me away from that terror.

What have I done, recently, about that nightmare? Well . . .

Now, very late in time, The Thing is standing up at the top of the stairs, still waiting. From 1926 to now, in the spring of 1986, is a long waiting. But at last, gleaning my ever dependable list, I have typed the noun out on paper, adding "The Stairs," and I have finally faced up to the dark climb and the Arctic coldness held in place for sixty years, waiting to be asked to come down through my frozen fingertips and into your bloodstream. The story, associated out of memory, was finished this week, even as I wrote this essay.

I leave you now at the bottom of your own stair, at half after midnight, with a pad, a pen, and a list to be made. Conjure the nouns, alert the secret self, taste the darkness. Your own Thing stands waiting 'way up there in the attic shadows. If you speak softly, and write any old word that wants to jump out of your nerves onto the page . . .

Your Thing at the top of your stairs in your own private night . . . may well come *down*.

Chapter 2

Plotting as Your Power Source

J. N. Williamson

1. DEFINING THE PLOT

The late teacher-novelist John Gardner said in his posthumously published *On Becoming a Novelist* that, in order to place a novel at *all,* one requires either "a coterie" or "profluence—the sense that things are moving, getting somewhere." We expect that quality in most books. Always, in novels.

It starts with the germ of an idea, is enacted and experienced by the people who populate your novel (or story), and is powered to a planned, satisfying outcome by the *plot*.

"Genre," wrote author-publisher John Maclay (*Wards of Armageddon*), "is the last stronghold of plot." By which Maclay meant "a *kind* of story—versus, I can't resist suggesting, no story at all."

Your writing success depends, to an extent seldom adequately stressed, upon powering your fiction by the tightest, most interest-sustaining plots of which you are capable. And a plot is *not* an idea, one fairly well-rounded character, a flurry of conversation climaxed by a quarrel, kiss-and-make-up, and a cheery platitude. That is a *vignette*.

Dean R. Koontz, a very experienced, best selling author who also has two chapters between these covers, defined plots exceedingly well in his 1981 Writer's Digest book, *How to Write Best Selling Fiction:* "Plot is the skeleton of the novel, the bare bones that keep everything else from collapsing in a formless heap." It supports all and it's what Gardner described—the "sense that things are . . . getting somewhere."

That's because a plot, in a way, is a means of transportation for the characters in your fiction; one that takes them from the inception of the yarn to the close of it. What they and the readers do not know is the harrowing, circuitous, but ultimately logical route the plot machine will follow. You, the writer, *must know*.

I say *logical* even though we're working with fantastic fiction, because regardless of genre, time, or space, a skilled writer's world always contains its own inherent reasonableness. Limitations have been placed early on, subtly, so that the cleverest elves may not become invisible unless the writer has established that variety of elfness. Vampires *do* die with stakes through their hearts, and may *not* become skyscraper tall! However things were *said to be* before you've written much of the tale is how they must remain.

Too many fiction instructors try to teach new writers that the primary consideration is that of theme or character. (Gardner called theme "elevated critical language for what the character's main problem is.") Some teachers never mention the need for fresh ideas and grudgingly identify the plot as a writer's third, or fourth, consideration.

But most people buy a novel or a magazine containing fiction in the expectation of being entertained. (Do creative writing teachers know people who read fiction in the hope of being bored?) Crafting a finely tuned professional plot, Koontz wrote, is the "most demanding task that a novelist must face . . . the supreme test of self-discipline, craftsmanship, and art."

The facts appear to be these: Nothing is more important than idea and plot for the writer who wants to be published. Theme *is* of consequence, but overemphasizing it can turn the writer into a preacher or missionary. Characterization is very important; its exaggeration is a series of unpurchasable, vignette-like character sketches—for the reader, boredom. It's always preferable that you have something to say, a viewpoint on the human condition.

But it's okay if all you have is an engrossing, involving plot founded on interesting ideas—because that may be sufficient to place your work.

A tangent to advice that isn't elsewhere in this book: Think fully of yourself, when you are able—automatically, unconsciously—as a writer. In the way an attorney is always an attorney, a pro basketball player is always that. What you *are* attracts the people, the appurtenances, the ideas, and the opportunities of that activity.

2. PLOTTING UNPREDICTABLY

It's mildly surprising that John Gardner believed there was "nothing wrong with fiction in which the plot is relatively predictable."

It matters a great deal to readers of fantasy fiction and to publishers who know that it does. A contemporary fabulist who wants to give his readers an entertaining reading experience must try to devise numerous unguessable twists and turns.

The recognition of this fact explains why the early portions of this book comprise chapters on idea generation; setting and character and naming your people; the emphasis upon originality; how to write suspense; and the importance of getting *your* novel or short story off to an alluring start. Viewed as ambience, superior works of horror, fantasy, and SF integrate all these elements. "Technology poses no threat to the future of the book," said a 1984 report from the Library of Congress; but dull, uninspired or safe fiction does. The first way you can be sure that you are not doing what technology has, happily, failed to do is by reading—as much as possible—in the genre of your choice. Discover what's already been done.

Your next step is deciding to outline, and learning how to do it.

3. PLOTTING WITH THE OUTLINE

Think of your next work of fiction as a meaty, lifeless but strangely viable monster sprawled on a lab table—and *you're* Dr. Frankenstein. The creature's made up of ideas patched together as seamlessly as possible. He has a (blank) face and a background (he's gentle; after all, he was dug up from the graveyard of unconscious thoughts); his theme involves the absence of a soul (a professional spark). You've planned for him to be a one-of-a-kind, but when you get him on his feet, he lumbers around, then collapses.

And lies there like a lump. Because—*"Class?"*—he isn't energized; lightning hasn't struck him yet. He lacks—*"Together, now"*—a *plot!* (Even, in horror, his burial plot!)

He needs—*you* need—"medical charts," or diagram-plots, to keep him from running around excitably all the time. Real people have an ebb and flow to them, as do plots. They don't lurch, crawl, gasp, and choke; they advance more or less evenly through life save for the times of pressure and tension. The way good plots do.

But your pet monster remains synthetic if the only way you can empower him is by introducing factual material—events culled from personal experience, or from TV or printed news. Too much reality threatens the complex structure of fantasy. Even with a more preposterous plot, we need to be involved, working from some deep, essential portion of ourselves, if what we write is to sound sincere and credible. And credibility in fantasy, horror, and SF is not only more important than in any other kind of fiction but also harder to create.

The degree to which we write freshly, insightfully, from discoveries made in our individual and intimate pools of truth often determines the emotional re-spect paid our work by our readers. Recording with total fidelity too many actu-al, real-life events is reporting, biography, or journalism. Not fiction.

Good plots that animate your lethargic monster happen, more often than not, because of well-planned *outlines*.

Not all professional writers work from outlines, but, as Gardner said (in *On Becoming a Novelist*), "sooner or later the writer has no choice but to figure out what he's doing." More directly, this widely respected teacher and working professional urged others to "start with a plan—a careful plot outline."

The one for my first novel ran thirty thousand words, that for novel two was nearly that long; the last six or eight have been written from outlines averaging some four thousand words, and I don't think they'll get much shorter. Why do I drag in this personal stuff? Being prolific won't guarantee greatness, but the twenty-four novels I've written and sold, to date, have enabled me to be-come a full-timer; constant practice—sixty- and seventy-hour weeks—have made me a *better* author; and I'm convinced that I'd never have written thirty-one novels in twelve years if I hadn't outlined them from the beginning.

But outlines need not be half the length of the book, obviously! And, by *outline*, I don't mean what your high school English teacher meant. I don't rec-ommend setting outlines up with Roman numerals, boxing them off with letters of the alphabet dutifully denoting each new chapter.

Here's what I recommend (and these steps can be applied to the writing of shorter fiction as well):

Carry your basic ideas around in your head until you begin seeing *All* and the major characters have begun to take shape. Do this until you effortlessly see the rough progress of the novel/story taking place and you know with some con-fidence where everything is likely to end.

Sit down at the instant of bursting enthusiasm to devise the outline (by whatever means). Record those lines which capture all the events of the pro-logue, the first chapter, or the story's first scene; then draw a line or turn the page and proceed to the next part. *While this happens,* hold in mind a visualized ending of the tale plus the realization that you need enough chapters (or scenes) to accomplish a certain length. As characters come to mind, use them; if they lack names, call them Mary and Bill or A, B, C—anything that helps you re-member what roles they play without interrupting your plotting.

A chapter-by-chapter breakdown gives you the chance to decide ahead of time when information should go into Chapter Two, Twelve, or Twenty-Three; if, later, you decide you want it elsewhere, cross it out and slip in the data where it now belongs. Nothing's permanent until you actually begin to *write.*

Then, basically, it *is.* Your plot is set—or that's what you pretend so that any modifications or diversions from your plot are made solely because you've *brilliantly* discovered a better way! Approach it this way and you are confident in both the plot and the few divergences you talk yourself into making.

A word—several, actually—on beginnings, middles, endings; about major crises, and going on from there; that sort of thing: Too many pieces of fiction—especially short stories, but it's also true in novel- and nonfiction-writing—start with too much exposition. An excessive amount of time is spent preparing the reader, who, most probably, is impatient to get on with the story. More times than I care to recall, and more recently, as well, editors have pointed out to me that my "*real* beginning" was buried several pages into the manuscript. Make it a rule to begin *anything* you write in the midst of something: dialogue, physical action, a character going somewhere or returning.

A fault repeated by many of my Writer's Digest School students clearly displays the difference between the amateur and the pro, and it is encountered midway through stories or midway through chapters: The writer, abiding by what he or she has read about (1) starting interestingly and (2) finishing strong, does something very human—the writer gets tired. Pointing this out to you and stressing the frequency of it in amateur writing should be sufficient to put you on guard against your own waning vitality—except that it happens a lot in the middle of newcomers' novels as well! Now you've had a blanket caution flag waved at you, with this further admonition: Proofread and doublecheck at such midpoints just as tirelessly and demandingly as you do with fictive starts and finishes. And be alert that at these points, you're also likely to expel a lot of hot air—to wander and to pad. (The finest of us do this at times. We do it *less* when we're reminded of such tendencies.)

One way to counter these problems with story and novel midsections is to remember them *while you are outlining* and purposely create moments, well ahead of the actual writing, that will stimulate your imagination. Doing this, you'll gain the added benefit of stimulating your readers' minds, since it is precisely then that *they* may begin to wander!

Ending a novel or a story, even when you are plotting it in the outline, is more difficult to describe and easier, for an experienced author, to execute. Remember, first of all, that you are a god to your characters. And in devising your plot, it won't hurt if you're not the most compassionate deity in the cosmos! By this I mean that even when your fiction's people think they have taken the right step, you must—for most of the course of the novel or other tale—prove them in error. They misjudge, preferably the way readers would have misjudged; increasingly, as the storyline advances—and a key to ending fiction well is found in the way you plot the work so that every development is intended to advance the story toward an envisioned time of climax—your protagonists encounter complications which seem to dash every hope, every valiant step. The worse things continue to look for the protagonist, the harder it is for him to find a way out, may happily stem from how difficult it is for *you* to discover an out!

It is when (1) the most important problems facing your primary characters are resolved, following times of ever-growing setback and suspense, and (2) they (ideally; not you) have disposed of or answered all the interesting details along the way, that your book or story is over. But at this moment, readers need to feel that the expectations *you* subtly gave them for your main characters have been fulfilled; readers can be left with mysterious or philosophical questions, but they should not, usually, be left with significant questions unanswered or doubt that you've dealt reasonably with protagonists—and with them.

Each main crisis experienced by your major people—and never forget that interested readers emotionally or intellectually experience them, too—should not only advance the plot but reveal (1) more about the protagonists and (2) more about the enigma that resides at the soul of your plot. Don't believe for a second that mystery fiction is the only fiction containing mystery! If there's nothing for your readers to wonder about, you've written something tedious and probably incomplete.

And as each crisis or confrontation is passed, by your hero or heroine (the terms are more apt in fantasy fiction today than they were when they applied to protagonists in mainstream fiction of the past), readers should usually feel that the hero is becoming a *better* or, at least, an *altered* person.

With these pointers in mind, try to end each outline chapter on a note of *rising curiosity* or *suspense generation, action,* or *imminent disclosure.* It's very hard to do this consistently without an outline. With one, you plan notes of gravity or fascination, and once you begin to write, you find yourself (a) looking forward to writing it and (b) meticulously *building* the moments of the chapter or short story until each ending is effectively climactic.

The payoff for such plotting is the confidence-generating feeling that any editor or reader reading *that* wind-up *has* to go on reading! While it doesn't always work out that way, it is incrementally harder for anybody to lay a manuscript aside when the finish of a scene or chapter almost shouts at you, "See what happens next!"

Plan, in your outline, to let us *see* most scenes of action instead of letting characters inform us offstage; the fundamental fiction writer's rule of "Show, don't tell" obtains most of the way and nearly always where action is concerned. Action, of course, may be nothing more exciting than an astronaut again getting back into his ship, a child once more mounting a mythical beast— but *show* your readers with *fresh terms* whenever you can. Involve them, in part by enabling them to see what your characters think and feel. While plotting, try to follow a long, expository talking scene with action; then try to return your readers to your protagonist in company with a different character, in another place, at another time of day, or in other weather conditions.

When describing people or action and creating atmosphere, keep a thesaurus within arm's reach and describe in new ways—vividly—that with which readers have grown familiar. Just as your outlined individual chapters ascend toward plateaus of intensity and involvement, succeeding scenes of progressive action should become ever more . . . *something:* more understandable to the protagonist, difficult, dangerous. And it is hoped that the high point with which you complete a chapter (or a key scene) is a case of your people's and your readers' simultaneously *recognizing* some *new strand of fact or truth.* No more than you can help it should the page-turning moments be merely a manufactured surprise, but it *will* be necessary, occasionally, during your outlining. Try hard to make those somewhat contrived scenes subtle, story-advancing—and infrequent.

4. THE ART OF PLOTTING

There are terms that annoy me and many of my writing friends, more than I can fully indicate to you. *Mainstream* is one; *horror,* to a lesser degree, is another, because it is called upon to cover so much. *Dark fantasy* irks me for two reasons: it seems to apologize for the older word, *horror,* and it is less than accurate when pinned to a yarn written as realistically as the writer is able (a story about a lifelike serial killer, for example, in which nothing occult exists save the antagonist's own awful mind). I'm certain that writers who are primarily SF or fantasy authors have their own troublesome words to contend with.

I think we all loathe the expressions *serious novel* and *serious writer,* with the loaded implications that the wordworker who stresses action, the sheerly imaginative, or the fully nonexistent is somehow playing at writing and decidedly less talented. Worse, *mainstream* and *serious story* are often meant to convey that fantasists, detective story writers, and so on are less concerned with the important things.

I won't dignify such pompous contentions beyond pointing to many of the wonderful tales of every length that are celebrated toward the close of this book and remarking that I, for one, am dead serious about my work—and so are all those who were asked to contribute the present chapters. More earnest than Hemingway, more grim than the Brothers Grimm. Anyone who strives to earn a living from writing *is.*

Those women and men who write novels and short stories of fantasy—of whatever variety—take great pride in it, and so may you. We may feel especially proud that, for us, storytelling remains as significant as it was for any writers who preceded us. We know that art is accidental; we know it is incidental to having told—*showed*—our story as well as we can. Working creatively, industriously, lovingly, we tend to reach the point of knowing what sort of thing we plan to go on writing. Although most ideas can be reshaped or modified to fit our individual, central truths, we have found writing to be the best education and culture-molding method available to humankind and our principle aspirations and concerns, hopes and dreads, sing from the core of all that we write just as affectingly and as effectively as any writers currently at work.

Dean R. Koontz wrote in *How to Write Best Selling Fiction,* ". . . Being read is the fundamental test of greatness in literature. The purpose of fiction is communication, and if the work is not read, the purpose is not fulfilled." It's considerably easier, as Koontz also observed, to write for the literarily pretentious or doctrinaire than attempting to reach, and entertain, the millions. But it is not nearly so challenging, so thrilling, or so profitable, for most. Such satisfactions may be your own when you have learned the profluence-giving power of well-plotted fiction.

Chapter 3

Reality and the Waking Nightmare: Setting and Character in Horror Fiction

Mort Castle

Undoubtedly, you have had the experience of picking up a novel at the end of the day, telling yourself you'll read a chapter before going to sleep, and then . . .

. . . A surprised glance at the clock. It's five in the morning!

Huh? What happened? You had taken no notice of time passing, not here in the *real* world. Instead, your time became the time of the novel, with perhaps a day depicted in 113 pages, or eleven months flashing by in three tightly constructed paragraphs.

Nor while time passed on Earth were you thinking about such here-and-now concerns as the cluster of mosquito bites on your forearm, that difficult choice between paying the car-repair bill or the pediatrician's child-repair bill, or your chances of winning the lottery.

As you read, your body occupied space in RealityLand—but you, the thinking, feeling, imagining, real *you,* were literally somewhere else. You were walking the suburban streets or city alleys, the forest paths or sandy beaches of a fictional world, as you shared the adventures and thoughts and emotions of that world's people, people you had come to know—and to care about.

The late John Gardner, a fine writer and teacher of writing, called fiction a "waking dream." When you sleep and dream, you experience the dream as real. And when you enter the waking dream of a well-written short story or novel, it is just as real.

Of course, you're reading this because you are interested in creating not waking dreams but waking nightmares. (*Daymares* is a term commonly used by horror fans and writers, but I don't care for it—too cute!) You want to set spines a-shivering, souls a-shaking—and sometimes stomachs a-spasming.

How do you do that?

Perhaps you expect me to answer my rhetorical question by saying something like, "Use your imagination. Dredge up the dreads in the corners and basement of the brain. Set free the imagination to go on a scythe-swinging, chain-saw slashing, Roto-Rooter rooting rampage—and you've got a horror story."

Sorry. Imagination will give you an idea for a horror story, but you're a long way from having the waking nightmare that will envelop and encompass readers.

It's reality's "What is!" not imagination's "What if?" that can transform horror premise into horror story.

It takes reality, heaps of it, to create and populate a story realm that gives readers the frights *royale*. It takes settings that have the reality of Lincoln, Nebraska; Tucson, Arizona; or Grenada, Mississippi. It takes breathing, thinking, feeling, story folks who are as real as your Uncle Albert, who always gets drunk and sentimental at family reunions; as real as Mr. Schlechter, your high school English teacher who nearly flunked you for not handing in your term paper on "Washington Irving's Use of the Comma in *Rip Van Winkle*"; as real as your first puppy-love paramour or your last meaningful-relationship partner.

Good fiction, by definition, is credible. It is a lie that can be believed. Readers should be able to say of a contemporary or mainstream work of fiction, "Yes, given these circumstances, this could really happen." Readers should be able to say that of a western, romance, mystery, suspense, you-name-it work of fiction.

And readers *must* be able to say of a story of the supernatural, the paranormal, the occult, the horrific, the weird, the wild, and the off-the-wall, "Given these circumstances, this could really happen"—if they are to enter into and be held by a waking nightmare.

The key to credibility in fright-fantasy fiction is setting and character.

Your readers, after all, are already meeting you more than halfway, as they implicitly say, "I want to be scared—and so I choose to willingly suspend my disbelief in order to accept your imaginative premise. A manacle-rattling, saber-waving, or ice-cream cone licking ghost, a werewolf, were-panther, were-bear, were-whatever, a 200-year-old transvestite vampire who needs root canal work on his fangs, okay, I'll go with that. I'll stretch my credulity that far. . . ."

But that's it! With *one* such leap of imagination/acceptance of the incredible, readers have given you all you have a right to expect. That means *everything else* in your waking nightmare must be true to life so that readers are never saying, "Uh-uh, I'm being lied to."

What's "everything else"?

Everything else = setting and characters. (Okay, fiction has setting, characters, *and* plot! Correct. But if your principal characters respond to their problem/conflict situations in credible ways, plot happens *almost* automatically. Besides, I wasn't asked to do a chapter on plotting!)

How do you make settings real?

Bring out the old chestnut: *Write about what you know.*

It's hardly a surprise that Robert McCammon's evocative and frightening-as-hell novel, *Mystery Walk,* is set in Dixie. A graduate of the University of Alabama, living in Birmingham, Alabama, McCammon knows the territory.

J. N. Williamson often chooses Indianapolis, Indiana, as the setting for his fictive frights. Indianapolis-born, Indianapolis-dwelling, sure to get all worked up over the Indy 500, Williamson knows Indianapolis—and depicts it so you know it, too.

A Maine native, Stephen King has *lived* in Castle Rock and 'Salem's Lot—even if those towns have other names on the Auto Club map.

I've lived in Crete, Illinois, one of Chicago's south suburbs, for nearly twenty years. I slide behind the wheel of my Chevette, and within twenty minutes, I'm at Lincoln Mall, an under-one-roof shopping center that always smells of caramel corn; or Prairie State College, which in two years can provide you an associate's degree in English or air-conditioning repair; or Suburban Heights Medical Center, a modern facility with a large staff who are rightly termed *professional* health workers. I can drive through Park Forest, a well-established, middle-class planned community; or East Chicago Heights, as poverty-stricken and dangerous a ghetto as you shouldn't be able to find in our proverbial land of plenty; or Swiss Valley, where my poor Chevette's ego dies as we pass driveways in which are parked Cadillacs, Mercedeses, and Jaguars.

You can understand, then, how I came up with a suburb called Park Estates for the setting of my horror novel, *The Strangers.* You know why my protagonist's wife signed up for a psychology class at Lincoln State College. You now have the inside info on the protagonist's daughter, struck by a car, winding up in the emergency room of the South Suburban Medical Center.

Here's a brief passage from *The Strangers:*

> Two uniformed officers from the Park Estates Police Department and the paramedics arrived without sirens, their whirling lights fragmenting the neighborhood into coldly iridescent expressionist objects and angles: a bird-bath, jumping shadows cast by the limb of a tree, an advertising circular blowing across a lawn, the eyes of a prowling cat. . . .

To write that, I employed *zero* imagination. Instead, I relied on memory and knowledge, and found words to let my readers see what I can see every day.

I hear a protest: "But I live in North Nowhere, Kansas, three churches, four taverns, and a trailer park. Our big cultural event is the annual VFW show when the guys dress up as women. . . . How's a fictionalized North Nowhere to grab and keep readers' interest?"

Sorry, I maintain that North Nowhere *is* interesting—if you set out to discover the interest. Maybe I'm not exactly a wild and crazy guy, but I note all sorts of local color events in Crete that grab me (and, fictionalized a bit, often wind up in my writing): The eclectic Old Town Restaurant adds something new to a menu that already offers Mexican burritos, Chinese egg rolls, Italian ravioli, and Greek *dolmaches;* Crete Hardware has a sign, "Thanks for your patronage for the past 30 years," not because the store is going out of business or anything—just to say, "Thanks"; the high school's cheerleaders slow traffic at the Main-and-Exchange intersection (the town's only stoplight), by holding a "Sucker Day" to raise money for new uniforms.

Granted, reality-based settings are prosaic and commonplace. The very ordinariness of such settings works *for* you in two ways.

First, readers are familiar with the ordinary; they live there. Readers relate to the ordinary without your having to work at establishing that relationship. And readers will find your settings *credible,* as they *must.*

Then, if you have an ominous, thickly atmospheric setting, the phosphorescent-fog-shrouded swamp, the torture chamber of a crumbling castle, the burial ground of a Satanic church, you will be hard pressed to spring a surprise on your readers, who rightly anticipate an awful or nasty occurrence in such a foreboding place.

But . . .

> Summer. A few minutes past sunrise. Birchwood Lane, a quiet suburban street. Mailbox on the corner. A parkway torn up to repair a broken sewer tile. A squirrel zips up a tree, fleeing a gray tomcat . . .

Ho-hum, hum-drum . . . *until* something sinuous, gleaming with slime, slithers from the mailbox's "In" slot . . .

Or . . .

The squirrel, safe on a limb, chatters defiance at the cat below . . . and then, from the thick leaves behind the squirrel, a furry arm shoots out and a knobby-knuckled, four-fingered hand encircles the squirrel's neck . . .

When the ordinary is invaded by the terrifying *extraordinary,* horror happens.

And thus it is the intrusion of the extraordinary, the terrifyingly unusual, into the *lives* of ordinary, credible, for-real characters that makes for compelling shock fiction.

A good horror story character is a fictional someone who is every bit as alive and as much a unique individual as anyone we really know—really well—out here in RealityLand. He must be for readers to care about him. If readers don't care, they will not give a rap about what the character does or what happens to him. You can make your readers like or dislike, love or hate a character, but you can *never* allow readers to feel only *indifference* toward him.

To illustrate this idea: Like you, I read the newspaper obituaries. I note the passing of 82-year-old Lorinda Strudel, for three decades third-chair viola with the Peoria Semi-Symphonic, or Andre Shuttlehans, inventor of the Pocket Fruit Juicer . . . and then I turn to the comics, the horoscope. I don't know these people. They mean nothing to me.

But I remember, remember so well, how I felt when I learned Jack Benny had died. Jack Benny, the fictional comic persona, whose money vault inspired Scrooge McDuck, who drove that sputtering Maxwell, who could turn, "Well!" into a bust-your-gut laugh line, who was immortally thirty-nine forever. Jack Benny, the man, the philanthropist, the concert violinist. Jack Benny, who visited my living room once a week on channel two. And so, Jack Benny died, and there was that scraped-out feeling within me, that gone-forever, hurting emptiness that is personal loss. Jack Benny. I knew him better than I knew a number of my relatives: he was a nice man and a good man and he made me laugh.

The real world of your waking nightmare must be inhabited by characters your readers know.

And that means *you* had better know those characters.

How well?

You've not only fathered and mothered these characters, you've been their closest confidant and their psychiatrist. There is *nothing* they've kept hidden from you—including things they might have been able to keep hidden from themselves. *That's* how well you know them.

That's how well I know my important characters, anyway. My readers might never need to know if my protagonist prefers real mayo to Miracle Whip, if his first car was a cherry-red '67 Ford Mustang, if he likes Willie Nelson's songs but can't stand looking at the singer, if he had a pet collie named Lizzie when he was five, etc.—but *I* have to know if I am to present this character as a three-dimensional, well-rounded human being, as I must.

In "And of Gideon," my novelette in the John Maclay-edited collection, *Nukes: Four Horror Writers on the Ultimate Horror,* my protagonist, Gideon, is a murderous psychopath. I wanted my readers to fear Gideon, to realize anew that such human aberrations do exist. I wanted my readers to pity him, this loser who'd been "programmed for pathology." But more than that, I wanted readers to see Gideon as a credible *human being,* one who would elicit the wide range of emotional response that only real people can evoke.

Here is some of what I knew about Gideon and what I wanted readers to know:

> . . . My father, a drunk, had no love for my mother, another drunk, she none for him, and neither for me . . . (From) my early years, I cannot recall a single hug . . . My father . . . would beat me, not with the flat of his hand or a belt but with his fists . . .
>
> In kindergarten, I could not color within the lines, could not catch a basketball thrown to me from a distance of three feet, nor hang by my knees from the monkey bars . . . I was always in trouble: for not coming to school on time, for not even trying on tests, for not doing this, for not doing that, always in trouble with the teachers, those despairing head-shakers, "Gideon, don't you want to learn? Don't you want to amount to anything? Don't you want to grow up and be somebody?"

Because your characters must have their own distinct personalities (just as you are the One and Only You and Nobody Else), you cannot people your story with stereotypes. Your credible fiction is based on reality, and if you've ever been friends with a truck driver in RealityLand, you realize there's so much more to him than can be described by "Truck Driver Type," more to the wife-beating drunk than "Wife-Beating Drunk Type"—more to *you* than "Writer Type." Stereotypes aren't permitted to have unique personalities as do real people; they are limited in thought, emotion, and action by the terribly confining mold which created them.

In an earlier era, we had such stereotypes, offensive lies thinly disguised as human beings, as the Irish cop with the whiskey nose and the "Faith and begorra" accent and the shuffling black who, eyes-rolling, yelled, "Feets, do yore stuff!" when confronted by "haints." You can think of many others, I'm sure.

I'm afraid horror fiction these days has its own stereotypes: The Ugly Duckling with the Paranormal Wild Talent; The Dedicated Psychic Researcher, so icily intellectual that he continues to take copious notes as Satan's personal imp cadre disembowels him; The Catholic Priest Suffering Doubt; The Twins,

One Good, One Evil; The Yokel Preacher, who speaks in tongues and would quote more frequently from the Bible if it didn't have so many multisyllabic words; The Helpless Female, who, although she is the vice-president of a New York advertising agency (a nod to women's lib!), nonetheless is totally incapable of dealing with a supernatural menace. (That's a job for Our Hero, who looks exactly like Harrison Ford, except he has the classic Batman square jaw and Paul Newman's never-a-doubt blue eyes.)

Don't use any of them! (Not that I'm being dogmatic. . . .)

Instead, apply that previously mentioned writing rule, *Write about what you know*. You know people. You have been a "practicing people" ever since you were born. That makes you a people expert!

You know what you think/how you feel when someone you counted on lets you down—so you know what your story character thinks/feels when someone he's counted on lets him down. You have experienced disappointment, joy, hate, love, and so you can create credible characters who experience disappointment, joy, hate, love. You've been embarrassed, you've felt pride, you have felt everything a human being can feel.

Your characters, animated by your knowledge of self, others, and the world, given your breath of reality as vital force, placed in authenticity-imbued settings, will come to life on the page. They will hold out a welcoming hand . . . and yank readers into your waking nightmare . . . and keep them there!

Chapter 4

One View: Creating Character in Fantasy and Horror Fiction

Steve Rasnic Tem

AN INTRODUCTION

I've long thought that one of the more complicated aspects of writing the "fantastic" forms of fiction is the creation of character. I'm sure quite a few people would question me on that point—after all, there are innumerable books and articles on the subject. So why the difficulty? Because those books and articles, for the most part, concern the creation of characters in realistic fiction.

What's the difference? The usual view is that the characters in fantastic fiction are really no different from the characters in realistic fiction—they are simply normal people who have been thrust into extraordinary situations (confrontations with unicorns, alien beings, alternative worlds, vampires). Although on the surface that view appears reasonable, I think it has its limitations. It ignores the central artificial quality of the fiction-making process: the fact that a story is a *made* object which must, although it makes reference to things outside itself, stand by itself as a complete thing. It ignores the fact that character in such a made object must be inseparable from the plot, setting, and atmosphere. The economy of fiction-making demands it. Each line must contribute and bind to every other line; otherwise cracks will be left and the object will fall apart.

In other words, a character is inseparable from the context in which he operates. That would seem to be a pretty commonsensical sort of idea, but its implications can be far-reaching. It makes the creation of character in fantastic literature different from the creation of character in realistic fiction, because the contexts are different.

The usual characterization techniques in realistic fiction (such as the enumeration of habits, physical traits, likes and dislikes, or the use of telling dialogue) work because their realistic context is generally understood. When we supplant that realistic context with a fantastic one of our own creation, similar techniques can be used, but the author must also establish the *links* between the two contexts. The educated reader has an intuitive understanding of what fashion, advertising, the media, and family values say about our culture and ourselves as individuals—in other words, how such things *characterize* us. Similarly, when fantastic elements are introduced, the writer must create a context that helps the reader intuit how these fantastic elements also characterize the protagonist of the story.

The importance of this sort of linking can perhaps be seen most clearly in the sort of tale similar to the *Twilight Zone* stories, in which the background and details are portrayed as realistically as possible. But then some anomaly, something wrong is dropped into the midst of this highly realistic context. The most skillful examples of this type—by writers such as Richard Matheson, George Clayton Johnson, and Ray Bradbury—use the opportunity of the strange occurrence to peer more deeply into the souls of the characters, and it is through this link to character that the strange occurrence becomes humanized and meaningful to the reader.

Although these ideas apply to all forms of fantastic writing, they are of particular interest to the horror writer. For it is the discovery of these hidden mirrors in the landscape of the story, the protagonist's sudden apprehension of other versions of himself in his surroundings, that in large part creates the atmosphere of paranoia so prevalent in this form of literature.

So that's the theory, my "one view." Now on to more practical applications of it.

DREAM CHARACTERIZATION

An analogy I've always found useful for the relationship between characters and their settings is the relationship those same elements have in dreams. A particular theory of gestalt dream interpretation suggests that every object in a dream is a piece of the dreamer. A chair, a table, a car, another human being—

each would represent some aspect of the dreamer. The theory is persuasive, I think, particularly when you consider the rather free-form, uncensored nature of the dreaming process. But whether you agree with its validity as a method of dream interpretation or not, I think it suggests a useful approach for fiction making, particularly for fantastic fiction, whose creations so often have the shape and color of dream.

Adapting this theory to horror fiction, we might say that all other objects in the story—the landscape, the other characters, the supernatural presence, even the individual events—represent some aspect of the protagonist (or *victim*). Each piece suggests or tells us something about our main character. Far more, I suspect, than a delineation of traits and opinions ever could. This dark moor reflects an inner terrain that is the character's alone. These people would not be here in the story except that the character needed them to be, perhaps because they embody essential aspects of the character, or represent the various points-of-view of his or her own internal dialogue. This horrifying presence is a child of the character's worst fears and suppressed imaginings. And somehow we know that these events could not have happened to any other person, in quite this same way, no matter how perfectly ordinary or innocent the character seems to be.

All the elements fit together economically to make a solid object. Character becomes inseparable from setting, plot, and atmosphere, simply because we are using setting, plot, and atmosphere to characterize.

I think many writers use this sort of dream characterization intuitively when they write in the fantastic mode. The very nature of writing in the fantastic mode, and its similarity to dreaming, forces writers to characterize this way, at least in part, whatever their chosen theoretical approach. What I suggest is that we become more consciously aware of its use.

I also suspect that this peculiar method of fantastic or dream characterization accounts for some of the criticism occasionally leveled at some writers of the fantastic concerning the supposed two-dimensionality of their characters. Because of long-ingrained reading habits, the critic has first artificially separated the so-called elements of characterization from the rest of the story, examined only these elements, and then declared the piece "wanting in characterization." As should be apparent by now, when such a methodology is applied to fantastic literature, such as the nightmare tales of a Kafka, the characterization will be missed simply because the critic is looking in the wrong place for it. Fantastic literature requires different expectations, a different way of reading.

When these pieces of the self are of the darker sort, concerned with hatreds and fears and masking long-suppressed thoughts and desires, an atmosphere of paranoia naturally evolves. To suddenly see, *out there,* what we have so carefully attempted to hide inside can be a terrifying thing.

CHARACTER AND DETAIL

The approach to characterization I'm suggesting here puts increased weight on the individual details that make up a story. Specific detail has always been of great importance to the tale of fantasy, science fiction, and horror. Writers as early as M. R. James elevated the gradual accumulation of atmospheric, foreshadowing detail to a central role in the structuring of their stories. In fact, a few of James's pieces take this to an extreme, his small, exquisite bits of description virtually crowding out all other elements in the piece. What is background in most genres of fiction becomes foreground in the story of the fantastic.

In the Middle Earth of Tolkien and the Mercury of E. R. Eddison, the protagonists are enveloped by all manner of strange backgrounds and exotic figures, all of which tell us more about exactly what sort of characters these are. The characters in the science fiction of a Gene Wolfe, a Samuel Delany, or a William Gibson are similarly surrounded by numerous details of strange artifacts, all of which tell us not only what sort of person our main character is, but also what sort of *community* of beings is being portrayed here. In science fiction, I think, people and communities are characterized by the *devices* (both cultural and technological) they choose to surround themselves with. The details of the machines become character details.

Only the mystery appears to have given these details a similar sort of emphasis—the reader learns to pay an unusual degree of attention to seemingly insignificant details because they may very well be the clues necessary to solve the mystery. Similarly, when reading the horror story, the reader needs to focus on the details because they may be the clues necessary to solve the *character*. In the individual details of the horror tale, we may recognize the pieces of self the protagonist has denied.

One of the finest examples of this sort of writing is the work of the British author Ramsey Campbell. At times his work is a virtual textbook of telling detail. Observe these two brief passages from his novel *The Parasite* (Macmillan, 1980):

> Outside, the sunlight seemed unreal. A truck with a jointed yellow arm brandished a man at a streetlamp. A car with a propeller drove by—no, with the foot of an office chair protruding from the boot. An old woman stumbled across a pedestrian crossing; as she gestured the traffic to wait she looked as though she was swimming. Everything looked bright but meaningless.

> The sky had brightened, but was stained by the grubby window. She knew it was a bright shell over infinite darkness. Muffled landscapes

sailed by. Distant trees resembled stitches struggling to pull free of the sky.

Twilight gathered like scum. The world looked drowned, an endless parade of feeble lights, of shapes that might have been composed of smoke. A few premature fireworks flew up. Their sparks clung to her eyes.

Frequently in Campbell's work, we are led through a gradual process of transformation, the commonplace details of a realistic world steadily mutating into the protagonist's inner landscape.

Writers such as Campbell have taken the technique of *pathetic fallacy* and renewed it, bringing expanded significance to its use. Normally, the discovery that the world surrounding us reflects our feelings and resonates to our concerns would be comforting. But I believe that horror fiction often turns that comforting illusion on its head: in these tales, what we cannot face within ourselves comes after us in the darkened woods or the shadows of an old house. We see underneath the traditional psychological definition of paranoia so that it is not other people we fear are watching us, sneaking up behind us, but instead it is ourselves. I think that in some stories the house is not haunted until we walk into it. Reading the work of certain authors, we discover that piece by piece the world takes on the shape and coloring of our own mind and body. And it is terrifying.

This particular approach to characterization blurs the distinction between the two types of characters which are traditionally seen as populating horror stories: the character whose personal psychology has somehow generated these horrors, and the character who is an innocent victim to truly outer evils. Dream characterization suggests that any differences between the two are only matters of emphasis and degree. I'm not saying that you can't write about true outer evil or true innocents—I'm simply suggesting that perhaps the very process of writing fantasy fiction creates links between these outer evils and the psychologies of these innocent characters. In this sense, as I see it, there are no completely innocent characters in horror fiction. Although innocent in a moral sense, I think they become partly guilty by virtue of the techniques of the story-making process. I believe that even the eminently likable protagonists of a Stephen King story are ultimately responsible for what befalls them. The disasters, the horrific events were inevitable because of *who* these people are.

CHARACTER AND PLOT

Using plot events to characterize is really just an extension of the old idea of showing who a person is by means of his actions—which may be the most effective, dramatic way to delineate character in any case. But with the framework of dream characterization in mind, I would also include those actions that happen *to* the character as well. By following to its logical conclusion the theory that story events are inevitable and intrinsic to each character, we might view horror plot as the careful mapping of the protagonist's fear or obsession. Not *everyone* has encounters with vampires or werewolves. In a story of the fantastic, the very fact that a character has such an encounter may well tell us something about her, something far more significant than the social history of realistic characterization would tell us. (This is not to say that the kind of dream characterization I'm talking about could not be used in so-called realistic fiction—it often is—its use may just be more necessary in fantasy fiction.)

Making practical use of this *characterization-by-encounter* is not easy, of course, particularly since it is difficult to analyze scenes for this quality with any precision (sometimes we have a feel for what a scene shows about a character, but can't put that feeling into words). But it starts, I think, with being conscious of the process, so that we can create such plot encounters with an eye toward maximizing their characterizing properties.

CHARACTER SEEDS

Once we have expanded our ideas of character delineation to include specific details of setting, atmosphere, and the descriptions of other characters, as well as the actual events or encounters which occur in the story, I believe we have opened up the actual fiction-making process. Our tools are prepared for concise, economic story creation—we are seeing description, character, plot, and atmosphere as part of a continuum.

This conciseness enables us to play and experiment. The short story becomes a fictional laboratory. With setting, atmosphere, and character so closely allied, we can put our characters through a number of strange experiences and transformations and still not stray far from their emotional center.

I think this allows us to discover new ways into a story, new seeds for generating narrative. Once we find such a character seed, we are ready to make the appropriate connections, gather the appropriate story materials around the character.

Once you have developed a process of characterization that is intimately connected to all the elements of a story, you will be able to find complete and compelling characters just about anywhere.

We may feel more at ease adapting autobiographical materials. Biographies of various possible selves can be used for character seeds. Examining our own and others' actual lives, and at crucial decision points, posing the question: "What if I had been a slightly different person then, and made a different decision?" can generate a number of story ideas.

Another seed might be free-floating anxiety—inspired by scraps of description—suddenly given voice. Some of M. R. James's more atmospheric fiction and much of Kafka's work have this feeling.

Character can be based on a single, overwhelming fear that becomes a driving emotion, as in a number of stories centered around fear of heights, fear of drowning, claustrophobia. Or an obsession can first be created, then a character found who is trapped and fixated by this obsession; in my own short stories "The Poor" and "Derelicts" I've attempted just that. Or the inner sources for dark folk tales may be explored, as in Thomas Tessier's werewolf novel, *The Nightwalker*. Or the salient anxieties of a time can be factored out and a search conducted to find the characters best suited to illustrate them. I see that kind of perceptiveness in much of Fritz Leiber's horror work, in particular the stories in *Night's Black Agents*.

But perhaps the highest form of horror fiction occurs when, rather than merely describing a known fear, the author exerts the power of *maker* and *creator* to produce new fears (or old fears in startling new forms) on the page. The writer is able to discover fears in characters which are almost unrecognizable in their shape and color, yet they still have the power to move and terrify us. Writers as diverse as Clive Barker and Dennis Etchison have had this effect on me. Their characters seem not so much beings with anxieties to count and explore, as dark, universally human landscapes—hidden from ordinary scrutiny—which have suddenly been given voice and body.

Chapter 5

"Oh, Just Call Me Cuthbert": The Naming Game

Thomas Millstead

"I heard a heavy step approaching behind the great door. . . . Within stood an old man, clean shaven and clad in black from head to foot without a single speck of colour about him. . . .

"He moved impulsively forward, and holding out his hand grasped mine with a strength which made me wince, an effect which was not lessened by the fact that it seemed as cold as ice—more like the hand of a dead than a living man.

"He bowed in a courtly way. 'I am Count Cuthbert L. Gooch, and I bid you welcome.'

"I heard as if from down below in the valley the howling of many wolves . . ."

Hold it! Cut! Muzzle the wolves!

What's that again—*Cuthbert L. Gooch*?

That sound you hear is a mood of impending horror being loudly and rudely shattered. The reaction you experience is not so much a frisson of terror as the faintest twinge of a snicker.

And the lesson for all of us is that we cannot ignore the vast importance of names in tales intended to chill, thrill, or enthrall.

A century ago, Bram Stoker knew well the impact of names, and so, while he wrote the above lines, he did not, thankfully, dub his vampire "Gooch." He called him "Dracula," a name that in and of itself oozes dank darkness, malevolence, and the stench of the Undead. Dracula: a name that twangs the reader's nerve ends and contributes much to a sense of being led irresistibly into the fetid vaults of eternal evil.

Of course, bestowing appropriate names is critical in every form of fiction, but much more so in fantasy, horror, and science fiction. Why? Because this genre, above all others, thrusts below the surface to touch the subterranean depths that lie within us all. It strives to bypass the representational, the mundane, the "reality" of the four senses. Instead, its quest is to awaken that which was hidden and secret: wonder, passion, astonishment, primeval dread.

In this effort, names have power—sometimes almost mystical power. They can be a formidable tool to reach those depths. When properly chosen, they can guide the reader insinuatingly and almost subliminally into the journey of illusion. Ineptly chosen, they can botch the trip and dispel the magic.

What makes the fanciful real, what gives it substance, is a name so apt that, in retrospect, it could be nothing else. To cite just a few examples:

Perelandra (C. S. Lewis)

Opar, City of Gold (Edgar Rice Burroughs)

Oz (L. Frank Baum)

Urras (Ursula LeGuin)

Azathoth (H. P. Lovecraft)

There is an inevitability here. What else could these places be called but what they were? Their names alone conjure up visions, fears, delights. To many they are as real as Peoria or Pocatello. Maybe more so.

At this point, a contrarian rejoinder: Yes, a neat-sounding name may be okay, but isn't it really the content of the story that defines the name, *any* name? In other words, suppose Oz had been named *Skumafeder,* and Dracula, *Cuthbert Gooch.* Today wouldn't "Skumafeder" stimulate happy memories of the Munchkins cavorting on the Yellow Brick Road? And wouldn't "Gooch" set off knee-jerk reactions of repulsion and fright?

A valid point, and true to some extent. But not totally. Doubtless these masterpieces would have been successful even without those legendary names. But I submit that the degree of success, and the degree of reader satisfaction, would hinge enormously on how well the new names evoked resonances similar to those of the originals.

Granted, responses to names can be subjective. If you were bullied as a child by a hulking brute called Cuthbert Gooch, the very whisper of that name might forever strike terror in your heart of hearts. Nevertheless, to a larger audience, to anyone receptive to the music of words and syllables, *Gooch* clearly carries fewer convincing intimations of threat than does *Dracula.*

It's true that Stoker did not invent the name. He took it from an unpleasant tyrant of some centuries earlier, Vlad Dracula. But certainly Stoker appropriated the name not because it was historically accurate but because of its palpably ominous overtones.

Since names are so crucial in this genre, what then are the criteria for picking the right ones? There are none, naturally. In a field of writing that aspires to break free from conventional constraints, few rules are graven on stone. That is as true of names as it is of plots.

Still, there is one abiding precept, and that is the imperative to keep the names compatible with the tone and texture of the story.

The most quickly spotted tipoff to the amateur is in the choice of names, according to one best selling horror novelist who also teaches creative writing. His students may put together a passable plot and tolerable dialogue, but he laments that their characters' names frequently blot out credibility. Too often they seem pinned on hastily, randomly, without purpose. They may be drab while the character is colorful. Or they may suggest ethnic or social backgrounds that have nothing to do with the characters or the narrative. Or several characters may have names closely resembling each other, sowing confusion.

Above all, they don't ring true to the spirit or mood of the story. They do not strum those subconscious chords that prompt the reader to suspend, unwittingly, all disbelief.

Admittedly, in real life our names may not ring true either. But in fiction too much disparity between name and persona can be lethally disruptive. The dominating precept is verisimilitude, a faithful wedding of narrative and name.

On occasion, this may require minting new and exotic names. *Yoda, Ishtar,* and *Erewhon* are superb because they suit the tales in which they are integral. In other settings, such unique creations would be out of place. Stephen King's rural Maine hamlets and J. N. Williamson's Indianapolis suburbs bear familiar and almost forgettable names that—very intentionally—belie the ghastliness waiting in the wings.

Consider that most ordinary of monickers, John Smith. It's perfect for the protagonist of King's *The Dead Zone* because Smith is a likeable Everyman until an accident equips him with psychic gifts and impels him on a highly unorthodox course.

The name game can be subtle and deceptive. With Dracula, we know almost from page one that we have an arch-fiend on our hands. But other names may, calculatingly, play against type. Example: another of King's creations, Jack Torrance in *The Shining.* What a fine and cheery fellow he must be, with a commonplace but somewhat jaunty name like that! Not so, but we were fairly fooled.

Or take Guy Woodhouse in Ira Levin's *Rosemary's Baby.* Guy is a New York actor, and his name projects a stagey, debonair flair. Is this the sort of chap to cut a deal with Satan?

He also illustrates the fact that names can be fun. I have no idea why Mr. Levin christened him Guy Woodhouse, but I suspect it's an amalgam of Guy Bolton and P. G. Wodehouse, who collaborated on the Princess Theater musicals in the early days of this century.

I also suspect, more than strongly, that the building in which the diabolical doings occur in *Rosemary's Baby,* The Bramford, was so named in homage to Bram Stoker. I would not be surprised if Stephen King was doffing his cap to the master, too, by giving the name of Straker to the vampire's amanuensis in *'Salem's Lot.*

If these suspicions are true, King and Levin got away with it because the names—even if contrived as an inside jest—still convey authenticity. They are nuances that add to, not detract from, the atmosphere of the stories.

To those with a less artful touch, however, flirting with flip put-ons can be risky. It can turn the reader's attention to the author's sly wit and away from the narrative. Additionally, it can easily slip into satire or high camp. If that's what's intended, so be it. But if not, names should be taken as seriously as every other major element in the creative process.

Perhaps this is the most essential thought about names to store away: Respect must be paid. Names may not make the difference between selling and not selling a particular work (although they certainly might), but they can make the difference between realizing a story's full potential and muffing it.

They should not be an afterthought. Always, some part of the writer's mind should be open to names: noting them, voicing them, savoring them, dissecting them, comparing them, combining them, remembering them.

Genesis tells us that "whatsoever Adam called every living creature, that was the name thereof." So it is with writers of imaginative literature. From their minds flow beings, kingdoms, and even entire universes never before seen or dreamed of. And each of these entities, like a squalling newborn, demands and deserves an identity.

It is the writer's challenge, responsibility, and joy to confer this identity via a name that is truly fitting and proper for every person, place, and (in the horror arena) Thing.

Call them by their rightful names—and see them come alive.

Chapter 6

Involving *Your* Reader from the Start

William F. Nolan

I'll begin with a public confession: In 1963, when I was managing editor of the SF/fantasy magazine *Gamma*, I would reserve one morning each week for the "slush pile"—the stack of unagented manuscripts from new writers who hoped to crack the pages of our magazine. I had a sure-fire method for getting through the slush pile quickly; I'd pull a typed manuscript halfway out of its envelope and read the first paragraph. If I liked it, I'd remove the entire story and read it through. But if that opening paragraph didn't grab me, I'd let the manuscript slide back into its mailing envelope and that would be the end of it. Another rejection.

Brutal, right? Unfair to those poor writers to judge their whole story from just the opening paragraph, right? Wrong. For me, the acid test of a story is its opening. A good story should leap off the page, grab you by the throat, and *demand*, "Read me!"

We're talking about hooking your readers with mood or character or incident or with a unique situation. Getting them *involved*, from the start. Let me cite several examples from my own published stories (first paragraphs only) to show you what I mean:

● From "My Name Is Dolly" (*Whispers VI*):

"*Monday.*—Today I met the witch—which is a good place to start this diary." I had to look up how to spell it. First I spelled it 'dairy,' but that's a place you get milk and from *this* you're going to get blood—I hope.

● From "The Final Stone" (*Cutting Edge*):

"They were from Indianapolis. Newly married, Dave and *stirring, flexing muscle, feeling power now . . . anger . . . a sudden driving thirst for* Alice Williamson, both in their late twenties, both excited about their trip to the West Coast. This would be their last night in Arizona. Tomorrow they planned to be in Palm Springs. To visit Dave's sister. But only one of them would make it to California. Dave, not Alice. *with the scalpel glittering.*"

● From "Jenny Among the Zeebs" (*The Future is Now*):

"What kicked off the hooley was: the zeeb contest had gone sour and *that's* when this zonked-out little chickie wanted to cast some bottoms. It was the two coming together that way, like planets in a collision orbit, that kicked off the hooley."

● From "Into the Lion's Den" (*Alfred Hitchcock*):

"Before she could scream, his right hand closed over her mouth. Grinning, he drove a knee into her stomach and stepped quickly back, letting her spill writhing to the floor at his feet. He watched her gasp for breath."

● From "The End with No Perhaps" (*Impact* 20):

"After he had parked his pink-and-cream Thunderbird at the end of the long gravel drive, Harrison Miller decided that he would like to step on his sunglasses. He got out of the car and removed the hand-tooled leather case his wife, Sylvia, had given him for his birthday; carefully he placed the tinted glasses at his feet. Then he stepped down heavily, grinding the expensive prescription lenses into powder."

● From "The Halloween Man" (*Night Cry*):

"Oh, Katie believed in him for sure, the Halloween Man. Him with his long skinny-spindley arms and sharp-toothed mouth and eyes sunk deep in skull sockets like softly glowing embers, charcoal red. Him with his long coat of tatters, smelling of tombstones and grave dirt. All spider-hairy he was, the Halloween Man."

● From "One of Those Days" (*Magazine of Fantasy & SF*):

"I knew it was going to be one of those days when I heard a blue-and-yellow butterfly humming *Si, mi chiamano Mimi,* my favorite aria from *La Bohème.* I was weeding the garden when the papery insect fluttered by, humming beautifully."

● From "Down the Long Night" (*Terror Detective*):

"The ocean fog closed in suddenly, like a big gray fist, and Alan Cole stopped remembering. Swearing under his breath, he jabbed the wiper button on the Lincoln's dash, and brought the big car down from fifty to thirty-five. Still dangerous. You couldn't see more than a few yards ahead in this soup. But he said the hell with it and kept the Lincoln at thirty-five because he wanted this mess over in a hurry, because he wanted to hold Jessica in his arms again before the night was done."

● From "And Miles to Go Before I Sleep" (*Infinity SF*):

"Alone within the great ship, deep in its honeycombed chambers, Robert Murdock waited for death. While the rocket moved inexorably toward Earth—an immense silver needle threading the dark fabric of space—he waited calmly through the final hours, knowing that hope no longer existed."

● From "A Real Nice Guy" (*Mike Shayne's*):

"Warm sun.
A summer afternoon.
The sniper emerged from the roof door, walking easily, carrying a
    custom-leather guncase.
Opened the case.
Assembled the weapon.
Loaded it.
Sighted the street below.
Adjusted the focus.
Waited.
There was no hurry.
No hurry at all."

● From "The Yard"(*Masques II*):

"It was near the edge of town, just beyond the abandoned freight tracks. I used to pass it on the way to school in the mirror-bright Missouri mornings and again in the long-shadowed afternoons coming home with my books held tight against my chest, not wanting to look at it."

- From "The Day the Gorf Took Over" (*Infinity Two*):

"There's a special office at the Pentagon called the Office of Stateside Emergencies. Dave Merkle is in charge, a thin, night-eyed man, haunted by a perpetual sense of failure. He was depressed on the morning of June 3, 1982, because there had not been a decent stateside emergency since early May. There had been three superb overseas emergencies, but they were handled by another office down the hall and didn't count."

- From "The White Cad Cross-Up" (Sherbourne Press):

"The Marshal's big automatic crashed twice, and two .45 slugs whacked into my chest. At close range, the force of the bullets drove me back like a boxer's fists, and I landed on the rug, gasping and plenty nervous."

- From "Fair Trade" (*Whispers*):

"He tole me to speak all this down into the machine, the Sheriff did, what all I know an' seen about Lon Pritchard an' his brother Lafe an' what they done, one to the other. I already tole it all to the Sheriff but he says for sure that none'a what I tole him happened the way I said it did but to talk it all into the machine anyhow. He figgers to have it all done up on paper from this talkin' machine so's folks kin read it an' laugh at me I reckon."

- From "The Grackel Question" (*Gallery*):

"Arnold Masterbrook I, II, and III was crossing the Greater Continental Federated United States for the sixteen-thousandth time in his customized hoverbug when he saw two lovely hitchies by the side of the road."

- From "Of Time and Kathy Benedict" (*Whispers V*):

"Now that she was on the lake, with the Michigan shoreline lost to her, and with the steady cat-purr of the outboard soothing her mind, she could think about the last year, examine it thread by thread like a dark tapestry."

See what I mean? These opening paragraphs make a reader sit up and take notice. You are pulled into the story, your imagination is stimulated, your curiosity aroused. You want to know *what comes next*. (Editors are *readers*, too, don't forget.)

Sometimes I do it with a one-line paragraph. A real hook to the gut. Examples:

- From "Dead Call" (*Frights*):

"Len had been dead for a month when the phone rang."

- From "The Public Loves a Johnny" (*Impact 20*):

  " 'Lightning!' shouted Ed Fifield, rushing into the kitchen."

- From "The Worlds of Monty Willson" (*Amazing*):

  "It *looked* like the same world, but it wasn't."

- From "The Mating of Thirdburt" (*Alien Horizons*):

  "When Thirdburt turned twenty-one, his father threw him bodily out of the family lifeunit in New Connecticut."

- From *Logan's World* (Bantam):

  "Argos died twice."

In the no-TV, no-video, no-comics world of Charles Dickens, readers were conditioned to deal with complex, dense, often-wordy opening pages in books and stories. It was an era of leisurely reading when the pace could be slow and unhurried. Not so today.

We live in a jet-paced, media-oriented society where everything happens fast. Quick, gaudy images flash across the TV screen to grab our attention. For a short story or novel to compete in this modern world, it must waste no time getting off the mark; it must engage the reader's attention *instantly*.

What elements are utilized to achieve such openings?

As a writer, you must ask yourself: How can I establish an opening mood which promises danger . . . or thrills . . . or death . . . or adventure? How can I inject the personality of my protagonist into the first paragraph? How can I create a fresh situation that points toward a unique dramatic resolution?

The modern writer's job is to set up his narrative in a clear, direct manner that says to the reader: Stick with me and I'll frighten you, or amaze you, or make you laugh or cry; I'll take you to places you've never been and involve you with characters you'll find hard to forget.

Go to your bookshelf (or to the library) and select fifty *recent* novels or stories. Read *only* the first paragraph in each. Then sit down and analyze what elements you've found in each opening. Think about what "hooked" you, made *you* want to keep reading. Look for the Big Four: situation, mood, character, and incident. One or more of these will be present in each of your fifty opening paragraphs. Take them apart word by word; find out *how* the writer achieved his or her effect. Then, when it's time to begin writing your next story, you'll be equipped to hook *your* readers.

Keep it fast, fresh, and simple.

Chapter 7

Freedom of Originality in Fantastic Fiction— and How to Use It

James Kisner

The reason I write horror, fantasy, and science fiction is basically rather pragmatic, but a most compelling reason for the beginner nevertheless: these genres give the freedom I need to be my most creative and to make the most of my imagination—to be as *original* as I dare. Given this freedom, I have also developed methods for maintaining my originality, which any new writer can apply to his or her own fiction. These methods can not only insure that your own writing will be as fresh as possible, but also can lead to more sales and greater success.

The freedom to be original seems to be the most attractive aspect of writing fantastic fiction for most professionals. In her insightful article, "What Horrid People!" (*The Horror Show*, Spring, 1986), Ardath Mayhar said, "Originality is one of the best things to be found in the [horror] field." This statement holds true for science fiction and fantasy as well. In these genres, you are treated to a smorgasbord of entertainment, a variety and range of subject matters, and a feast of ideas that simply are *not* offered in romance, mystery, and other genres. Or, for that matter, in most mainstream fiction! True, these other categories provide a degree of diversion, on an escapist level, often in a mindless sort of way—but for the startling, for the different, for the shocking, you must turn to the genres which are the subject of this book.

More specifically, the fantastic-fiction categories give the writer greater *opportunities* to be original and creative, and to say something that is, quite often, entirely *new*. That's an exciting concept, but it can also create pitfalls for the newcomer. It's not always easy to know if what you're writing *is* new—or if it's been done so many times before no editor will consider it. Fortunately, there are ways to avoid such pitfalls.

In his introduction to Clive Barker's *Books of Blood,* Ramsey Campbell observed, "When it comes to the imagination, the only rules should be one's own instincts. . . ." However, instincts can lead you astray if you don't first *train* your imagination to recognize and sort out the mundane, the overused, and the trivial. You can learn to cultivate your own originality, then, by fine-tuning your thinking processes to reject certain concepts, so you can be free to develop those ideas that are unique to your own creativity.

Why is this training necessary? Because the mind is easily fooled into grasping the obvious and claiming it for its own. Everyone is born an original thinker, but after years of exposure to other people's ideas, the mind can lose its independence. Children, for example, see things in entirely original ways; adults show them the traditional or accepted ways of seeing things and teach them to reject their original perceptions. The best writers, then, are still children in their minds, seeing things anew again and again.

Beginning writers are also misled by the notion that there *is* nothing new under the sun, or "it's all been done before." This is the kind of stultifying bromide often heard in high school and college writing classes. It is a chilling denial of our creative instincts that effectively stifles originality. It leads too many beginners to believe everything *has* been done—so they go after the easy stuff and don't try hard enough, to the detriment of their writing.

A writer's goal should be to recapture that native, childlike ability to see things in original ways and eschew the "easy stuff" in the process.

Of course, it's one thing to tell you to be original; it's another to show you *how* to do it. The first step, as I've found in my own writing, is to learn how *not* to be *un*original. This is not a flippant tautology; it is important advice and what it really means is: *read.*

Read and *study*—not just anything, but recognized works of imagination by the more original writers in not only the genre you wish to write for, but in other realms as well. Your purpose in this pursuit is not to imitate these writers, however, but to discover what is *possible* and thereby determine where the best potential for your own original ideas lies.

A good starting place is the list of works you'll find at the end of this book—novels and stories recommended by other successful writers. You can often learn more by reading any one of these books or stories than you would from dozens of lesser works selected by random browsing through a bookstore. Indeed, one particular book, simply by pointing the way to possibilities you might not have considered otherwise, can totally change how you approach your own writing.

A few examples come quickly to mind. In horror, there is *Hell House,* by Richard Matheson; *Ghost Mansion,* by J. N. Williamson; *Ghost Story,* by Peter Straub (the *one* book you must read if you are going to write supernatural stories); and the anthologies *Masques* and *Masques II,* both edited by J. N. Williamson. In science fiction, the most original works include *UBIK,* by Philip K. Dick; *Traitor to the Living,* by Philip Jose Farmer; *The Jagged Orbit,* by John Brunner; and the anthology *Dangerous Visions,* edited by Harlan Ellison, a collection of original brilliant stories that was also a major force in bringing maturity to science fiction in a way never thought possible before. In fantasy, there is *Time and Again* by Jack Finney, a time-travel story set in a romantic milieu that separates it entirely from science fiction. Each of these books establishes a *new* approach to genre story-telling by means of plot, characterization, style, or treatment.

It is also helpful when reading such books to keep a file of notes analyzing what makes each one original or different. Is it the use of sexuality in *Hell House?* The special evocation of despair and hopelessness in *Ghost Mansion?* The unique delineation of an afterlife in UBIK? By examining what makes these books original, I can be more certain my *own* work is original. I can see how it's done, without imitating, and thus can better generate my own ideas.

Each of the titles cited above, as well as most of the books in the lists at the back, represents a different approach to its subject matter, yet it still fits its particular genre niche as well. There is very little traditional fare here—no BEM's, no vampires, no space operas.

I also highly recommend two nonfiction books that offer insights into what makes originality and how to achieve it, *Writing Popular Fiction* by Dean R. Koontz, for approaches to writing in all genres; and *Danse Macabre,* Stephen King's horror manifesto, which has a great deal to say about fantasy and science fiction as well. Both these instructive books also include numerous examples of original works of fiction to be aware of in all the fantastic genres.

Koontz, in an interview for *The Horror Show* (Summer 1986), also advises against reading too much within *one* genre. He goes on to say, "To have vitality, to have *juice,* any form of fiction has to be built upon an awareness of *all* contemporary fiction and of the possibilities and techniques that writers in other genres have explored." Reading Spillane, John D. MacDonald, or John Gardner may give you just the original insight you need to create a startling new work in your own genre of choice. "Classic" authors can give you new directions too; Koontz cites Dickens as a major influence in his work; my own writing has been shaped by Steinbeck and Sinclair Lewis; and most contemporary writers of *any* genre owe a great deal to Fitzgerald, and, of course, Mark Twain.

A word of caution is in order here: Originality, to some degree, is in the eye of the beholder. The first time *you* read a time-travel tale, it may seem the most original concept in fiction. You don't want to discover, after doing your own temporal fiction, it's already been done a thousand times before. Don't let one book, or the works of one author, be your sole guideline as to what has already been done. And notice when the impressive or influential work was *first published*.

After you read your first haunted-house novel, or a vampire tale, immediately find another by someone else. See *what makes it different*—or what makes it *like* every other story in the same genre. (It might not be original at all!) Don't rely on only one favorite author; for all you know, his work may be the most derivative fiction being published. Read as many different authors in a genre as you can, including the bad ones (and learn by *not* imitating *them*).

There's also a danger of overkill in all this reading. Eleanor Sullivan, writing in *The Mystery Writer's Handbook* (Writer's Digest Books), noted, "rather than reading too little, these [mystery] authors were reading too much and relying for direction on what had already succeeded."

Obviously, you cannot read everything that's been written anyhow. You can supplement your knowledge of what's been done (and overdone), however, by sending for any writer's guidelines available from many book and magazine publishers. (See *Writer's Market* and *Fiction Writer's Market,* both published by Writer's Digest Books, for addresses.) Editors often include in these guidelines "laundry lists" of overworked subjects and plots to avoid. You'll soon discover, to cite a few examples, that stories in which the main characters turn out to be Adam and Eve, or in which the character is being born, or is in hell, or it's all a dream, are so timeworn as to be unacceptable in virtually any form, no matter how well written your particular variation might be. (To these examples, I would add stories about word processors or computers that are possessed and/ or have gone berserk; stories about killer fogs; stories with trains as metaphors; and stories about possessed vehicles or machinery of any kind. The first several times these were done, they *were* original; now they are passing into the realm of the hackneyed. How do I know? By my own continued, extensive reading in the genres.)

Also remember that television's *The Twilight Zone, Thriller, Alfred Hitchcock, The Outer Limits,* and various other anthology shows used and reused most of the common ideas more than twenty years ago. So did the E. C. Comics, the Warren publications, the pulps, and, to an extent, the movies. You should try to *avoid recycling* ideas from these media, even on an unconscious level.

In general, if an idea comes too easily to mind, it probably *has* been done before, so assume that it has until you've trained your imagination to weed out the tired and the stale automatically. Then that easy idea will be true inspiration.

At this point, you might be saying to yourself, "Why bother? This reading, this note taking, this constant awareness is a lot of hard work! You don't *have* to be all that original to be published." That's true. Some of the most popular, best-selling stories sometimes fall just short of being outrageous plagiarism. Being original is not a requirement for publication at all! But publication alone is not success. As Wordsworth said, "Every great and original writer, in proportion as he is great and original, must himself create the taste by which he is to be relished." Translated into modern terms, that means you owe it to yourself and your readers to be as original as you can. Because *only* by developing your originality will you establish a true, specific audience for your work and avoid producing generic, run-of-the-mill books, the titles and authors of which mean nothing.

In short, if you continually go after facile writing, you will eventually be found out. Your work will not endure. It will reside, instead, in the boneyard of used bookstores, with countless other volumes of the same old stuff.

Despite what you see published, editors *are* seeking new, original ideas, and they will often overlook bad grammar, poor spelling, or even a poorly typed manuscript to acquire that gem of creativity, that *original* work of art.

The original artists do endure. The most creative writers, like Richard Matheson, Ray Bradbury, William F. Nolan, and others of their generation are producing original works today, just as they did thirty years ago. That's true success. All it takes for you as a beginner—if you have the basic talent, have developed your writing skills and achieved a personal style—is a lot of work and a willingness to take advantage of the vast opportunities that exist in the fantastic genres.

Then, before you know it, people will be imitating you!

> Originality does not consist in saying what no one has ever said before, but in saying exactly what you think yourself.
>
> —J. F. Stephen
> *Horae Sabbaticae*

Chapter 8

Creating Fantasy Folk

Ardath Mayhar

Of the three main categories of imaginary beings, the first that comes to mind is the *monster* (à la Cthulhu). The second is the semioriginal being with its roots in folk and mythological sources. The third, the one to concern us here, is the *alien* . . . the completely imaginary creature.

Monsters need no comment here; they're almost endemic in the human mind. Our primordial ancestors invented their prototypes. Elves and trolls have been around as long as we have and require no discussion here.

Instead, let's discuss the creation of an entirely *new* sort of being. It can be done in either of two ways. One of these is beginning with another world and its characteristics. From that basis, we can contrive a being *capable* of living there. This requires a careful thinking-out of the planetary or fantasy-world context, and we work backward from that to find what characteristics an inhabitant must have. Common sense wedded to logic, with a modicum of research into planetary phenomena, can make this quite possible.

For instance: I was using a world that was distant from a rather cool sun. It was glaciated over most of its surface, except at the equator, subject to blizzards through most of its extremely long year. Its growing season was counted in weeks. Yet it had to be inhabited by creatures capable of surviving and of helping stranded human beings to survive there.

I knew that I needed creatures with considerable physical bulk. (Extra size provides more body warmth.) They absolutely needed, of course, thick fur—and triple eyelids to protect the eyes from both glare and blowing snow.

The creatures lived in caverns in the chains of volcanic mountains running north to south in parallel ranges. Living so for many months, trapped with their own kind in close quarters, had worked the hostility out of their species through sheer demands of survival. The aggressive and short tempered had simply been forced out into the winter to die, removing those genes from the pool.

They were intelligent. Their calm kindliness extended even to a kind of being completely unfamiliar to them. Their technical expertise (they controlled hot water springs and lava vents in order to warm their caverns, as well as to grow edible fungi in sheltered conditions) was something the stranded human beings could learn and profit from.

The demands of the story, as well as the demands of the planetary context, helped to form this kind of being. Common sense, I repeat, is the main ingredient necessary to invent such fantasy folk. The alien *must* be believable. Its description must satisfy the critical faculties of the reader.

But there is another angle of attack: You begin with an alien that *has* to be a certain sort. You go deeply into its nature. Then you devise a context that could logically have produced it.

An instance is one of the characters in *Khi to Freedom* (Ace, 1983). It is an energy-gas intelligence, without any physical being except a weak electrical field that is, in fact, its mind. But it *is* intelligent—enough so to devise a telepathic code that provides a link with the human being imprisoned nearby. This being cannot withstand heavy gravities or any humidity whatsoever.

What sort of world might generate such a creature? Devising such a world involved working backward from the known to the speculative. He would come, first of all, from an extremely dry world—one with constant winds sufficient to generate static electricity among the dust particles covering it. It would probably be near a very hot, blue-white sun and be bathed in electromagnetic energy every day.

When enough of the intelligences came into being, they would, by the nature of intelligence, begin to interact. And at that point they would become a society—one without the capacity for coercion, without physical needs to drive it, with pure thought as its entire reason for being.

To find a common ground for communication between such a being and one of our sort, hag-ridden by hunger and thirst and cold and heat and fear of pain, is a most interesting challenge. Only the processes of rational thought need apply. It was fun to do, and I think it worked out well.

These are, of course, science-fictional characters. But, like it or not, science fiction that deals in any extraterrestrial intelligence is purest fantasy, as are these two examples. Elves have been done to death. Dragons and such must be weary and ready to lay down their burdens.

Wonderful new creatures are waiting to be invented: ones with three legs (from a world with constant earth tremors? Rough terrain? Work it out!); ones that live in such dangerous environments that they surely have a ring of eyes right around their heads!

Stories about winged people, which are usually interesting, and in the main, physiologically feasible, already exist. The characters are jointed differently at the knees. Their bones are far lighter than ours. Their hearts are heavy-duty organs, capable of sustaining their weight in flight for long periods of time. And their metabolisms are most efficient.

It helps, too, if they come from worlds with lighter gravities than ours. Matters of diet, habits, procreation, and such require intelligent handling by the writer to make them logically satisfying.

The secret lies in working your new being and its habitat together neatly, matching requirements and phenomena with the needs of story. You must *visualize, analyze,* and *understand* this creation of yours.

Remember that you can't sacrifice your plot to explanations of your invention. It must fit into your story line without stress and without extra verbiage. As when introducing a human character, you will need to bring out the oddities of your alien gradually; remember that long strings of adjectives are more like inventories than descriptions. As does a human character, the alien needs to *act out* its nature. Its appearance and habits must come through observation of the being in action, or else it is only a snapshot, not a living creature with its own manner of existing and operating.

Note the acting out of the alien in the following example:

> LinKee moved across the field, his three legs moving in oddball synchronicity, giving him much the gait of a drunken spider. As he reached the trees beyond, he unfolded his sitting-stalk and perched, waiting to talk with his opposite number from the human enclave.
>
> Admiral Ellerbee ambled out of the rubber-leaved forest. He stared into the purple eyes of the Keelian representative. LinKee stared back, entirely unperturbed, it seemed. But one of his legs was twitching slightly.

I made this up as I went along, simply to demonstrate how you can grow into an alien, *learning* about him as you go with the flow of the story. Note that the description grows organically from the progress of the story. This is good practice, no matter what or whom you may be describing.

Create entirely new beings—it's fun! It isn't easy, but it is most challenging, and it helps to make a wonderful difference in a story. Just remember that in fantasy more than almost any other field, keeping your characters logically *consistent* is a necessity. The more fantastic the elements of your tale, the more precisely consistent and sensible must be those who inhabit it.

Chapter 9

Keeping the Reader on the Edge of His Seat

Dean R. Koontz

Suspense. It is what you feel on the uphill start of a roller-coaster ride. It's what you feel at a blackjack table as you sit with a pair of kings and wait to see if the dealer's hole card will give him a blackjack or give you the win. It's what you feel at the ballpark when the home team is only one run ahead in the bottom of the ninth—and the other team is at bat. This kind of suspense—call it *"light"* suspense—is fun, desirable, and probably good for you as well; it gets your heart beating, squeezes a little extra adrenalin into your tired bloodstream, exercises your emotional responses, and makes you feel *alive*.

Life is also filled with moments of darker suspense. You have felt that kind of suspense if you have ever sat in a doctor's office, waiting to hear what the lab tests showed about that strange lump you discovered the previous week. It's what you felt during the sickening seconds when, driving in a snowstorm, you lost control of your car and started sliding broadside toward oncoming traffic. It's what you felt all too sharply while waiting for a loved one to come out of emergency surgery. Nobody would argue that this darker brand of suspense is good for you; it strains your heart, breaks your spirit, and every minute of it that you endure probably shaves an hour or two off your life.

Only in fiction do we seek—and benefit from—both light and dark suspense. In books and movies, all suspense is vicarious, so we can experience every shading of it and walk away unharmed. Light suspense—the kind found in movies like Spielberg's *E.T.* and novels like Gregory McDonald's *Fletch* series—is the passive equivalent of taking an especially wild and unusually long roller-coaster ride. Grimmer stories that strike deep into the core fears of the human unconscious—*Aliens* and *Psycho*, Blatty's *The Exorcist* and Stephen King's *The Shining*—may be beneficial because they purge us of the psychological muck that is a residue of getting through life's bad moments. And if the lead characters in such stories have honor and courage—and are portrayed with depth—the tales may also serve as examples of how one can face death, loss, loneliness, and other real-life tragedies with dignity. In other words, suspense fiction can provide both thrills and subtle—heed that word *"subtle"*—moral lessons.

Techniques for building suspense are acquired with practice and developed only over years as the writer learns his craft. However, the following few suggestions, lessons I have learned from more than two decades as a novelist, can save the new writer valuable time as you strive to make your stories more suspenseful.

Don't mistake action for suspense. A good novel must be filled with action, and the characters must be kept in meaningful motion; however, a tale can be composed of one gunfight and wild chase after another yet be totally lacking in suspense. Action becomes suspenseful only if you write with a full understanding of the following two truths: (1) suspense in fiction results primarily from the reader's identification with and concern about lead characters who are complex, convincing, and appealing; and (2) anticipation of violence is infinitely more suspenseful than the violence itself.

One-dimensional characters do not engage the reader's empathy, and if the reader does not worry about what might happen to them, suspense is aborted. For some ideas about how to create compelling and appealing characters, see my other article in this book, "Why Novels of Fear Must Do More than Frighten." As I argue in that piece, well-drawn and likable protagonists are essential if the writer hopes to frighten his readers. Likewise—and for the same reasons—good characterization lies at the heart of suspense.

Anticipation—that is what makes carnival funhouses so popular. Shuffling along pitch-dark corridors, edging across canvas-walled rooms queerly illuminated by black light, the funhouse patron has more fun anticipating the sudden appearance of a ghoul or a demon than he has when the thing actually pops out of a niche in the wall or up from a trap in the floor. Why? Because in the labyrinthine chambers of the human imagination, more bizarre terrors can be conjured than anything one is likely to encounter in real life. The pop-up ghoul, no matter how hideous, can never compare to what one pictures in one's mind while *anticipating* the fiend's assault.

James Cameron's superbly crafted film *Aliens* spends considerably more screen time building the audience's anticipation of monstrous violence than it spends depicting that violence. Tension is heightened every time a character turns a corner or edges warily through a doorway into a new shadowy chamber. Time and again, the slavering beast is not there, but we know that sooner or later it *will* be waiting, and we relish our anticipation of its appearance. When the aliens do attack, the action is furious, intense, electrifying—and quickly finished.

In some ways, the rhythms of exquisitely crafted suspense are akin to the rhythms of good sex: long, slow foreplay . . . followed by gentle and almost lazy lovemaking . . . building steadily and deliciously toward the climax . . . then The Big Moment with its swift and intense release.

My novel *The Voice of the Night* contains a long scene in an auto junkyard that builds suspense by delaying a confrontation between the fourteen-year-old protagonist, Colin, and the fourteen-year-old (and evil) Roy. Pursued through the eerie night landscape of wrecked cars and old rusting trucks, Colin locates an apparently safe haven. I could have had Roy find him within a sentence or two, but I allowed the reader plenty of time to anticipate that development. Poor Colin cowers in his dark hiding place while he listens to Roy hunting for him, and he strains to convince himself that he is safe. Paragraph by paragraph, the reader's tension is heightened because he *knows* that Colin isn't safe and will surely be found. Because the reader likes Colin and fears for him, this is the kind of scene that brings the reader to the edge of his seat.

Consider Stephen King's *The Shining*. In what may be the scariest scene in contemporary horror fiction, five-year-old Danny enters the forbidden Room 217 of the Overlook Hotel, where a rotting but malevolently animated corpse is waiting for him. Does King start the scene with Danny in the room? No way. The scene begins with Danny outside 217, the passkey in his pocket, and he takes more than two hair-raisingly tense pages *just to open the door and step inside*. Anticipation. King makes us sweat. But when Danny finds the dead woman in the bathtub, and when she opens her eyes and reaches for him, the rest of the scene moves like a bullet and climaxes one page later. We are given more time to dread the encounter than to experience it.

In fact, in spite of a wealth of scary scenes and horrendous encounters scattered throughout the book, *The Shining* is essentially one long anticipation sequence. In the very beginning of the book, we know that Jack Torrance is sooner or later going to go after his little boy, Danny, with an ax. But King withholds that ultimate scene of terror for more than four hundred pages, building toward it with such care that it is excruciatingly tense when it finally arrives.

Style is as important as good characterization and anticipation. Stylistic excellence—good grammar, unfaltering syntax, and (most important of all) a strong sense of the rhythms of prose—is an essential ingredient in the creation of the highest-quality suspense. The very flow of the words on the page can lead the reader ever more swiftly toward the climax and generate in him a barely conscious but effective feeling of plummeting through empty space.

Some stylistic techniques for creating that effect are obvious. As the antic-ipation sequence builds toward the moment of violence or the dreaded encoun-ter, the writer sometimes will employ more short sentences, simpler words, shorter clauses and phrases—all of which give the reader a sense of headlong, hellbent forward motion. Likewise, throughout the anticipation sequence and especially as The Big Moment draws near, brief mood- and scene-setting de-scriptions—generally never more than a line or two—can be crafted to generate anxiety in the reader without his quite seeing how it is done. For example, a fall of moonlight could be said to resemble "the milk-pale skin of a drowned wom-an" and a nest of shadows in the corner might be called "sepulchral" or "graveyard-deep." By using words and images of death, you are subliminally encouraging the reader to think that perhaps the lead character is about to die.

In *The Vision,* I used a technique in one scene that was exactly the opposite of shortening sentences to heighten tension. When my lead character encoun-ters the killer, I try to convey the chaos and psychotic frenzy of the attack by writing a large part of it in a single sentence:

> . . . the knife ripped into him, rammed out of the darkness and into him, felt like the blade of a shovel, enormous, devastating, so devastating that he dropped the gun, feeling pain like nothing he'd ever known, and he re-alized that the killer had tossed the flashlight aside as a diversion, hadn't really been hit at all, and the knife was withdrawn from him, and then shoved hard into him again, deep into his stomach, and he thought of Mary and his love for Mary and about how he was letting her down, and he grappled with the killer's head in the dark, got handsful of short hair . . . and the flashlight hit the floor ten feet away, spun around, cast lunatic shadows, and the knife ripped loose from him again, and he reached for the hand that held it, but he missed, and the blade got him a third time, ex-plosive pain, and he staggered back, the man all over him, the blade plunging again, high this time, into his chest, and he realized that the only way he could hope to survive now was to play dead, so he fell, fell hard, and the man stumbled over him, and he heard the man's rapid breathing, and he lay very still, and the man went for the flashlight and came back and looked down at him, stood over him, kicked him in the ribs, and he wanted to cry out but didn't, didn't move and didn't breathe, even though he was screaming inside for breath, so the man turned away and went to-ward the arch, and then there were footsteps on the tower stairs, and, hearing them, he felt like such a useless ass, outsmarted, and he knew he wasn't going to be able to recover his gun and climb those stairs and res-cue Mary because stuff like that was for the movies, pain was pulverizing him, he was leaking all over the floor, dripping like a squeezed fruit, but he told himself he had to try to help her and that he wasn't going to die,

wasn't going to die, wasn't going to die, even though that was exactly what he seemed to be doing.

Stylistic devices can be employed in countless ways to heighten tension and build suspense. To outline only those with which I am familiar, I would need an entire book. The new writer must be aware that style matters, that full control of the language and a profound understanding of its possibilities have at least as much to do with the creation of spellbinding suspense as do chase scenes and battles.

Finally, suspense hinges on the villain. He—or it—must be powerful, a fitting match for the lead characters, possessed of such a great capacity for evil that the reader cannot see how such a beast can possibly be defeated. The villain must be implacable, relentless, unstoppable. Think of Arnold Schwarzenegger in *The Terminator.* Think of Count Dracula. In my *Whispers,* Bruno Frye is a psychopath of almost superhuman dimensions, an embodiment of the chaos that lies at the heart of the universe; he is capable of absolutely anything, so the reader is instantly edgy when Bruno appears.

At the same time, your antagonist must be complex, not a comic-book villain, not Snidely Whiplash; he must possess human dimensions, perhaps admirable qualities as well as flaws. (Unless, of course, you are writing a dark fantasy in which the villain is a demon or some other supernatural entity; but even then, a textured demon is preferable to a one-dimensional funhouse cardboard devil.) The best villains are those that evoke pity and sometimes even genuine sympathy as well as terror. Think of the pathetic aspect of the Frankenstein monster. Think of the poor werewolf, hating what he becomes in the light of the full moon, but incapable of resisting the lycanthropic tides in his own cells.

Suspense cannot be created in a vacuum. It is generated only as a by-product of good characterization, good pacing, an awareness of the value of anticipation as a prelude to action, strong stylistic control, and an ability—and willingness—to write complex characters and complex scenes that encourage the reader to suspend his disbelief and enter fully into the world of make-believe.

Chapter 10

Stepping Into the Shadows

Charles L. Grant

The primary purpose of dark fantasy is to tell a story that will, somewhere along the line, give the reader a chill, a shiver, a good scare. More than one if you can do it. If that doesn't work (and aside from the obvious literary considerations), the story doesn't work; it can't get much simpler than that.

The problem is setting up that situation in order to deliver what you've promised, and it's in the method of delivery where some of us part company. I prefer the threat of the razor to the blow of the bludgeon; I like shadows more than daylight.

To describe *in loving detail* the results of an attack either by a madman or a critter is, to me, an insult to the imagination. I can picture very well, thank you, what a victim looks like with his head chopped off, his arm mangled, his insides spilling out all over the floor. So can most people. It's been bludgeoned, if you will, into us over the past decade by singularly unimaginative television and film directors, and by those writers who have become their unimaginative and untalented slaves.

The reaction such a scene produces is not fear—it's revulsion. And revulsion is not what dark fantasy is all about.

This is not to say, of course, that a well-done shock doesn't belong in your story. It does, if the story's done properly. But it should not be, as it is in many films, the sole reason for the story's existence. Shock, like everything else, is only a tool that you use to create that chill, that shiver, that good scare. When it's appropriate, you use it; when it isn't, don't bother.

There are, I think, three major ingredients for a good dark fantasy, none of which are expendable.

First and foremost are the people you've used to populate your world. The fear you've instilled in your reader then is the result of knowing with or without proof that something terrible *might* happen to someone he likes, or at the very least, doesn't hate. If that character is a thoroughgoing sonofabitch, who cares what's lying in wait for him in the attic? He deserves it. Big deal.

But if you've created sympathy, if not empathy, for one person or another, then you've taken the first major step in developing a nail-biting situation. The key word is *person*; this is a, for the moment, living, real human being, not just a character—a spear-carrier whose sole purpose is to die when the author's ready. In fact, there will be times when someone you really like *will* die, even when you haven't planned it. That's called the story's telling itself, and you're just along for the ride.

So when it happens, planned or not, the emotions react accordingly. And when the reader *cares*, the chills come naturally.

And the chills come because of tension.

Consider a thunderstorm. Watching the sky darken, watching the clouds move in, listening to the thunder working over the horizon, seeing the lightning flare over the tops of far trees—all this creates tension. The air changes, the wind changes, the light changes. You can *feel* a storm. You *know* it's coming your way. And there isn't a damn thing you can do about it.

That's tension, and that's what you want to inflict the reader with. That's what you have to create if you want the reader to feel that chill.

If all hell breaks loose right away, from the opening paragraph, from the opening scene, what's left? Not much, because sooner or later the reader gets used to it; and once that happens, the storm loses all its power.

Lastly is the fantasy itself.

The *dark* fantasy.

I have lamented in more than one place, and at more than one time, the passing of my favorite old-time monsters. They've been trivialized, castrated, psychoanalyzed to oblivion, and otherwise have been pretty much rendered impotent. And while exceptions exist, they are rare.

That doesn't mean that monsters don't exist. You just have to find them. And that's not as difficult as it may seem.

After all, what are monsters but literalizations of what we're afraid of? So . . . what are *you* afraid of? What makes your stomach knot up, your skin turn cold, your throat dry up, your pulse race? What wakes you up in the middle of the night, sweating? What makes you want to crawl under the bed?

Death is the easy answer, so easy it's almost a cop-out, because once it comes there's no coming back. Usually.

But what about those things that don't come just once in a lifetime? What about those things you have to face at least once every day of your life? How about bills, love, relationships, failure, exposure, being different, being conformist? How about sex, machines, growing up, growing old, weakness, motherhood, fatherhood, having power you don't want, not having power you think you want?

It's the easy answer made complex: it's the *unknown*.

And the unknown is, for me, far more frightening when it's a shadow than when it's a Thing. Shadows never stay where they belong, are never the same shape, can go where you go, and come from where you can't go. They can provide shocks as well as any critter, but they also provide a major ingredient of any dark fantasy—tension, which spills into fear.

Literal shadows can, of course, be a cliché. But suppose, for example, you have a young boy, deaf from birth, who wants more than anything to be able to hear his girlfriend's voice. There might be an operation, but his parents can't afford it. And suppose that one evening he "hears" his name. Impossible, but he does. Why? Because the pressures of deafness, and the pressures of simply being a child, and the wishing, and the love . . . well, something's going to give somewhere, especially if the boy gets mad.

Or suppose there's a young man who, like most adolescents (most of us), sooner or later feels that the world is against him, that there are too many rules he doesn't have a say in creating. He's been taught to be a "good boy," and he's also been taught that expressing certain emotions just isn't manly. The more he struggles, then, the greater are the pressures and the more magnified are the injustices he perceives are aligned against him. It doesn't matter that most of these injustices aren't true; they *are true* for him. So he rebels in the only way he can—by creating someone to fight his battles for him.

The first example is a story called "Listen to the Music in My Hands"; the second is a novel, *The Pet*. Both, immodestly, are mine, but they're what I mean when I talk about shadow-pieces, *dark* fantasies, stories that grow out of the fears of their characters. In the short piece, the thunderstorm quite literally remains at the horizon; in the novel, the thunderstorm finally breaks overhead and all hell breaks loose—but not until the end, not until (if I've practiced what I preach) the tension, the people, and the shadows have done the groundwork.

The story, in other words, dictates where you're going to have not only the chills, but also the shocks; and the people dictate what the story will be.

If you work on the people, then, the shadows will do the rest.

Chapter 11

Innocence and Terror— The Heart of Horror

Robert R. McCammon

Let's talk about the tale of terror.

And about one particular tale of terror: in this story, a spirit of the dead hauls its chains up a long, dark staircase, images of the past and future flicker like wind-whipped candlelight, and a man falls wailing upon his own grave.

Of course you've read that tale of terror called "A Christmas Carol," haven't you? Oh, you hadn't ever considered that a horror story? Why not? Because it had a statement to make about the human condition, and tales in the horror genre don't? Well—*wrong!*

In "A Christmas Carol," Charles Dickens used the elements of horror fiction to emphasize characterization and to explore the life of one man in the space of a night. What would that tale be without its three ghosts, its spectral time-traveling, or its unflinching glance beyond the grave?

Unwritten, that's what.

I'm a writer of tales of terror. To me, the beauty and power of horror fiction is that every tale is a reinvention of the struggle between good and evil—and by that I don't mean necessarily the fight between angelic and demon hosts, though God knows that goes on often enough, but also the inner struggle in the heart and mind of everyday people just like you and me.

In horror fiction is the essence of struggle. You create characters and cast them into the wilds of imagination. Some of them fall into tarpits, others are lost in the thicket, but the characters who keep struggling to the final sentence will be smarter and stronger, and so, hopefully, will be the reader. So, is horror fiction just a bag of bloody bones, or does it have meat and brains? I think it's both meaty *and* brainy. If I didn't, I wouldn't be writing this, would I?

I once participated in a seminar called "Morbid Literature." I went knowing what it was going to be like. I wasn't disappointed. The audience was full of people who wanted to know why writers of horror fiction persisted in slopping gore on the page and calling it either entertainment or even readable. They accused me of killing kittens and hating orphans and being an all-around, demented, *bad person* who should not be allowed within a mile of a schoolyard, lest I infect their children with green mindslime. Nothing I could say would make a difference. I talked about "A Christmas Carol," and they screamed "Friday the 13th!" See, those folks had come to talk about morbid literature, and that's *just* what they were going to do.

But they were reacting to a label, confusing fiction with film—and they're two different dragons, believe me—and considering that *horror fiction* by its own tag exists simply to scare the jellybeans out of people, or make them sick, or cause them to run riot in their neighborhoods and wear white socks with black trousers. Horror fiction *is* more than mindless emotion—*isn't* it?

I think it is. The best of it, that is. What other type of writing involves life, death, good, evil, love, hatred, the base and the best, decay and rebirth, sex, God and the Devil? I mean, horror fiction is *IT*! If you consider the authors who've used the elements of horror fiction in their work, your list is going to include H. G. Wells, Edgar Rice Burroughs, Rudyard Kipling, George Orwell, Mark Twain, Sir Arthur Conan Doyle, Edith Wharton, Flannery O'Connor. . . .

Well, you get the idea. I have to use the label *"horror fiction"* for the kind of work I and so many others write simply because we live in a world of categories. But the term *horror fiction* implies writing that socks the bejeezus out of the emotions while leaving the intellect untouched. Horror fiction is perceived as going for the gush of blood and the quick shriek, as a superficial exercise in typing, instead of logically constructed writing; in other words—and I think publishers are at fault for promoting the lowest common denominator—horror fiction is perceived by its critics as about as much of an art form as those sound effects records of screams that appear in the stores every Hallowe'en.

But . . . isn't it kind of *fun* to be scared? I mean, there's nothing *wrong* with writing fiction simply to terrify, is there?

I like to read a good, go-for-the-gory-gusto horror novel every now and then, but they don't stay on my shelves. I read them and toss them out. The novels that stay do *more* than terrify. They resonate with human emotion, thought, and—yes, a kind of innocence—long after the pages are closed.

Some of the horror-fiction titles on my shelves include Charles L. Grant's *The Pet*; Peter Straub's *Shadowland*, and *The Talisman*, written with Stephen

King; Anne Rice's *Interview With The Vampire;* Clive Barker's *The Damnation Game;* and Joan Samson's *The Auctioneer.* There are many, many more, and they stay there because, to me, they're complete worlds between covers, worlds I want to return to and explore again and again. The best of horror fiction contains chills and frights, but it's not constructed around a scream but rather around a solid core of human experience.

Humanity is what's missing from bad horror fiction. How can a reader feel the delicious anticipation of fear if the book has no humanity, if the characters aren't real enough to reach out and touch, if the world that book represents is not detailed and colored and lavished with attention?

When I begin to construct an idea for a novel, I begin with a problem to be solved—not with a list of scares and scenes to be included for the sake of the horror-fiction tag. I began *Mystery Walk* with the thought of flipping the traditional idea of what constitutes good and what constitutes evil. *Usher's Passing* is about a young man's struggle for identity. My newest, *Swan Song,* is about the aftermath of a nuclear holocaust and the subsequent fight for survival. My work-in-progress is about the inhabitants of a southwest Texas town whose way of life is rapidly coming to an end—but, of course, there are horror fiction elements in it because that's what I enjoy reading and that's what I enjoy writing. But I do *not* begin work by outlining a list of scare scenes; those scenes—the good-vs.-evil confrontation scenes—come about in a natural flow of events, not because I've designed the events to satellite around the scenes. Plot, character, atmosphere, setting—all those should be thought out and judged on their merits apart from whether the book is horror fiction or not.

Fiction is, after all, fiction. Good writing is good writing, and bad writing kills a book on page one.

I mentioned *innocence* a little while ago. Innocence in horror fiction? Yep. And by "*innocence*" I mean the author's sense of wonder, at the characters and the setting and even the spooky elements. Without that sense of wonder, a novel goes nowhere. I think most good authors in any genre retain the innocence of a twelve-year-old kid just on the verge of finding out what the world is all about. Those innocent authors can take a reader anywhere, and the reader willingly goes wherever the sentences lead because wonder can *reinvent the world*—and isn't that what reading's all about?

Horror fiction must be more than scares. Yes, it's great to create a good scare, and that can be difficult enough in itself; but the best of horror fiction is about human experience. Maybe it's a kinked view of humanity, and maybe gore splatters the pages here and there, but that's because we're horror writers and it leaks out of our pens on its own. The best of horror fiction is not that bag of bones I spoke about earlier; it's a whole body, complete with beating heart and questing, introspective mind.

So: I think it's neither right nor wrong simply to terrify; yet the works that have no more ambition but *just* to terrify are sorely lacking. You can spot them from the first chapter. The characters are hollow shells designed to ramble around a maze of scare scenes, and they have nothing to say about the human experience because, of course, their creator has nothing to say.

I say, don't sit down to write *horror fiction*. Sit down to write *fiction,* pure and simple. If your voice has a horrific edge, that will come out in your writing and the story will flow naturally. But I've never, never sat down to write a horror novel. I've always simply sat down to write, and what came out is what came out.

And don't be afraid to address complex issues, either. The demon-possessed child, the old dark house, and the crazed-killer-in-a-small-town-hacking-up-prom-queens have lurched off the plot line horizon—and none too soon! I say, dare to be different! Politics, the phone company, computers, urban sprawl, frozen yogurt, *whatever*—a plot is stronger if the writer *feels* strongly about it, if he or she feels something *must* be said before the brain explodes. Urgency, immediacy, strength of conviction—all play a part in designing a plot, no matter what kind of novel you're working on.

Gee, I just heard myself, and I sound like I know everything. I certainly do not. I'm a working writer; that means I'm still learning. I used to think the writing would get easier, the more I did it. I was wrong, It's harder now than ever because I keep pushing myself to write on a deeper, more instinctive level. My first book, *Baal,* was a snap to do. It also is extremely superficial. And aspiring writers, hear this: Your books may stay around a long, long time. In some cases, longer than you'd like them to.

But, of course, there must be beginnings. Without those, where would we be as writers?

Human experience. Detail. Deep characterizations. The innocence of wonder. The risk of writing from the soul. The essence of struggle. All these are important in writing, and all of them elevate a horror novel to the status of a world between covers, waiting to be discovered and rediscovered. They are elements not easily mastered—maybe *never* mastered—but surely worth the effort if we're to continue to learn our craft.

I'm proud to be a writer. My books are called *horror fiction* because no one has yet come up with something more descriptive of what can be humanity's most powerful and expressive literature. I want to do what I can to benefit that body of work.

Writing simply to terrify? Sounds morbid to me. I know where a seminar's being held on that subject, if you care to go.

Chapter 12

World Building in Horror, Occult, and Fantasy Writing

Marion Zimmer Bradley

One of the first things to be done before your write any story that steps out of the most severe, mundane reality is to set the limits of the rules by which your particular game is to be played—the logic of your particular corner of the world, the geography of horror, if you will. The horror writer invades a world of thought which is no less strange (and no less necessarily logical) than the world of the detective story—although the territory of the writer of horror, occult, or supernatural fiction is the territory of the policeman, the priest, or the psychiatrist. Horror can vary from the amusing friends of Oz to the archetypal dreads of Grimm's fairy tales. Horror need not even be fiction. A taste for crude horrors is the stock-in-trade of such tabloids as the *National Enquirer* (Pregnant girl kept in pigsty by parents; Girl of seven years bears Siamese twins; Nine-year-old boy dies in exorcism rites).

Obviously, a horror story need not deal with the supernatural at all; some of the most frightening horror stories have been written entirely excluding supernatural horrors; and we need not call in ghosts or vampires or werewolves to evoke very dreadful horrors indeed.

Dean Koontz's excellent *Whispers* (Putnam, 1968) calls up only the horrors of man's inhumanity to man—rape, multigenerational child abuse, the buried secrets of a psychotic family. Norman Mailer's *The Executioner's Song*, Truman Capote's *In Cold Blood*, the various tales of the Nazi concentration camps, and the various books dealing with the investigations into the mass murders of Theodore Bundy are one well-established field of horror.

No book could be more truly terrible (in the precise sense of the word) than Emlyn Williams's *Beyond Belief* (Random House, 1968), a very graphic account of the Moors Murders in Manchester, England, in the early sixties. Of course, here it is not the book that is dreadful—on the contrary, it is well and even tastefully written—but the matter of which he writes, the original case, makes most psychotic murderers seem pale in contrast. A British friend who covered the trial of Ian Brady and Myra Hindley told me that hardened constables, forty years on Her Majesty's Forces, wept or rushed outside to be sick, on hearing some of the testimony; he assured me that Williams's book had softened the facts considerably. Considering that Brady and Hindley were two young psychopaths who, among other things, murdered children and tape-recorded their dying screams and pleadings of terror, there are some things almost inconceivable to humanity. For that matter, the sensitive person who reads accounts of Chinese foot-binding, or of still-extant pubertal rites in Africa, needs look no further for horror.

These incidents are quite horrible enough, and many writers go through a lifetime of writing horror fiction without calling up any horrors more shocking than those calling for the attention of a policeman or a psychiatrist.

With all of these mundane horrors, demons, ghosts or the supernatural would seem almost superfluous. Yet people have always loved ghost stories; perhaps because they are at liberty to disbelieve in the Devil or the vampire, while the psychotic murderer and the foot-binder, not to mention the Nazi Stormtrooper, are regrettably matters of history.

Horror in everyday life, perhaps, is sufficiently dreadful; all you need then for the purpose of building your world is to do your homework. If your story is, for the sake of argument, set in Providence, Rhode Island, you need obey only the limits of time and space; if your story is set in 1910, it goes without saying that no vehicles except steam trains, suburban trolley cars, and bicycles may be used to move your characters from place to place, and very rarely (for the average citizen) the model A Ford or the monoplane. Commuter jets, television, and rapid transit are still in the future; even radio is a rarity. This creates *isolation* (a prime requirement for many horrors, but hard to accomplish in the eighties). This is why the gothic novel, which flourished up through the forties, is now vanishing; this kind of story, whether horror or merely suspense, relied heavily upon isolating the distressed heroine; the strange old house on the edge of the moor loses much of its horrifying effect when the governess or companion can climb on the first Greyhound out of the place, or call 911 for anything from an ambulance to a SWAT team.

On the other hand, once the unknown enters the story, a new world must be created with its own parameters. Every world has its own rules. To put it as simply as possible, we do not use the wonders of modern technology (except perhaps for the contrast of shock) in a story that deals with ghosts and witches; a scientific background destroys the credibility of such beings, and if they are to coexist in your story, either the scientists must be convinced of the existence of the supernatural (that's one good story), or the apparently supernatural must be explained away as the result of a fraud or confidence trick (and that's another kind of good story). It's been done by John Dickson Carr (*The Three Coffins* is the classic example, but he'd written that same story many times).

But even if you decide that your story will deal with the supernatural, that a "real" ghost, poltergeist, vampire, werewolf, or what-have-you will play a part in your story and *not* be explained away as an illusion or a fraud, you don't simply throw the door open to unreason and abandon all the rules; if that were so, the story would suffer from the insurmountable problems.

Take, for instance, the early "Superman" comics. I remember reading, years ago, that they had a great deal of difficulty finding stories because they'd established that Superman could literally do *anything;* there was no real conflict in the stories because nobody else had a fair chance against him! Only by introducing something that set limits on Superman's power, introducing some real suspense—"How will he get out of this one?"—with the element Kryptonite, which could endanger or kill him, did it become feasible to write real stories with real challenges for Clark Kent and his awesome alter ego.

Because the original Superman, like the Devil—and that will be discussed later—was omnipotent; the cards were inexorably stacked against *anyone* who went up against him; and while of course nobody wants the bad guys to win, if it's absolutely predetermined that "Nothing's going to happen to him; he's the hero," it does destroy suspense. One of the horror-inducing things of the traditional horror story dealing with the supernatural as the province of the Devil is that in traditional tales of diabolism, the Devil is literally omnipotent in human terms and there is no recourse except by direct intervention of God—and this makes for poor fiction.

So if you are going to have, say, vampires, you must know the rules under which the vampire, or your particular vampire, operates—the logic of the existence of vampires.

About the best way to understand this (at least, about vampires) is to read the splendid chapter in *Dracula* in which Dr. Van Helsing explains that, far from being a free spirit, the vampire is "even more prisoner than the slave in his galley, the madman in his cell." All writers or would-be writers of supernatural subjects should read this chapter; it is as carefully reasoned a piece of work as ever came from the rational pen of Conan Doyle constructing the logic of Sherlock Holmes.

In *Dracula,* after an awesome summing-up of Dracula's supernatural powers, Van Helsing concludes:

He can do all these things and yet he is not free; he is more prisoner than the slave in his galley, the madman in his cell. He cannot go where he lists; he who is not of nature has yet to obey certain of nature's laws—why, we know not. He may not enter anywhere at the first unless there be some one of the household who bid him come, though after he may come as he pleases. His power ceases, as does that of all evil things, at the coming of the day. Only at certain times can he have limited freedom. If he be not at the place whither he is bound, he can only change himself [presumably from wolf or bat form] at noon or at exact sunrise or sunset . . . whereas he can do as he will within his limit, when he have his earth-home, his coffin home, his hell-home, the place unhallowed, as when he went to the suicide's grave at Whitby, still at other time he can only change when the time come; it is said too that he can only pass running water at the exact slack or flood of the tide. Then there are things which so afflict him that he has no power; the garlic that we know, and as for things sacred, this symbol, my crucifix, . . . to them he is nothing, but in their presence he make himself small, he take his place far off and silent with respect . . . the branch of wild rose on his coffin keep him so that he move not from it, the sacred bullet fired into his coffin kill him so that he be true dead.

This kind of setting of limits is *indispensable for all supernatural, or apparently supernatural, beings;* an understanding of *the laws by which they exist.* For instance, if your ghosts can (and do) walk through walls, what is the explanation for why they don't fall through the floor?

Chelsea Quinn Yarbro in her excellent series about a modern and apparently immortal vampire, St. Germain, has given *her* vampire a number of powers the original Dracula never enjoyed; but she too has played by the rules; the vampire St. Germain can, for instance, cross water if he can find a bridge or boat, but he lines his shoes with a layer, inside the soles, of his native earth. Even vampires live by their own laws, and so do wizards. A wizard who can solve every problem by waving his magic wand and saying "Poof—you're a frog" is unsatisfying. A splendid explanation of wizards and the limits of their powers is set forth in Ursula LeGuin's *A Wizard of Earthsea* (Atheneum Press, 1962).

Whether you use traditional werewolves or African leopard-men (and they do not live by the same laws of magic), they too operate under whatever laws give rules to their existence.

The most satisfactory way to create supernatural fantasy is, paradoxically, by taking a pragmatic stance; if these things *exist,* they are therefore, q.e.d., not supernatural; rather, they belong to a part of nature whose laws we do not yet *understand.* This attitude can lend strength and credibility to almost all the creatures of the so-called supernatural.

It is in fact the only defense against the too-common attitude that anything unknown or mysterious is absolutely from the Devil and therefore invincible in human terms. It must not even be investigated or inquired into by the faithful, nor may any defense be sought against it except prayer.

This, of course, is one way to build a special world for your horror or fantasy fiction; the simplistic one that the unknown, supernatural or extraterrestrial, is directly Satanic. For readers who do not wish to stretch their minds very far, or who have very strong religious convictions, this is the safest way to write. If it is outside what's loosely called "God's laws," it is, of course, from the Devil and there can be no compromise for writer or reader, no moral choice; this unknown represents *evil,* and there's no use discussing it.

This is the world in which we find such very popular novels and films as *The Exorcist* or *Rosemary's Baby.* There is no question here of moral choices; the unknown represents *absolute evil.* One simply does not play with or inquire into anything coming from the Devil or take any attitude about it except fear— or prayer. Like a monster in the 1940s science-fiction films, it is there for only one purpose—to be destroyed. In these films, there is never any question of finding out what or who the monster is; nobody asks questions; as a rose is a rose is a rose, a monster is a monster is a monster, and it's evil because it's evil because it's evil, and that's *that.* There's no compromise or investigation; the answer is to call out the Marines and kill it—quick!

On the other hand, this approach has always been unsatisfying to me. As a further quibble, at least one reader was deeply offended by the confusion, in *Rosemary's Baby,* of witches with Satan-worshippers. In this modern world, many people choose to believe or take the stance (perhaps more appealing to modern reason) that witches were (and are) simply followers of a pre-Christian (not necessarily anti-Christian) nature worship, who, far from worshipping the (or *a*) Devil, don't even believe such things exist.

Once you throw out the concept that the unknown is always diabolical, you are free to make what rules you choose. For instance, if your house is haunted, instead of believing that the only answer is to call up a priest and cast out Satan (with or without the rites of exorcism) your characters can attempt other means of solving their problem. In the classic ghost story of Dorothy MacArdle, *The Uninvited* (written about 1936), a brother and sister whose house is still occupied by the former tenant, choose instead to find out *why* this unhappy spirit is staying in their house, and how to persuade her to leave. This approach has also created the excellent novels of Barbara Michaels and many others, including my own novel *The Inheritor* (Tor Books, 1985).

Of course, only the author can choose whether his characters are to live in a world of absolute reality, where the only demons are those within the minds and hearts of man in the material universe—or in a world where God allows Satan to torment his creation—or in what Stuart Edward White, writing on parapsychology, chose to call *The Unobstructed Universe.*

The major choice, then, for the writer of horror, fiction or nonfiction, is to choose between limited and unlimited views of reality—the horrors of the tabloid writer, the true-crime addict, or the specialist in abnormal psychiatry, whether or not the unknown belongs to a different order of reality—to choose between the worlds, in fact, of the policeman, the priest, or the parapsychologist.

Or you may choose to invent a world beyond any of these; but it too must have its own rules, and you must make them clear, or your story will never convince anyone—far less scare them.

As one of the greatest of all supernatural-horror writers stated—in fact, he wrote the book about it—(H. P. Lovecraft, *Supernatural Horror in Literature;* Arkham House, 1927):

> Any magazine-cover hack can splash paint around wildly and call it a nightmare, or a witches sabbath or a portrait of the devil; but only a great painter can make such a thing really *scare* or ring true. That's because only a real artist knows the anatomy of the terrible, or the physiology of fear.[1]

And this is true of the horror writer; if he is to chill or convince, he must know the anatomy, the physiology, and the psychology of the terrible, the frightening; the geography and sociology of fear, what will make the spine prickle rather than merely making the gorge rise. The more realistic your horrors—in fact, the closer the reader comes to believing that your werewolf, ghost or vampire could really exist, as we all know the Nazi concentration camp guard or the chainsaw murderer could exist—the more effectively the world of your own horror tales will be constructed.

---

1. H. P. Lovecraft, "Pickman's Model," *The Outsider and Others* (Arkham House, 1927).

Chapter 13

Sword and Sorcery, Dragon and Princess

Darrell Schweitzer

Sword-and-sorcery fiction is to fantasy what the western is to the historical novel, or, perhaps more precisely, what the hardboiled-private-eye story is to mystery fiction. It is a subgenre based on a prefabricated image, without which it cannot be identified at all: the cowboy in the middle of the dusty street, ready to draw; the private eye in the trenchcoat; the brawny, scantily-clad swordsman, glaring defiantly at menaces supernatural and otherwise, with an even less-clad, shapely wench cowering somewhere in the background.

Any writer needs to approach this sort of fiction with caution and with some sophistication. If you aren't already an enthusiast, if you have to be *told* what is meant by a western or a hard-boiled-detective novel or sword and sorcery, then you probably have no business writing in those fields. If you have no specific *use* for the subgenre-defining characteristics of these particular varieties of popular fiction, then you will be hard pressed to produce anything more than just recycled clichés, which no editor anywhere wants.

But the reader expects and demands these clichés when turning to westerns or hardboiled detectives or s&s (as aficionados are wont to abbreviate what Sprague de Camp calls "the Sacred Genre"); so even if you know what you're doing, it's a tricky business indeed.

The comparison with the hardboiled detective story bears closer examination. There were mysteries, series detectives, and crime stories before Dashiell Hammett created Sam Spade; but somehow, afterward, with a lot of help from

Raymond Chandler's Philip Marlowe, a new kind of detective story was born, defined by the *type* of *detective*. We could crudely say it is a genre about guys like Sam Spade.

Similarly, sword and sorcery is about guys like Conan. There had been fantasy fiction for a very long time before Robert E. Howard (1906-1936) first wrote of his famous Barbarian, and even fantasy with heroic heroes, imaginary lands, dragons, princesses, evil wizards, and all the rest. These ingredients can be found in the beautiful, art nouveau fantasies of Lord Dunsany published before the First World War, but it is only with Conan that the sword-and-sorcery story became a distinct phenomenon.

Conan is a romantic primitive, like Tarzan, save that his homeland of Cimmeria is on about the level of the Scandinavia of the Vikings. He is a huge, brawling warrior, who ventures into the quasi-medieval, civilized realms of his Hyborian Age, occupying himself first as a thief, then a mercenary soldier, and finally seizing the throne of a kingdom for himself. In the course of all this, he has vast numbers of supernatural adventures, rescuing maidens, slaying monsters and wizards, filching treasure from demon-haunted tombs, and so on.

Robert Howard's early death did not bring an end to reader demand for this sort of thing. Fritz Leiber played the role of Chandler, raising the new category to a more sophisticated level with his Fafhrd and Grey Mouser series.

Fafhrd is Leiber's barbarian, a similarly hard-drinking, hard-wenching lunk, but by no means stupid; he has a sidekick in the smaller, city-slick Mouser. Their adventures are great fun, cynical, filled with startling events, from which the duo usually manage to emerge unscathed, if not always the wiser or the richer. (*An important point:* If your series character manages to *keep* that vast hoard of loot he's been chasing after, then he'll settle down, not have any more adventures, and that is the end of the series. So sword-and-sorcery characters tend to be footloose, irresponsible, and, in the end, financially unlucky.)

The sword-and-sorcery story depends on three elements, which *must* be in every story: (1) an imaginary, pregunpowder setting, usually based on medieval or ancient societies; (2) magic; and (3) a vigorous, heroic warrior as a central character. He or she *must* be a warrior. You could have a story about magic and imaginary lands in which the protagonist is a shoemaker, but while that would be fantasy, it wouldn't be what most readers and editors mean by *sword* and *sorcery*.

This is not to say that all heroes must be large, barbaric sorts like Conan. Michael Moorcock, L. Sprague de Camp, and others have greatly extended the boundaries of the genre. And, despite the presence of obligatory, stock elements, there is no pure sword-and-sorcery *formula*.

If you want to write the truly clichéd sword-and-sorcery story, remember the following sequence of events: barbarian encounters wizard; barbarian is temporarily overcome by wizard; barbarian kills wizard and wins loot/the princess/or just freedom from wizardly meddling. But that's a sure way of getting rejected! Be original within the standard framework. Tough-guy detective stories don't all have the plot of *The Maltese Falcon,* now, do they?

Here are a few pointers for swordly-and-sorcerous fiction:

Use plain language. Sword and sorcery attempts to combine the vigor of the slam-bang adventure story with the heroic grandeur of the old epics: *Beowulf, The Song of Roland,* and the like. William Morris (1834-1896), one of the great predecessors of the genre, came very close to approximating the language of medieval romance in such fantasy-quest novels as *The Well at the World's End.* But for most writers since, the use of *high* or deliberately archaic style has been a trap. Aye, if ye do scribe like this when chronicling the days of adventure, mayhap thou'lt sound more like a Monty Python impersonation of Long John Silver than a barbaric bard of yore.

Robert Howard wrote in clear, vigorous prose, with colorful descriptions and a lot of action verbs. This remains the more useful approach.

Make sure you know what a barbarian is. On a broader note, make sure the societies you depict make sense. A common fault of such stories is that they seem to take place in a world consisting of swordsmen, sorcerers, maybe a king or two, shapely wenches, *and no one else.* Who forges the swords? Who grows the food? Who builds the castles? More specifically, de Camp defines a *barbarian* as someone in that stage of cultural development between hunter-gatherer and city-building. Barbarians are usually farmers or herdsmen. They live in taboo-ridden, tribal societies, usually in villages. They are typically attracted to the richer, more interesting lands of civilized men, for all civilization may be bewildering to them. If they arrive at the right moment, when the civilization is breaking down, they can take over. The model barbarians from history—usually evoked by sword-and-sorcery fiction—are the Germans of various sorts, Ostrogoths, Visigoths, Vandals, and the like, who overran the Western Roman Empire in the fifth century A.D. The best historical model for Conan himself is the third-century Maximin the Thracian, a gigantic, illiterate herdsman who came to the attention of the Roman Emperor Septimius Severus because of his strength, got a job in the imperial bodyguard, rose through the ranks, and, when the time was ripe, seized the throne from one of his sponsor's weaker successors. Maximin, like the usurping Conan in Howard's writings, soon found the imperial couch no bed of roses. Reviled because he was a crude foreigner and a usurper, nearly everyone soon plotted against Maximin. Unlike Conan, he did not survive.

Ancient and medieval history abounds in examples like this, which the sword-and-sorcery writer can barbarously loot for greater realism! The important element here is not *detail* but the character portrait. Maximin, the huge barbarian, probably became increasingly cynical as he lived among decadent, civilized men. (Indeed, Howard makes much of the alleged pure and simple virtues of the barbarian.) For all he dressed like a Roman, spoke Latin, and had a Roman name, he could not *be* a Roman, which is why he was never accepted by the people of the Empire. He ended up with a pathological fear of ridicule. Since sword-and-sorcery fiction tends to be upbeat and escapist, an obvious possibility would be that the usurping barbarian-emperor somehow manages to chuck it all and revert to his former state, the plot of the story growing from the resultant complications. Howard's King Conan *thinks* about reverting, but ultimately accepts his responsibilities.

Learn the rudiments of swordly combat. In other words, get the physical details right. Poul Anderson wrote a whole essay on this subject, "On Thud and Blunder," in which he explains why no one swings a fifty-pound sword or rides a horse at a full gallop all day. It is required reading. But for basic research, a book on the history of arms and armor would make a good beginning. If your story is to feature hand-to-hand combat, or maybe even battles between armies, you must make these things convincing. Learn the difference between a broadsword and a rapier. Learn what a pike is for. Mark Twain, in lambasting Fenimore Cooper, once stated that one of the Rules of writing "Romantic" (i.e., adventure) fiction is that "crass stupidities shall not be played upon the reader." This applies to sword and sorcery, too.

Make sure the magic is an integral part of the story. A sword-and-sorcery story, as the name implies, is about *sorcery* just as much as it is about swordsmanship. It is not a sloppy historical swashbuckler with the history left out, but a tale of wonders. As with any other sort of fantastic fiction, the fantastic element should be so central to the plot that, if the fantasy were removed, there would be no story left. A sword-and-sorcery story consisting of mundane adventures and murders, then one brief fight with a giant snake at the end, is sure to be unsatisfying. In one of the very best Conan adventures, the novel *Conan the Conquerer,* disgruntled noblemen plot to depose King Conan by resurrecting a long-dead sorcerer of awesome power. But complications ensue. The sorcerer has ideas of his own and plans to restore his own ancient kingdom; the magic jewel employed by the plotters, like Tolkien's One Ring, seems to have ideas of *its* own and moves from owner to owner, propelled by an obscure destiny. The novel is thus far more than mere politics in an imaginary kingdom.

Keep the magic both limited and consistent. Someone commented wisely that if *anything* can happen in a story, no one cares what does. While it isn't necessary (but sometimes can be interesting) to work out the rules of your magic as if it were an alternate science, it still has to make sense. If the Flaming Jewel of Fnong works its magic only after someone has been killed, you can have a suspenseful scene when the hero and friends *have* to use that jewel and there is no one convenient to kill; but the suspense would be completely destroyed if, just this once, the jewel did its thing without help. Similarly, magic-wielding characters must have limitations. If the wizard-villain is all-powerful, how can the hero plausibly slay him?

A word about heroines. The stereotypical sword-and-sorcery woman has always been a wilting thing, good for nothing except rescuing. Howard himself opposed this convention and created several very capable female characters. About the same time, Catherine L. Moore wrote a popular series about a medieval swordswoman, Jirel of Joiry. Today there exists a whole school of feminist sword and sorcery, featuring brawny swordspersons who are just as much female wish-fulfillments as Conan is a male one. Follow your own inclinations on this. If your story needs a wimp to be rescued, then so be it. But don't feel obligated to so characterize females.

You need an action plot. Sword and sorcery is not a field of deep psychological introspection. This is not what the readership comes to sword-and-sorcery stories for. Try for overt conflicts, plenty of physical action, and rapid plot movement. That is, if they're plotting to overthrow the barbarian king in chapter one, by chapter two, the palace should be invaded by Serpent Men of Valusia, and in chapter three, the hero is magically whisked away to the Black Crypt of N'Kai. You get the idea.

Sword and sorcery is essentially daydream fiction. There is nothing wrong with that. (The only people opposed to escape are jailers.) Its appeal is that of bright, colorful action, with menaces, marvels, and larger-than-life characters. At the same time, it doesn't have to be brainless. Often a little levity is in order, as in the witty writings of de Camp and Leiber. If you don't enjoy it, don't try to write it cynically, because the result *will* be brainless, not to mention dull. The best sword and sorcery is exciting, flashy fun. The field is by no means exhausted. There is room enough for your own, original contribution.

Chapter 14

Science Fiction: Hard Science and Hard Conflict

Michael A. Banks

I've long suspected that the reason there are relatively few active science-fiction writers in the world (as compared with, say, romance writers or mainstream or action/adventure writers) has very little to do with market conditions or writing ability. Certainly the basic elements of fiction apply to all genres equally, and the successful mainstream or other *genre* fiction writer ought to be able to do equally well in science fiction by applying his fiction-writing craft to the field.

It doesn't work that way. Otherwise-fine writers just won't touch science fiction because the first word in *science fiction* scares them off. It's difficult enough to put together a short story or novel without having to worry about technical background, right? That's work, and many writers would rather leave those research-required projects to the likes of Arthur Hailey or James Michener.

There's no doubt that science is a necessary element in science fiction—be it as background or the source of conflict. Today's market all but demands believable high-tech and hard science. This is not to say that the science part supersedes the fiction part, but you aren't going to write successful science fiction without science.

Oh, sure—Harlan Ellison succeeds without resorting to detailed explanations of (and sometimes without justification for) the science in his stories. Ray Bradbury's work is much the same way. These authors, however, write with such fine style and technique that readers *want* to believe their worlds are possible.

There is limited room in the science-fiction marketplace for stories and situations that lend themselves to a nontechnical approach. And few writers write at such a level. So, if you're going to write science fiction, you'll most likely need science.

Whether you're a beginning writer or not, you may well be intimidated by the prospect of having to research the technical and scientific background in your work. You shouldn't be, for this reason: science is *simple*.

To which you may well reply, "Yeah. That's easy for you to say. You probably have a degree in physics or some such."

Surprise—I don't. My post-secondary *formal* education consists of a few credit hours in a pre-engineering program, followed by a lot of hands-on engineering and technician-level training. The bulk of my scientific knowledge is self-taught. Nor do many of my science-fiction-novel-writing friends who routinely knock down five-figure advances have heavy scientific backgrounds. I won't blow their covers here by naming names, but several of them also work in auto assembly plants, teach high school English, or sell.farm equipment.

It is no accident that a significant number of the several hundred science-fiction writers in print today are working engineers or scientists, or academics with the proper resources for researching the science in their fiction. But you don't have to *be* a scientist to write hard science fiction.

You *do* need a technical orientation. Your interest in writing hard science fiction implies that orientation, so you should have no problems in that area.

And how do you get the science into your science fiction, without having a technical background? There are three stages, two of which, you'll be happy to know, have little to do with scientific training or knowledge.

STAGE ONE

The first stage is determining how technical you'll need to get in a story or novel. This is partly intuitive and partly dependent upon whether the science is to be background or a part of the conflict. If the science is simple background, you needn't stress it much more than you would, say, local color in a story set in New England, or airplanes in an aviation setting. You need just enough to give the story the proper flavor.

And how much is enough for flavor? Well, every story (or novel) is different, so there are really no procedural guidelines. I suggest that you look for works with situations and settings similar to yours, and follow the lead of those works.

I also suggest that you mentally translate your *approach* to presenting futuristic science and technology to a contemporary milieu. To illustrate, if you are using space travel as a background, you are probably safe to detail space travel about as much as air travel might be detailed in a contemporary novel—with a touch more detailing. More detail is necessary because you are frequently showing the reader things that don't exist. You'll have to depend on intuition to tell you just how far you can go without being a bore. (For an excellent example of this type of detailing, read Robert A. Heinlein's novel *Friday*. Heinlein not only gets the science into the story, but also does it in a nonintrusive and truly entertaining manner.)

If the science is to be part of the conflict, you'll have to take it quite a bit further. Because conflict is so closely tied to characterization, motivation, and the overall success of plot, you will have to give the science behind a conflict as much attention as you would any of the other basic story elements.

I learned this when I was writing a series of stories involving some madcap inventors who accidentally invent antigravity devices, matter transmitters, and other devices. In this series, it was important to explain the scientific elements clearly, because without them the conflict could not exist. When I submitted the first two stories, the editors returned them with requests for more scientific detail. Not coincidentally, after I had fleshed out the basis for the conflicts with scientific detail, both stories had more depth.

These two stories (and the others in the series) happen to be the ones that readers remember when they meet me for the first time. What makes them so memorable is not the science but the characters and the plots—which, of course, are partly derived from conflict, which in turn depends heavily on the science.

(For the curious, the stories are "Horseless Carriage," which first appeared in the June/July 1978 issue of *Isaac Asimov's Science Fiction Magazine* and has been reprinted several times since; and "The Tie That Binds," which appeared in *Analog* in August 1981.)

STAGE TWO

After determining just how much scientific background is required, you must acquire the knowledge necessary to create that background. This is the area in which the scientists are one up on you. Fortunately, gathering scientific information can be a relatively painless undertaking, given the proper approach. It can also be less time-consuming than you might think.

If you read as voraciously as I (and most science-fiction readers) do, you may already have the knowledge you need. The human brain can be a storehouse of oddball facts in a variety of fields, and it functions as a relational data base, stringing this information together in a variety of ways. Thus, it frequently happens that we know more about a topic than we realize. For me, this means that I have somehow picked up the knowledge I need, in many cases, and don't need to research a scientific topic. At the very least, I find that I usually have enough background to guide myself through the research and to understand the results.

As far as the actual research is concerned, there are two ways to get it done—do it yourself, or have someone do it for you. I prefer the latter method.

Being active in attending science-fiction conventions, writers' workshops, and scientific meetings, I meet a lot of people, more than a few of whom are scientists or engineers. When I need to do some research, I flip through my mental address book (and my collection of business cards) in search of someone who might know what I need to know. If I don't find the expert I need among my acquaintances, I may check the appropriate department at the local university.

I then visit, telephone, or write the expert and outline what I'm doing. I don't ask the expert to tell me everything about his field; I can get that out of a few months' reading. Rather, I let my consultant know exactly what I'm doing so that he can see my points of inquiry in context and thus isolate exactly what I need to know. With this approach, I usually learn more than I thought I wanted to know—which always turns out to be exactly what I *needed*. A few questions clear up any gray areas, and that's that. If my expert can't tell me everything I need, he tells me just where to find it, saving me a lot of time and effort and freeing me to concentrate on the story itself.

Reading contemporary hard science fiction is another convenient way to have part of your research done for you. You will want to check to make sure that this year's science hasn't dated last year's science fiction, however.

I undertake a full-blown research project only as a last resort. If I can't find the appropriate expert, if the topic does not lend itself to query-type research, or if the project requires a truly in-depth understanding of the field, I head for the local library. With the help of the card catalog, *Books In Print, The Reader's Guide to Periodical Literature,* and the librarian, I generate a reading list and take it from there. My list leads me to professional journals and societies, on-the-spot investigation, and eventually, back to the experts.

I also try to get my hands on any technology involved, and if the project is a big one, visit any research locations. Consulting an expert can open doors in this area, too.

STAGE THREE

Now for the prize question: How do you work the science into the fiction without being obvious? Well, it's a lot like developing a character, which is to say the reader should learn about and/or experience story background in the same manner as he would in real life.

The ground rules are simple: Don't tell the reader everything you know, and don't dump the information you do use on the reader all at once.

There are two reasons you must not tell the reader everything you know. The first is simply that no one reads science fiction just for the science. The second is that a story is told from a character's viewpoint, and that character is very unlikely to be thinking about the scientific and technical details of his environment (unless the plot calls for it).

Quite simply, if you overload a story with detail, you are going to lose the illusion of fiction. So, if you are writing about an Earth-to-Moon shuttle flight, don't go into how Newton's laws apply to space flight, or how hydrazine and liquid oxygen interact. That would be as out of place as discussing Bernoulli's Principle in describing an airliner in a mainstream story. Use only detail that adds necessary color, moves the plot, or helps the reader understand story events, characters, or background. (The Stage-One process of determining how detailed your background will be will eliminate quite a bit of extraneous information in advance.)

The folly of pushing all of the science on the reader at one time should be obvious. Stories and novels follow certain forms, and none of those forms include unbroken descriptive background. The reader wants to learn, to be sure, but he wants to be entertained along the way.

Full narrative backgrounding, with a suitable transition, is possible, but it should be a last resort. Although it's easy to do, it is like the infamous background chapters in Victorian novels—deadly dull. (Robert A. Heinlein uses narrative backgrounding to good effect in *The Day After Tomorrow;* an entire chapter is devoted to a primer in genetics. This example, however, is a rare exception.)

As for actual backgrounding techniques, they are many and varied. The most obvious technique is to have one character explain a scientific process or procedure to another. Unfortunately, the technique is easily spotted by readers (and thus disruptive to the story), especially if you write something like this: "Well, Bill, you already know how the teleportation system works, but allow me to refresh your memory. . . ."

If at all possible, avoid contriving a scene to explain things to the reader. If you must fall back on this technique, make sure your characters have more reason to discuss details than merely informing the reader. You might, for instance, have a character who is being trained in the use of certain equipment, or an important scene might involve a demonstration of a new scientific device.

A better technique is the narrative flashback, in which a character's recollections segue into a minihistory by association. For examples of how this is done, read Larry Niven's *Ringworld* or Frederik Pohl's *Gateway.*

Perhaps the best technique of all is to bring your science into the story the same way you do other background—by *showing* it, rather than describing it. Have your characters use the science and technology surrounding them, and allow them to react to and discuss it naturally, as story situations dictate.

Science + Fiction = Science Fiction

Unless it generates conflict, the science in your story should be no more visible than are televisions, houses, airplanes, or weather in a mainstream story. After all, one of the major elements that draws readers to science fiction is the thrill of dealing with strange, new, and exciting concepts on an everyday basis.

Keep your science on that level. Don't flaunt it too heavily, and don't hide it out of ignorance. Science fiction that merges science into the story, rather than using it as a prop or putting it on display, is the most satisfying to write and to read.

Chapter 15

Researching Science Fantasy

Sharon Baker

Imagination is a crucial ingredient in a science-fantasy novel—any novel. But imagination's complement, I think, is a plausible background. Together they give fiction the weight and shape and edges of reality.

Sometimes, one can sink into a story and accept very odd happenings because they take place in a familiar framework. My second science-fiction novel, *Journey to Membliar,* has the hoary form of the picaresque tale. It's also a love story in which the charming, untrustworthy hero, fairly innocent heroine, and a small boy go from point A in the highlands to point Z in the lowlands, seeing many strange people and things along the way. Also according to literary tradition, the three are changed by what they see.

How can science fantasy's odd events (and sometimes odd people) be made acceptable whatever the form of their story? I check them against their earthly parallels. What I find often changes and enriches my tale, though I may need to temper reality to avoid horrifying the reader. I use secondary sources when I must, primary ones when I can, and try to look at pivotal facts from at least three angles. Here's an example of how I work:

Since the heroes of my first novel, *Quarrelling, They Met the Dragon,* are slaves, as are the hero and heroine of my second novel, *Journey to Membliar,* I investigated slavery. Slaves being in short supply in Seattle, I looked through books like Stamp's *The Peculiar Institution* and Patterson's *Slavery and Social Death;* I talked to acquaintances of the slaves of our Pacific Northwest Indians; still, I needed someone to answer other questions. (How does it feel, how does it taste, how does it smell? Do you ever despair? What kind of dreams do you have? What do you love about your life? What makes you angry? How does it feel to be you?) Then I thought, There are white slaves—prostitutes.

So I followed a Seattle vice cop on his rounds. I talked to street kids as young as ten who sold themselves to live. A friend who had hustled gave me an adult's view of what they told me. Touched by these runaways' plight and fascinated, I questioned outreach social workers, an anthropologist doing a study on juvenile male prostitution for the National Institute of Mental Health, read her bibliography, and did a MedLine search on male prostitution. My story changed. *Quarrelling's* hero became a street kid and a hustler but half a galaxy away; *Membliar's* hero, a courtesan.

These people's realities went into my books. A college-educated man whom I talked to in jail said that after his first act of prostitution he went home, washed, shaved, and combed his hair. Then he met his own eyes in the mirror. In *Journey,* my hero tells the heroine, "The following dawn when my—admirers—returned me to the great sleep chamber I shared with the other students, before I crawled onto my pallet I bathed. I dressed. Last, I met my eyes in my new, polished gold mirror."

I used similar techniques for *Quarrelling's* physician, whose husband and child were killed by countrymen of the boy she is forced to heal. I used them with *Quarrelling's* rape. But as T. S. Eliot has remarked, "Human kind cannot bear very much reality." So I skimped on detail. And only five men attacked my hero on Naphar. Here, an imprisoned Quaker war protestor had sixty assailants.

More than characters need to be made real in science fantasy. Their languages should sound authentic, too. So their words will seem related, I choose words that *are* related. Since my world is like our ancient Middle East between ice ages, as described in the Cambridge Ancient History series, I use our ancient Middle East's Semitic languages and add research's partner, my imagination. Culled from archaeological monographs, books, and lectures, the words I find often have no vowels. I add my own. If one is complete, I'll use my own spelling, pronunciation, and interpretation.

For example, *Naphar,* the name of my planet, is from the Cretan for *total.* When the Cretans used that word in the palace at Knossos, they meant the total number of jars in a storage bin. I mean, *Total. The world, complete. Ecosystems and souls in harmony.* An ideal, in other words, on Naphar, as on earth, that perhaps not all of its inhabitants live up to. *Kakano,* my word for the small people of Naphar, comes from the Cretan for *small* or *star. Rabu,* my word for the large people twice their size, is from the Babylonian for *big.* The Napharese drink wine. In Minoan it's *ya-ne,* in related civilizations it's *yayn* or *yen,* and in Ugaritic it's *yan.* I prefer the Ugaritic form, but since Napharese wine is different from earthly wine, I spell it *yiann.*

The difference in Napharese wine is, perhaps, typical of the differences in all my planet's vegetation. Though it may be unusual, an earthly botanist should not find it impossible.

Yiann is blue and filled with sparks that shoot from the mouths of freshly broached jugs. Squeezed from songfruit grown at the edge of a luminous river, the juice is fermented with a yeast that picks up luciferin from the river's chemiluminescent organisms osmosed by the songfruit plants. When the jug is opened, the luciferan combines with oxygen with the help of an enzyme, luciferase, to spark (with almost one hundred percent efficient radiant energy) with cool blue lights. Since Napharese air, like ours, holds a lot of oxygen to keep the organisms winking, undrunk yiann, unlike champagne, doesn't go flat. (The *Encyclopaedia Britannica* helped with this explanation.)

Not all of Naphar's plants are so benign—it also has the Death Flowers of Membliar. Man-sized, they're really fungi. When I found them in *Smithsonian Magazine* (where they're a few centimeters high and prey on bugs and rodents), I immediately invented a lovable alien to use them on. The alien is a kotellue—an affectionate but not-very-bright black-and-white lizard built like a chubby Boston Terrier. Here are the Death Flowers:

> In the center of the moonlit glade stood a ring of pale, motionless flowers. A breeze sighed across the grass, flattening it to silver, but the luminous blooms and their stems never moved.

The flowers call with pheromones. I imagine their victims smell their favorite foods and try to eat the flowers:

> The kotellue braced its forelegs against a white slender stem. It broke with a tiny pop. Its bell-shaped flower tipped; spores showered into the moonlight, covering the little lizard and the ground like snow.

The eaten and inhaled spores mature swiftly:

> Each stiff white blossom grew from a skull. . . . Bleached, eyeless, they stared at the sky, ribs pushed wide by the roots of the lovely, insatiable plants.

Besides being deadly, some Napharese flora is useful. It can be eaten—and used for poison. In *Journey,* the villain makes a contact poison similar to ricin, the castor bean derivative in the umbrella that killed a Bulgarian defector in the late 1970s in London. Oddly, neither my book on future weapons nor my toxicology book had ricin's effect. I found it in the *Merck Manual,* a physicians' encyclopedia of symptoms and their treatments. Here's part of its recipe and impact:

The troops ground and pressed blackened seeds to remove their oils, then soaked the resulting cakes of contact poison in salted water, filtering them through silken cloths held gingerly by the hems. . . . Sickened, Cassia watched as a soldier clawed his burning mouth and throat, vomited, soiled himself while shrieking that he could not see, caught his breath, stiffened, and died.

Useful as the plants of Naphar can be, they have their limitations. They don't have enough protein. Selenium in the soil makes the animals' flesh inedible to the Napharese, who inherit their digestions from their alien ancestors. As the little boy in *Journey* recites his lessons, he describes the earthly diseases of selenium poisoning (which a physician and his textbooks described for me), and Kwashiorkor (a protein deficiency disease mentioned by a hospital nutritionist who lent me her textbook). I added the Napharese's unearthly remedy.

Blinded mothers wept over monstrous babes. . . . They staggered, convulsed, and died [selenium poisoning]. . . . A new death found us . . . grew lizard skin, hair striped and loosened, we bloated, and again we died [Kwashiorkor]. We found the gods' own cure: through ritual Sacrifice, we eat each other.

If the boy's recitation sounds like an attempt at poetry, it's because I assume that Naphar's northern continent, like our own Middle East, has an oral tradition. I have written Naphar's tales (like the one above) in the style of the religious poetry of the ancient Middle East and adapted some of our Middle East's own stories to fit Naphar's past. I have drawn most heavily on the traditions of Ugarit, a city that flourished four thousand years ago on the Mediterranean coast of northern Syria. Its temple and secular libraries burned; the clay tablets baked hard and have recently been refound and deciphered.

I use bits of Cyrus Gordon's translations in *Journey.* Here's the little boy's preface to a story which the heroine only half-hears because she's falling asleep:

Tadge crossed his legs in a storyteller's pose and began, ". . . phrases to sing you . . . I understand the lightning . . . all tongues . . . Come listen. . . ."

I rhyme some of the Ugaritic poetry in the heroine's dream of being a priestess:

"I speak for Sassurum's three: the song of the stars, the wisdom of the Stone, the strength of the tree. Star, Stone, and tree are yours to command. What would you ask Sassurum through me?"

Next, the man quizzes the child on stories I took from Babylonian myth about Marduk's part in creation. I rhymed it too, twisted it to fit *Scientific American's* version, and changed Marduk to Kumar (to me, Marduk sounds too much like Donald Duck to be suitably awesome):

> ". . . From the slain god's body, Kumar drained the blood away,
> Mixed it with the Apsu's waters and its clay.
> Thus from the sacred caverns he emerged with . . ."
>   "Man!" Tadge's triumphant chortle and bounce rocked Cassia over
> the edge into sleep.

More than man inhabit Naphar's legends; black-winged immortals (like earth's vampires) do, too. Since they also inhabit Naphar, I must account for them. Especially since the heroine is turning into one. Here's the mechanism of vampirism, as reasoned by an allergist with an interest in immunology.

> Sipping his pale green broth of neuro-transmitters, Jarell listened to the lecturer illustrate the Neo-Classic Evolutionary Theory that large structures are created from smaller ones, by describing the workings of Night Demon Poison.
>   . . . While drawing blood, the Night Demon's virus-like parasites go into the victim's bloodstream and take over the cells' deoxyribonucleic acid. During a "honeymoon" of no more than sixty days, if the subject has not died, these cells change, producing a life form—half human, half Night Demon—with which the parasites may enjoy the same symbiosis they had with their original host.

Not all the background for my novels comes from others' experience. I also use my own. Some of my babies have died. Here, my heroine remembers her stillborn child:

> . . . She tossed once more in her straw, breasts aching and swollen with useless milk, keening for her babe born dead, unkissed, unheld, unloved. Again the cold tears slid down her cheeks as she sealed it in the reed coffin she had woven, covered it with black wax, and cast her motionless babe into the River Lathon. Her babe, so little, so alone, forever. . . .

As my heroine's surroundings hint, Naphar has buildings. I modeled them on some in the Cambridge Ancient History sections on Ugarit, adding structural details from other archaeological texts, the California building code (Naphar has a lot of earthquakes), a history of architecture, and (as always) my imagination. Here's the outside of an earthly ziggurat decorated with a cone mosaic and transposed to Naphar:

At first she thought she saw dancers in the changing shadows. Between bands of brownish red and black, kilted figures connected by scarlet ribbons capered in elaborate poses. Looking more closely she saw that the scarlet ribbon connecting the dancers issued from gaping holes in head and heart and neck. . . . She looked again at the dancers. They were not real! They had only seemed to move when the trees swayed in front of them, changing the light. But now Cassia saw that the apparent movement came from the play of shadow on painted fingerlength cones of clay packed together base to base."

This temple to the goddess is the site of *Journey's* climactic curse, taken mostly from Ugarit's Epic of Kret, Epic of Aqhat and Danel, and the Baal cycle. I used the old poetic form of rhymed thoughts, not sounds, the reason for so much repetition in the Bible. Here are examples from Gordon's translations:

(Kret's description of his army) "Like locusts they occupy the field / Like grasshoppers, the corners of the steppe."

(Kret's people lament their starvation) "Spent is the bread from their jars / Spent is the wine from their bottles / Spent is the oil from their cruses."

(Kret is ordered to abdicate because) "Thou dost not judge the case of the widow / Nor adjudicate the cause of the broken in spirit / Nor drive away those who prey upon the poor! / Before thee thou dost not feed the fatherless / Nor behind thy back the widow. / For thou art a brother of the bed of sickness / Yea a companion of the bed of disease."

(Anath threatens her father) "I shall make thy grey hair run with blood / The grey of thy beard with gore."

(Anath regrets killing Aqhat) "Like the song of the harp of his fingers / Like the whiteness of the stones of his mouth . . ."

(Anath at war) "Knee-deep she plunges into the blood of her soldiery / Up to the neck in the gore of her troops . . . /

Here's how these and other antique verse came together:

"Oh, you hungry little people, I will show you Sacrifice, and it will be yours. You wish your fields to bear? Worship me thus falsely and I shall command the hot winds of perpetual summer to turn your fields to howling wastelands. You demand blood? I bring your blood! Your gray heads shall run with it, gore shall redden your beards. I will take your young men for my army until they are like an infestation upon the hillside and I will bathe in their blood, I will stack their bones for my footstools. There will be moaning and crying in the land as your young men and your children sicken of the war plagues and die. For you are corrupt, siblings of the pallet of sickness, companions of the pallet of disease. . . .

"I, Sassurum, have seen how you profit from despair. Do you sell your sons and daughters for coin so you may eat? Behold the inhumane who hear the cries of the broken in spirit and heed them not. I, Sassurum, shall avenge them. The high mountains shall weep for you, the peaks of the gods shall cry. Spent is the bread from your ovens, empty are your jars of yiann, gone is the oil from your cooking pots and your lamps. In mourning for your dead and enslaved children and your fields, homeless and without a city shall you roam until you are sated with weeping and you quaff tears like strong drink. . . .

"Oh, you who deny the teachings of the goddess and believe lies and allow yourselves to be seduced into Choosing the Old Ways, your bones will be scattered and left for the carrion lizards to gnaw. Stilled are the harps of your fingers, silent the stones of your mouths. Empty, oh empty is your land like your hearts, oh sellers of children, defamers of the goddess. For I, Sassurum, curse you and your children and your children's children until your seed is cleansed from the earth."

Besides erring people, Naphar has creatures such as the Beloved, half human and half bat, some vampire, most not, who live in cavern cities, and commune with telepathic Song. I based them on books about bats, visits to the Night House at the zoo, and (again) my imagination:

The Beloved were hopping on rocky shelves, their wings outspread for balance, others flew or sat at ease. Some hung upside down, combing their fur with thoughtful claws; others glanced at Cassia, touched her with their thoughts, and brought her into their Song. . . .

Most had human faces—their eyes were large and black, their expressions tranquil. A few had white fur and faces as pink as those of the Snow People in the marketplace tales. Others were striped or mottled in red or yellow. Twittering, they clung to walls or ceilings. Some slept, wrapped in their wings; others sucked globes of redfruit or took dainty bites from golden melons. A few passed a drinking jar studded with tubes that smelled of summer flowers. And everywhere was pastel light and the scent of moss and fruit and stone, woven with love into the Song.

Finally, here is the one creature in *Journey* that I simply made up. It appears in the middle of the story in draining farmlands after a flood:

Shards of blue flashed in the fields like spare summer skies. Between them, color frothed.

With a smile, Cassia pointed to it and the familiar springtime miracle at their feet. "Look, Tadge. Bubble riders."

A break in the dirt pouted into a mound. Antennae, little feet, then an insect's drab brown shell broke through. Grains of loam still clinging to its back, the bug started blowing a translucent bubble, bright as flame. It inflated to palm size; the beetle clambered aboard.

A breeze took it, bouncing it along the tussocks and skimming it over puddles, its creator sprawled on top, still blowing. On the next bound, the wind from the river caught the scarlet and orange sphere and lifted it high to join its fellows of green, amber, blue, on its chancy journey to the highlands.

"Have you not seen this before, child?" Jarell spoke from behind her.

"Oh, yes! Always, at home on the first warm day after a rain. It's the same!"

. . . she watched Tadge run past the steaming fields where bright balls, each with its little passenger, bounded through ramparts and palaces of fog.

Even when I'm reduced to using imagination alone, Naphar seems alive to me because so much of it is founded on fact. Like earth, it is woven from others' realities—people I've talked to, those whose words and histories I've read, as well as my own experience, which seems authentic to me because I've lived it.

I hope that for readers turning the pages of my books, this combination of imagination and reality breathes life into Naphar so, for a few hours or days, they too can mentally walk the living mountains and plains and corridors of my world.

Chapter 16

Avoiding What's Been Done to Death

Ramsey Campbell

You can't avoid anything unless you know what it is. This idea alone would be sufficient reason for me to recommend that anyone who wants to write worthwhile horror fiction have a working knowledge of the tradition of the field. The finest single introduction to it is *Great Tales of Terror and the Supernatural*, edited by Wise and Fraser, and still, I believe, readily available. If you find nothing to enjoy and be awestruck by in that book, then it seems unlikely that you have any real feeling for horror fiction. On the other hand, you may be taken aback by how many of the themes in the book have recently been bloated into best sellers. I would hope that realization may make you deeply dissatisfied, because that kind of dissatisfaction is the first step in creating something new.

Some people (generally critics with no fiction to their name and writers near the end of their careers) claim that there's nothing new in horror. In a *sense*, that may be true. Most of sixty years ago, H. P. Lovecraft drew up a list of the basic themes of weird fiction, and I can think of very little that the field has added to that list. But that's by no means as defeatist as it sounds, because the truth is surely that many of the themes we're dealing with are so large and powerful as to be essentially timeless.

For instance, the folk tale of the wish that comes true more fully and more terribly than the wisher could have dreamed is the basis not only of "The Monkey's Paw" but of Steve King's *Pet Sematary* and of my own novel *Obsession*, yet the three stories have otherwise far more to do with their writers than with one another. That suggests, if I may be forgiven for emitting a homily now and then in the course of this essay, that one way to avoid what has already been done is to be true to yourself.

That isn't to say that imitation never has its uses. Here, as in any other of the arts, it's a legitimate and useful way to serve your apprenticeship. Though it may not be obvious to readers who know only my recent work, I began my career by imitating Lovecraft. No writer has orchestrated terror in prose more carefully than Lovecraft, but you won't learn how to write dialogue or deal with character from him. Such skills are best learned by reading writers outside the field (in my case, Nabokov and Graham Greene, among others). If you're writing in a genre, it's all the more important to read widely outside it in order to be aware what fiction is capable of. It's less a matter of importing techniques into the field than of seeing the field as part of a larger art. Depending wholly on genre techniques can lead too easily to the secondhand and the second-rate. There's only one Stephen King, but there are far too many writers trying to sound like him.

It's no bad thing to follow the example of writers you admire, then, but only as a means to finding your own voice. You won't find that, of course, unless you have something of your own to say. I did, once I stopped writing about Lovecraft's horrors and began to deal with what disturbed me personally. I began to write about how things seemed to me, which was more important and, at first, more difficult than it may sound. I tried and still try to take nothing on trust, to describe things as they really are or would be.

I'm sure I don't need to tell you that the horror field is riddled with clichés. The house that's for sale too cheaply, the guy who must be working nights because he sleeps during the day (must be a handyman, too, to judge by that big box he keeps in his cellar), the attic room the landlady keeps locked, the place none of the topers in the village inn will visit after dark—we can all have fun recognizing these and many others, which is by no means to say that they haven't been used effectively by masters of the craft. But I think there are more fundamental clichés in the field, and I think today's writers may be the ones to overturn them.

Take the theme of evil, as the horror story often does. Writing about evil is a moral act, and it won't do to recycle definitions of evil, to take them on trust. Horror fiction frequently presents the idea of evil in such a shorthand form as to be essentially meaningless—something vague out there that causes folk to commit terrible acts, something other than ourselves, nothing to do with us. That sounds to me more like an excuse than a definition, and I hope it's had its day. If we're going to write about evil, then let's define it and how it relates to ourselves.

All good fiction consists of looking at things afresh, but horror fiction seems to have a built-in tendency to do the opposite. Ten years or so ago, many books had nothing more to say than "the devil made me do it"; now, thanks to the influence of films like *Friday the 13th,* it seems enough for some writers to say that a character is psychotic; no further explanation is necessary. But it's the job of writers to imagine how it would feel to be *all* their characters, however painful that may sometimes be. It may be a lack of that compassion that has led some writers to create children who are evil simply because they're children, surely the most deplorable cliché of the field.

Some clichés are simply products of lazy writing. Tradition shouldn't be used as an excuse to repeat what earlier writers have done; if you feel the need to write about the stock figures of the horror story, that's all the more reason to imagine them anew.

For instance, we might have believed there was nothing new to be written about vampirism until Karl Wagner wrote "Beyond Any Measure," whose stunningly original idea was always implicit in the vampire tradition and waiting for Karl to notice. Again, generations might have thought that the definitive haunted house tale had been written, but it hadn't been until Shirley Jackson wrote *The Haunting of Hill House* (a statement guaranteed to make some of you try to improve on that novel, perhaps). Put it another way: one reason some folk recoil from my own novel *The Face That Must Die* seems to be that it confronts you with what I imagine it might be like to be a psychotic killer, rather than keeping a Halloween face or ski mask between him and the audience, and depicting him as a bogyman we could dismiss as being nothing like ourselves. It's only fair to warn you that many readers and publishers would rather see imitations of whatever they liked last year than give new ideas a chance. But I've always tried to write what rings true to *me,* whether or not it makes the till ring. If you don't feel involved with what you're writing, it's unlikely that anyone else will.

There's another side to the field, which is overdue for attack by a new generation—its reactionary quality. A horror writer I otherwise admire argued recently that "it has been a time-honoured tradition in literature and film that you have a weak or helpless heroine"—implying, I assume, that we should go on doing so.

Well, tradition is a pretty poor excuse for perpetrating stereotypes (not that the author in question necessarily does); time-honored it may be, but that doesn't make it honorable. In fact, these days, so many horror stories (and, especially, films) gloat over the suffering of women that it seems clear the authors are getting their own back, consciously or not, on aspects of real life that they can't cope with. Of course, that isn't new in horror fiction, nor is using horror fiction to define as evil or diabolical whatever threatens the writer or the writer's lifestyle; but at the very least, one should be aware as soon as possible that this is what one is doing, so as to be able to move on. I have my suspicions, too, about the argument that horror fiction defines what is normal by showing us what *isn't*. I think it's time for more of the field to acknowledge that, when we come face to face with the monsters, we may find ourselves looking not at a mask but at a mirror.

Now all this may sound as if it requires some discipline and dedication, and my experience is that it does. After all, the best way for a writer to compete is with oneself, to do better than one did last time. I'm not the first to say that the most important thing for a writer to do is to write, but I'll add that you should work on whatever you're writing every day until it's finished; to do otherwise is to court writer's block, every blank day adding to the hurdle that prevents you from getting back into the story and making the task seem more impossible. When I was writing my story "Litter," six months elapsed between the first day's work and my return to the story, which I took up by writing the line "That's how he enters the story, or *this* is." I should have rewritten the story to improve its shape, of course.

Now I rewrite more and more severely, and I take great pleasure in cutting thousands of words out of first drafts; I think that's a pleasure worth learning as early as possible in one's career, not least because realizing that one can do it helps one relax into writing the first draft, in which it's better to have *too* much material for later shaping than not enough. Learning to relax enough with the technique of writing novels comes easier to some than others; you may feel you need to plot a novel in advance (maybe all the way to breaking it down into chapter synopses) before you begin the first chapter, but it's worth trying to regard the synopsis merely as a safety net once you begin writing, trying to let the novel develop itself as it takes on more life. I did that first in *Incarnate,* and since then, I've avoided plotting or constructing too far ahead, trying to know only as much as I need to know to start writing and head in the right direction. It can be fearsome to find yourself losing your way halfway through a novel, all by yourself in the unknown, but I find that the solutions are usually somewhere in what you've already written, and I can tell you that the bad days are worth the days when you feel the novel come to life.

I'm still stressing the arduousness, but let me see if I can pass on some tricks I've learned. We all have an optimum period of creativity each day, and it's worth beginning work then if you possibly can. Mine is from about seven in the morning until noon or so. It's easy to get distracted from your desk, but music may help; my desk is between the speakers of the hi-fi, on which I play compact discs (which last longer than records and keep me there longer) of all sorts of music from Monteverdi onwards. (Steve King uses rock; Peter Straub, jazz.) Don't be too eager to feel you've exhausted your creative energy for the day, but if you sense you're close to doing so, then don't squeeze yourself dry: better to know what the next paragraph is going to be and start with that next time. Scribble down a rough version of it rather than risk forgetting it. Always have a rough idea of your first paragraph before you sit down to write, and then you won't be trapped into fearing the blank page.

If you must take a day or more out from writing a story, break off before the end of a scene or a chapter, to give yourself some impetus when you return. Always carry a notebook for ideas, glimpses, overheard dialogue, details of what you're about to write, developments of work-in-progress. If an idea or something larger refuses to be developed, try altering the viewpoint or even the form: if it won't grow as a short story, it may be a poem. Sometimes, two apparently unproductive ideas may be cross-fertilized to give you a story. Then again, you may not be *ready* technically or emotionally to deal with an idea, and it can improve with waiting.

What else can I tell you? Only to write. Surprise us; show us things we haven't seen before or didn't admit that we knew. Write the stories that only *you* can write. Some of the best horror stories have yet to be written. I have no idea what they'll be about, but maybe you *will* have.

Chapter 17

Why Novels of Fear Must Do More than Frighten

Dean R. Koontz

Every Hallowe'en, at least one newspaper somewhere in the country polls its readers to find out what they think are the ten scariest novels and movies of all time. Since my *Phantoms* was published in 1983, it has made these lists, frequently in the number-one slot, never lower than number three. On one such list topped by *Phantoms,* another of my books, *Whispers,* occupied the fourth position.

When readers write to me, they tell me that, after finishing one of my books, they sometimes have trouble sleeping in a dark room and need a night light. Others tell me they can't bear to read one of my novels if they are alone in the house. Still others relish reading while alone but confess to overreacting to every innocent noise.

Reviewers comment on all aspects of the novels, of course, but among their most common reactions are: "Will give you goosebumps," "will stand your hair on end," "not to be read until you're sure all the doors and windows are locked," and "makes your blood run cold."

The result of raising all those goosebumps and standing all those hairs on end and freezing several million gallons of blood is that, by the end of 1986, worldwide sales of my books were approximately forty million copies. Evidently, people enjoy a good scare.

New writers breaking into the suspense and dark-fantasy genres frequently write to me seeking advice or send manuscripts for my reaction. As *I* do, they take pleasure in wringing a cold sweat out of readers. Too often, however, they fail to achieve the effect they seek because they are trying to do *nothing else but scare the reader.* Fear cannot be generated in a vacuum. To induce fear, one must evoke other emotions as well. A writer of suspense and dark fantasy who is concerned only with creating fear is like a concert pianist attempting to play Mozart on just one-fourth of the keyboard: it cannot be done.

The initial reaction that a story *must* elicit from the reader is empathy—the vicarious experiencing of the feelings, thoughts, and attitudes of another person. The first person with whom the reader should have empathy is the novel's lead character, the protagonist.

To quickly induce empathy, a character's thought processes and motivations must be clear and understandable. For example, in my novel *Strangers,* the lead male is Dominick, a writer who, after years of struggle, has just written a potential best seller and desires only to do more good work and enjoy the fruits of his labors. Ginger, the lead female character, is a resident in cardiovascular surgery and, after many years of arduous study, wants to finish her residency and become the best doctor she can be. Their desires and goals are clear, admirable, and any reader can identify with them on that level. Or consider Stephen King's *The Shining,* in which young Danny, only five years old, functions as the novel's protagonist. Danny wants nothing more than to love his parents and be loved in return; the reader who cannot understand and empathize with those motivations is someone who needs counseling!

A protagonist who is a neurotic mess, who is motivated by greed or lust or one of the baser emotions, is not going to engage the reader's empathy swiftly. Certainly, we all have those darker desires and motivations, and on one level we *can* identify with a basically malignant character, but we do so only with great reluctance because we do not like to admit that such feelings exist in us. A great writer with tremendous talent can pull off this trick, as James M. Cain did splendidly in *The Postman Always Rings Twice* and nearly as well in *Double Indemnity.* In *Clemmie,* the incomparable John D. MacDonald writes of a lead character consumed and ultimately destroyed by lust, and the reader has almost painful empathy with him. But Cain and MacDonald are masters of the novel, and the new writer who sets himself the challenge of a "bent" protagonist is starting with a huge disadvantage that his nascent talent most likely cannot overcome.

Having created a protagonist with whom the reader can easily empathize, you are still not ready to instill fear. First, you must seek to elicit another important emotion—sympathy. The reader must *like* your lead character, care about him, and be concerned about his fate.

Many ineptitudes of characterization can prevent the development of sympathy in the reader. However, the following five are those errors most often committed by new writers:

1. Your character must not act irrationally and must not get into trouble merely because he makes stupid decisions. For example, if he moves into a haunted house with his family, and if lovable old Grandma is subsequently eaten by a monster that crawls out of the cellar, your protagonist will not enjoy the reader's sympathy if he stays in the house to prove his courage or because he's a stubborn individualist. Anyone with a brain would get the hell out after Grandma was consumed, and that would be the end of your haunted-house story. To keep the story alive, you must provide logical and convincing reasons that this man and his family cannot leave. Consider the movie *Poltergeist:* the family dared not depart because their little girl had been snatched away by a demon and was being held in an other-dimensional plane of the house; if the family left, they would be abandoning their child to the Dark One.

2. Your character must not be passive. He must not simply wait for things to happen to him and then react. As his situation grows more desperate, he must take strong and logical actions to deal with the antagonists who are plaguing him, whether they are human adversaries or, as in some dark fantasies, supernatural forces. He must seize the initiative. In *The Exorcist* by William Peter Blatty, the mother of the possessed girl and the young priest, Father Karras, diligently pursue myriad medical and psychological explanations and treatments for the child's condition. Ultimately, when all rational explanations are eliminated, they are forced to confront the likelihood that demons exist and are present in the girl, whereupon they call in the elder exorcist. They do not just sit around biting their nails and waiting for the next bogyman to jump out of the walls. Remember: Nobody likes a wimp.

3. On the other hand, your lead characters must not be supermen and superwomen whose actions always succeed. That would eliminate all prospect of genuine suspense. Some of their responses to the antagonists will improve their situation, and some of the things they do will make their dilemma worse than ever. In fact, the classic plot of nearly all fiction involves a steady worsening of the protagonists' situation until, at the penultimate moment, they save themselves and solve their problems—or die trying. The important thing is that they learn something from both their successes and failures and that they apply those lessons when deciding on their next course of action.

4. Your characters must not be explored solely within the main plot of the novel; they must have lives outside of the central story. Each character must have a past that is not merely a dry summary of where he was born, raised, and schooled; that past must have affected him, and we must see how it shaped him. In my book *Watchers,* Travis Cornell has lost everyone who has ever mattered to him: his mother died giving birth to him; his brother drowned when Travis

was ten; his father died in an accident a few years later; and his first wife died of cancer. As a result, Travis is reluctant to enter into close relationships, fearing that new friends and loved ones will also be snatched from him. As well as having to deal with the antagonists of the story—and a murderous lot they are!—Travis must also learn to conquer the fear of emotional dependency that has made him an unbearably lonely man. Ideally, all your lead characters have problems of an external nature (those imposed on them by the villains) and internal problems (those imposed by life and hard experience). Otherwise, they are cardboard creations incapable of inducing sympathy, and their travails will never move the reader to fear for them.

5. Each of your lead characters must not be concerned solely about his own fate. If your hero is running for his life, his major motivation is naturally going to be self-preservation, and any reader will easily empathize and sympathize with that. But your lead must also care about someone else within the story—a wife, girlfriend, son, daughter, parent, friend—for whom he is willing to put himself in emotional, spiritual, and/or physical jeopardy. More than anything else, fiction is about *the interaction of people,* about their complex relationships. A reader will be more inclined to like a character and to cheer for him if that character has a trace of altruism, if he is willing to risk all for someone he loves or for an ideal. Love is the emotion that readers—even readers of horror novels—find the most compelling in life and in fiction. If a character's love is so strong that he will sacrifice himself for another, and if you can make that love and sacrifice believable, readers will be moved.

A word of warning is appropriate here. You must not let your character's altruism get out of hand. He must not become a bleeding heart who wants to save the whales, bring about nuclear disarmament, end world hunger, and usher in the millennium at any cost. For one thing, such a broad spectrum of aching idealism will make him seem unfocused. Furthermore, while there is certainly a place in fiction for the exploration of broad social issues—witness the work of Charles Dickens—no fiction can *last* if it mistakes trendy political issues for great and enduring social concerns. Political issues involve simplistic one-answer solutions, while genuinely important social issues are complex and seldom find solution through political means; if your lead is to be sympathetic and tough minded (as he must be), he should know at least *that* much about the way the world really works. Keep his altruism focused on a small-scale, one-to-one, very *human* level, and it will be believable and admirable and engaging. A perfect example of doing this correctly is Dicken's *A Tale of Two Cities,* which contrasts the emptiness of political ideals with the enduring value of more personal and human ideals; it is a book filled with credibly altruistic acts, culminating in what may be the most moving final scene of any novel in the English language.

Now, you are ready to induce fear in the reader and make him sweat. If you have engaged the reader's empathy, encouraged him to be sympathetic with the lead characters, have made him witness to their love and friendship and joy and hopes and dreams, he will feel that these fictional people have something to lose, and he will not want to see them lose it. He will be afraid that they will lose not only their lives but their love, their happiness, and their hope for a better future. He will identify with each character not as a real person to a fictional person, but as one human being to another. The reader will be sweating with them each time that the villain walks on stage, and he will dread every encounter that might lead to their deaths. This is the *magic* of fiction.

In the dark-fantasy or suspense novel, fear by itself is empty and unaffecting. In context, however, when evoked with a panoply of other emotions, fear is one of the most compelling secondhand experiences that fiction can give us. This is because, at root, all fears have the same source: that you will have to stand alone against some adversary—something as external as a murderer or as internal as cancer—and that you will die alone, with no one to hold your hand as life fades away. Alone.

Chapter 18

The Supernatural? Naturally!

J. N. Williamson

1

It may surprise you to learn that the affirmation contained in this chapter's title is controversial. No, tempers haven't been lost (to the best of my knowledge). Yet gifted professionals within the horror-writing community are starting to line up on one side or the other of such questions as these:

1. Some paperback publishers lump fiction as diverse as horror, weird or *Twilight Zone*-style novels, ghost stories, and psychological terror tales under the heading *occult*. Isn't this contrary to the writers' intentions?

2. Apart from such scientifically plausible, *post*nuclear holocaust accidents as mutated people, shouldn't we eschew monsters from now on (if, by the term, anything is meant except biological humans whose warped minds perpetrate monstrosities)?

3. Since most psychologists agree that evil is only the product of dissension or aberration—of unfortunate environment or upbringing—don't we err if we invent tales that imply evils other than the antagonists' bent motivations?

4. Because, by acclamation in some circles, God is dead, isn't the creation of any evilly supernatural being or action ignorant fancy and beneath the concerns of a truly contemporary and intellectually knowledgeable author of horror or fantasy fiction?

The fact that I do not feel threatened by the first point and I'm opposed to and shout No! to the final three questions does not mean that those who agree with all four should head immediately for the nearest church or seance and begin writing a ghost story or even a novel in which Satan-motivated hordes crawl from the moist bowels of the earth. (It shouldn't mean, either, that writers who do are covertly ostracized from some inner circles, but that has happened.) Clearly, if you are uncomfortable working with the supernatural, you'll probably lack the conviction necessary to make occult books or tales credible to your readers.

But just as clearly, I think, a total commitment to the rationalistic or scientific approach can deprive both writers and readers of the sheer *fun* of exploring a make-believe world of raging monstrosities—or of the other world (I've called it the *afterdeath* in my novels), in which sizable quantities of both writers and readers continue to believe.

What the down-to-earth-but-not-beneath-it approach may lose sight of is the seldom-disputed fact that, by common accord, horror and supernatural fiction *is* fantasy. Make believe, if you will, or won't! Grown-up fairy tales, regardless of how chock-full of mature ideas our work may be.

What I fear I see in a recent horrific preoccupation with fictive existentialism is more than a self-indulgent and sometimes pompous, cool-school, *post*collegiate sophistry, more than horror's version of the same sort of thing that has happened to elements of science fiction. A single-minded emphasis upon psychological terror, which denies our readers the chance to suspend credulity for the time needed to read a novel or story, seems to suggest that today's readers are imaginatively deficient, no longer able to enjoy fantasy itself! Not only can such an approach lead to a restrictive publishing atmosphere but to horror which stresses hard-boiled crime with a pointed emphasis on amateur psychoanalysis and sociological crusading.

But be careful; take heed! Don't rush to agree with me too hastily—not if your ambition is to write horror that's readily sold (if no more widely read than before). While pointing out additionally that trends in this vast genre come and go, I'd be doing you a disservice if I did not acknowledge that—just now—magazine editors may be seeking horror that is aberrative but realistic, graphically violent but super-believable more than the other kinds. Even Stephen King, the best-selling writer of best sellers ever, sometimes seems not to explore the supernatural as much as he does humankind's difficulty with survival in an unjust "rational world," today's "chaotic universe" (to use terms of King's from an anthology introduction).

Yet consider some of the novels and shorter fiction drawing heavy voting in the poll near the close of this volume. Shirley Jackson, gone for years, garnered her highest totals for ghost stories; so did Peter Straub, whose *Ghost Story* says just what it is. The occult permeates *Rosemary's Baby, The Exorcist,* and Dick Matheson's wonderfully frightening *Hell House*—as it does King's *Pet Sematary* and *The Shining,* if not his *Cujo* (the only King book which did not fare spectacularly in the voting). In a refreshingly new way, Rick McCammon's successful "Nightcrawlers" is a contemporary ghost story; other short works receiving numerous votes give a firm nod toward that which is occult— which means *concealed,* beyond human understanding.

For my introduction to the anthology called *Masques II* (Maclay & Associates, Inc., 1987), which I edited, I quoted from an afterword the late and personally lamented Charles Beaumont wrote for a 1962 Ballantine anthology called *The Fiend in You.* That author of more than a dozen beloved "Twilight Zone" tales argued that, for the great portion of human history, cultures and nations have been *based upon* the supernatural—"powers beyond," Beaumont said, our understanding. Because, he explained, what mainly motivates us is fear of the unknown—a fear which I no more believe has run its course than the majority of our better known archetypal fears.

Saying that we wouldn't continue to enjoy any form of horror if we believed "that evil is not an entity and a force in itself," Beaumont speculated about a human, core premise that "not all things in this world are of this world," and declared that what writers of the supernatural do is to expose the "cheap overlay of modern civilization" for the comforting veneer it is.

2

Aside from the fact that, with Lewis Carroll, I sometimes believe a dozen wonderful new things before lunch, most of my own fiction has heavily relied upon supernatural/occult elements for the oddest of reasons:

It enhances the credibility of the story or the novel.

I'm astounded that relatively few regularly published horror authors—Ray Bradbury, Dean R. Koontz, and Ira Levin are some exceptions, as indeed they are in their fictional output—seem to have perceived the apparent truth of what may appear a dubious anomaly.

Whether Jung was correct or not in his reflections about our minds containing the collective fears of our most long-lost ancestors, it has always seemed obvious to me that most people *want* to believe what the majority of other persons believe or have believed. It's why the majority continues to vote a straight party ticket and remains members of the religion of birth. It is less challenging or trouble making that way, more companionable, even when we do not deeply believe or necessarily feel an absolute commitment to a given belief. Consequently, if I, as an author, can buttress the otherwise-improbable premises of my work by what was accepted as *real* or *true* by a large number of my fellow human beings, it stands to reason that I am more acceptable in my fictive intrigues, prepared to arouse, convince, and hold the attention of readers for the time it takes to read that fictional work.

Nothing is harder to write than fantasy of any kind. No writer has it tougher because, by definition, we deal not with the day-to-day commonplaces but with the largely unfamiliar, even alien—that which may very literally appear *in*credible.

In fewer than nine years, I've published well over twenty novels. That argues more for the suspended credulity—the willing, endlessly and richly imaginative capabilities—of my readers than for my prolific nature. But to *get* readers to that stage at which they will believe in those amazing or improbable tenets of my work has meant that I needed tools with which to persuade readers, to trigger that willing suspension to which I've referred. Following is a list of the beliefs that became available to me as a consequence of considerable research. Each number lists the ideas or themes present in each of these twenty-two books.

BELIEF BY A BODY OF PEOPLE, PRESENT OR PAST, IN:

1. *Reincarnation; evil's embodiment (the Antichrist); friendship and individualism.*

2. *Voodoo; self-sacrifice; individualism over corporate autonomy.*

3. *Thought projection/generation; the sanctity of the family.*

4. *ESP, the paranormal; occult soul living in burial mound; love.*

5. *Apparatus with which to contact the dead; sacrifice for the common good.*

6. *Judgment Day; the Second Coming; spontaneous human combustion; God's intervention.*

7. *Mythology; feminism.*

8. *Ghosts and seances;* ephialtes *and* bruxa; *family life/survival.*

9. *Transmogrification and immortality; rights of the living taking precedence over those of the dead.*

10. *Fairies (leprechauns, banshees, the nuckalavee); ancestor worship; romantic love.*

11. *Vampires; psychic archeology; levity as means to sanity.*

12. *Psychic combat; telepathy; well-applied human courage and know-how.*

13. *UFO; hypnotic regression; invasion by another world; individual human brain power over arrogant underestimations.*

14. *Ghouls, ghosts; levitation; parental self-sacrifice.*

15. *Astrology; the* lamia; *witchcraft; living statues.*

16. *Mind manipulation; alien invasion; familial unity as strength.*

17. *Biologically engineered vampire infants; primal source.*

18. *Egyptian magic; the talisman; parental bravery.*

19. *Zoroastrianism; Atlantis; innocence of small children.*

20. *Mummification; androgyny; sibling sacrifice; the question of intellectual superiority.*

21. *A ghost's human loneliness; errors of Heaven and Hell; ESP; tunnel to the other side.*

22. *Earthbound spirits, good and evil; ice-beasts; methodology of the dead returning to life; man's victory over himself.*

While I've always believed in God and reincarnation and have found astrology and Unidentified Flying Objects marvelous sources of intellectual investigation, the basic occult material I used for books 2 through 11, 13 through 16, and 18 through 22 was the product of my usual reading. Unquestionably, those volumes I have found most consistently useful—some easily located, others requiring a search of old bookstores (lucky you!)—are, in the descending order shown, the following:

Mysteries, by Colin Wilson; Putnam's, 1978

An Encyclopedia of Occultism, by Lewis Spence; University Books, 1960

Encyclopedia of the Occult, the Esoteric, and The Supernatural, by Benjamin Walker; Stein and Day, 1977

The Supernatural, published by Robert B. Clarke; The Danbury Press, 1976 (in eighteen volumes)

Dictionary of the Occult and Paranormal, by J. P. Chaplin; Laurel/Dell, 1976

The Directory of Possibilities, edited by Colin Wilson and John Grant; The Rutledge Press, 1981

The Mysterious World, by Francis Hitching; Holt, Rinehart & Winston, 1978.

Plus other nonfiction works of Colin Wilson (*The Occult; Poltergeist; Order of Assassins; The Outsider*)—and the Bible. I would no more think of starting a new horror novel without researching most of these works than I'd consider writing it by hand.

Did you notice that some of the pet icons of horror fiction—voodoo, vampires, ESP, hauntings—became subjects of mine? *What,* I'd wondered while writing my first novel in 1975-'76, *could make my novels different enough to draw the attention of acquiring editors and readers?* The answer was immediate—a mixture of entirely original ideas and unusual twists on old ones. Since I had been reading metaphysical and UFO literature for years, I already owned a number of books that go beyond a repetition of the generally known theories and facts concerning the pursuit of great longevity, psychic phone calls, miracles, spells, etc. My familiarity with such subjects explains why, in my prize-winning voodoo novel, *The Houngan* (reprinted as *Profits*), *no* reference is made to devil dolls used as pincushions. My research informed me that the practice was rather rare in Brazil, from which the Houngan came—and there was so much fresh material that there was no room for the trite!

And by the time I'd read the first four cited publications, I knew there was no reason for ever running dry of basic premises. A glance at the index followed by ten minutes of absorbing reading made *immediate* imaginative connections, then provided my usually desperate characters with facts to discover, which readers would experience as an enhancement of credibility, probability—even in the more improbable areas!

Beyond all this, when you glance over the twenty-two novels' titles whose belief systems were just summarized, kindly note that only three—numbers 7, 15, and 17—do not end in a corresponding gentler, more philosophical or traditionally humane or religious realm of faith. I wonder now if it's happenstance that two of the three ended a rather worn-out four-book series, while the third is the only novel I've written that I dislike. Hence, the point arises that many authors are moralists, covert preachers or advocates of this or that principle and way of life. Should that be true of *you,* your story line obviously can be designed in such a way that your personal views are broadcast *without* the kind of open proselytizing no pragmatic publisher can be expected to accept.

Finally, I have not said I believe in *vodun* (voodoo), mythological monsters, mummification, or the cosmic rightness of androgyny—because I do not.

But I *did*—often intensely—while I was writing about them. It's called *creative imagination,* and it precedes the same suspension of credulity that is passed along to one's readers.

I believe the Hoosier poet James Whitcomb Riley said it well: the "gobble-uns'll git you / Ef you don't watch out."

> Deep down, we look at the world through the eyes of wishes and fears and gratifications. It is independent of control . . . calculations of possibility or impossibility. It has nothing to do with time and space. . . . It can make things come to pass without doing or acting, simply by fantasy.[1]

---

1. Abraham H. Maslow, *The Farther Reaches of Human Nature* (New York: The Viking Press, 1971).

Chapter 19

Sexist Stereotypes and Archetypes: What to Do with Them/ What the Writing Woman Can Hope For

Jeannette M. Hopper

Women cannot write effective horror, science fiction, or heroic fantasy. In mild fantasy, which deals with elves and fairies, they excel because these are gentle characters, and women are a gentle sort. Since women are perfectly suited to fanciful creatures, it makes no sense for them to tackle the unfeminine demands of contemporary speculative fiction.

Now that I've got your attention . . .

There's a single grain of truth in that; women and men are different kinds of creators. The late psychologist Abraham H. Maslow, in his book *The Farther Reaches of Human Nature* (Viking Press, 1971), writes: "I have learned recently (through my studies of peak experiences) to look at women and to feminine creativeness as a good field of operation for research, because it gets less involved in products, less involved in achievement, more involved with the process itself, with the going-on process rather than with the climax in obvious triumph and success."

According to Maslow, women write not so much for publication, but for the simple joy of creation. But women *do* seek publication, and *some* of us feel as if we're being held back by sexism and stereotypical prejudices.

Is there sexism in publishing? Women just starting out suspect it; editors deny its existence. It's like venereal disease—some people have it, but no one wants to talk about it. And anyone who writes about it is going to catch a lot of flack. But if it didn't exist, there would be no reason to include the subject in a book for writers. The real question should be, Where *is* sexism in publishing?

WHAT TO DO WITH THEM

Writers, male *and* female, reveal sexist beliefs through stereotypical characters, most commonly in the form of female characterizations. The traditional roles of the female are emotional and psychic provider for the male; helpless victim; and nonphysical antagonist.

A clear example of all three is found in the original anthology, the Bible. Eve is the antagonist and supporter to Adam, and the naïve victim to the snake (Satan). In the ancient Greek and Roman myths, women were almost always evil, and those who were neutral or helpful were goddesses. Of course, the men were heroes or gods and are examples of male archetypes, which are still common in adventure fiction.

Fairy tales introduced most of us to fantasy and horror; their evil old witches, princess victims, and charming princes introduced most of us to stereotypes.

With these archetypes at literature's roots, it's little wonder that most beginners' fiction follows their basic patterns.

Stereotypes, however, *can* be used advantageously. Depending on how they're presented, traditional traits can make us like or dislike a character, instantly identify with them, or make them totally alien. If we believe in the stereotypes as writers, it will show in our work. So, in learning to recognize stereotypical characterization is the first step toward harnessing it as a tool.

From Eve has grown "Woman as Evil." With her feminine guiles and obligatory beauty, she lures the male into danger, which he must then battle to prove his masculinity. And, of course, he overcomes her, for he is male; weakness is *the* stereotypical female trait.

The most common stereotypical woman in contemporary horror and speculative fiction is nurturing, emotional, and supportive of her mate. She is a "Mother-Goddess" nonperson whose only purpose in the plot is affirmation of the male lead's prowess. When danger nears, she screams, then runs and hides until her male rescuer arrives. Written in reverse, many readers, conditioned to expect the stereotype, would find it ridiculous; few best sellers involve heroic women saving weak men.

When the clichéd woman-victim does offer resistance, she fights "tooth and nail," "scratching and biting," or in some other feline way. She's beautiful and female, therefore catlike and graceful. Anyone who has seen real women fight knows that this is rarely true.

Peggy Nadramia, editor of *Grue,* gives us something to think about. "I don't like stories wherein the writer sets up a problem from which the protagonist *cannot possibly* escape," she writes. "In too many such situations the victim is a woman; this is the tradition of the splatter movie, and the probable source of the critical position that horror is a sexist genre that exploits and persecutes women. I always sit up and take notice of any story where the writer has created an interesting, resourceful main character—but I'll admit I take even more careful notice when that character is a woman, simply because such women are much more rare in horror fiction."

Those of us who were reared amid ideas that girls grew up to be wives/mothers and boys grew up to take care of them may have trouble learning the easiest way to break the clichés: Reverse the stereotypes. This is done skillfully in two novels by women, C. J. Cherryh's *Cuckoo's Egg* and Jessica Amanda Salmonson's *Tomoe Gozen.* Cherryh presents a fierce male warrior who nurtures a young man from infancy. The warrior, Duun, is a veteran of countless battles, but he feeds, cuddles, and diapers his charge with parental tenderness. Salmonson's series of tales takes the other route; her title character is female, but also a deadly Samurai.

Reversing the stereotype doesn't mean you should make *all* your female characters swaggering butch types. To do so would lower your fiction to farce. Neither does it mean your hero should necessarily be effeminate.

The intensely physical *Conan* series might never have been so popular had it been written by women. Conversely, Mary Shelley's *Frankenstein* might have been labeled "just another monster concept" had it been handled with less feminine understanding. Women, say the pioneer psychologists, are more openly emotional than their male counterparts. To give a male protagonist feelings, and the ability to express them, is to add dimension to his character. Some male writers, having been taught early that showing strong emotion is unmanly, are reluctant to endow their characters with those very emotions which bring readers closer to the story. Stereotyping places emotional reactions on the feminine (weak) side of the board, but the skillful writer uses them to flesh out characters no matter what their gender.

Pat categorizations can also be used to evoke humor, which, if effective, is a refreshing relief from the dramatic. A valiant elf-king who fights his way through obstacle after obstacle to save his elf-queen, then finds her waiting impatiently with her sword embedded in the dragon's breast, turns the tables on some standard stuff. Using such twists in the body of the story can alert the reader that the character will seldom act as expected.

Be careful that your reversals aren't too far-fetched, or in themselves comical (unless that is your intention). When asked for examples of new stereotypes that writers should avoid, Marion Zimmer Bradley gave two: "The big, tough woman who is a spaceship captain but ALSO can cook, sew, and be completely orgasmic as soon as the Right Man comes along," and "Cutesy little girls who have learned to cuss and have sex, but are still Podkayne of Mars at heart."

Writers working with futuristic settings have the perfect opportunity to shatter stereotypes. We're moving toward a world in which, ideally, women will no longer have to *out*perform their male peers to prove their worth. Women of the future will assume less traditional roles and fit more naturally into present "male" occupations and attitudes. At least in fiction.

To disregard completely stereotypical traits is to ignore a whole range of possible characterizations. There *are* saintly women, whose lives revolve around home and family to the exclusion of all else. There will always be those whose only reaction to danger will be to run and hide. But just as there must be justification for a character's sudden change in disposition or for the compulsion to kill anyone wearing white shoes, there must be justification for the stereotyped female; don't assume that, just because the woman is a woman, she has sufficient excuse to behave in a stereotypical manner. The same holds true for male characters; not all men are hero material.

Your characters' personalities must each be as unique as your own, possessing some traditional traits of both sexes. Anything less results in two-dimensional, dull characters, and bored readers.

WHAT THE WRITING WOMAN CAN HOPE FOR

Women stand out when they achieve what has previously been expected only of men. Audrey Parente, 1986 President of SPWAO (See note following chapter), relates, "I was invited to speak at a conference of horror fantasy aficionados. The remark was made: 'You will be the first woman speaker we have ever had.' Also, it has been noted that I am the first woman president of Small Press Writers and Artists Organization." She goes on to note, "As part of my research for the biography of Hugh B. Cave, who wrote more than 800 stories for the pulps, I discovered that he wrote a story for February, 1935's *Terror* which was one of the few pulp stories in which women were allowed to dominate."

Things have improved. Women in speculative fiction now command space fleets, lead armies into bloody battle, oversee the building of cities on other worlds, and rescue entire civilizations from impending doom. But these dynamic women, with all their power, are not written solely by women. Men, too, have recognized the demand for strong female protagonists.

But it's the *writer* who must struggle in the marketplace for recognition. Story characters may have hordes of soldiers or supernatural powers at their command, but all the writer possesses is her ability and imagination.

Contemporary horror fiction requires rapid-fire chills; skillful, believable characters; and a style that will grab readers by their throats, throw them against the wall, and refuse to let go until they've bled through their psychic pores. That calls for grit on the writer's part—without it, readers will be left with lukewarm shudders instead of the heart-stopping terror they've come to expect from modern horror. Afraid of appearing unladylike, some women who truly *want* to shock avoid strong, direct language and graphic description of violence, death, or whatever disgusting things they've chosen to inflict upon their characters. Writing horror today, in a world where the stuff of the pulps is part of the nightly news, demands guts.

Modern science fiction requires knowledge of true science. No longer may a writer simply say a ship can go into space; the reader wants to know the method of propulsion, its speed, its trajectory, and the type of fuel it uses. The genre is a minefield of clichés—time travel, humanoid robots, space opera, UFO's, and invasions, to list but a few. Even those publications stating the need for strong characterization also demand correct scientific principles that are also interesting, if not novel. Many women (and men) will have to brush up on their physics and other sciences.

Fantasy, both high and contemporary, is a good starting place for any beginner who wants to deal in matters outside reality. There is no need for the timid to approach the grotesque or the technical (although much good fiction has a mixture of genres), but the freedom remains to build their own worlds and create their own beings. For women who might have resorted to romances or mainstream women's fiction earlier, the popularity of fantasy has been a godsend. But when even free governments are reluctant to pass laws banning discrimination based on sex, many writing women still feel hindered by their femaleness.

"I've achieved a level of success where my name is worth something," writes Jessica Amanda Salmonson, "and that helps overcome gender bias in editors; but it does remain that more women editors buy my work than do men. For the newer woman writer, however, without a salably established Name, it becomes extremely difficult to be taken seriously for serious work. In the horror field, where work of literary merit is rare, any writer, male or female, with uncommonly literate approach, will have some trouble." Salmonson, who also edits small-press publications, won't find much agreement among her fellow editors, but she cites some facts that support her opinion: "If one peruses anthologies of short stories . . . one soon discovers that male writers outnumber women, very often, ten to one. This is NOT because women don't write much horror. *1986 Year's Best* features numerous newcomers who are men, but the only woman included is best-selling Tanith Lee."

Perhaps author/editor/instructor J. N. Williamson has one explanation for this. When asked if he made an effort to balance male and female authors in his anthologies, he answered, "Not to balance, but to *include* female writers, along with at least one or two *new* writers. Sometimes it seems that that amounts to the same thing, partly, I suspect, because I can't remember an established woman writer whom I hadn't already asked into a book of mine who, entirely on her own, made contact and boldly asked me to read her story. That's happened *repeatedly* with male writers."

Some editors aren't influenced one way or the other. Ellen Datlow, fiction editor of the prestigious *Omni,* states, "I balance my issue by subject matter, theme, tone, and other criteria, never by gender of author. I believe gender is an artificial division in science fiction—as in much other fiction."

It's all too easy for a woman just starting out in the male-dominated fields of science fiction or horror to blame her lack of success on others' prejudices. But there are plenty of men struggling just as hard to get their work into print. In time, the woman writer should gain perspective on her work, and she may come to find that what's held her back has been her own ineptitude, inexperience, and/or lack of self-confidence.

Good editors don't see women as inferior writers; good editors see women as writers, period. When asked if they made an effort to balance male and female authors in a single issue of their publications, the overwhelming response was No. When asked the same question regarding the gender of protagonists, the answer was the same.

David B. Silva, editor of the critically acclaimed *The Horror Show,* writes: "I haven't made any effort at all to balance male and female protagonists, although it may be something to keep in mind. Characters a reader can identify with certainly are the foundation of good writing. But I like to believe a good author can make both male and female protagonists effective."

On being able to write from either point of view, J. N. Williamson has this to say: "There is, I believe . . . the natural tendency on the part of most writers to include autobiographical emotions or attitudes; unless the writer, then, is transsexual, his or her yarns will tend to involve protagonists of the same sex or preference (as a rule)."

Why, then, do so many women write more strongly from the male point of view? Perhaps it's because the combination of feminine byline and female protagonist often results in a label of "self-indulgent" being attached to our work. Or perhaps we're just *scared.*

Some sexism is brought about by writing women themselves, not editors. Marion Zimmer Bradley, whose sexually ambiguous name has confused some readers writes: ". . . A feminist writer, said that she had to vanity-publish everything because 'everybody knew no woman could be published in fantasy and science fiction.' When I stopped laughing, I told her she was crazy; she said that I had 'sold out' to the (male) establishment. I doubt that; my editors have been very supportive." Some women with obviously female names use them simply because they *refuse* to sell out.

Women with ambiguous names have their own problems. Some find them advantageous, while others use the titles Miss, Ms., or Mrs. to avoid confusion. The opinions of editors on this were divided; half said they didn't care what a writer's gender was, while the other half said yes, they appreciate a title in case they need to correspond with the writer. Marion Zimmer Bradley said she wants a title to distinguish a mister from a "mizz." "It was embarrassing," she said, "when I once said we were 'by accident all women in this issue'—interesting that Terry Tafoya turned out to be a young man." So it's as much a problem for men who have nonspecific first names.

Some writers opt for using only their initials. Not that it matters whether L. Sprague De Camp and C. J. Cherryh are male or female, but assumptions will be made by readers. J. N. Williamson takes it lightly. "I am amused," says he, "by the handful of people who have assumed that, since I use my initials, rather than my first name, I am a woman writer. It's no insult."

The decision to use a pseudonym is often made by a well-meaning agent rather than by the author herself. Sometimes, too, a writer will publish in divers fields under different names; she may write horror under her own name, children's fiction under a variation, and erotica under a male pen name. But those who change their names thinking it will increase their sales soon find out otherwise; the majority of editors buy good writing, not good names.

Whether you see publication of your work as a game that must be played by unfair rules or as a challenge to be met head-on, certain things *will* keep you from ever seeing your byline in print—sloppiness, awkward style, trite or boring ideas, and characters who seem to have walked off the pages of a thousand old, stereotypical stories. The gender of you, the author, will have little to do with the editor's decision to print or pass if you're not good enough.

Instead of moaning about sexism—whether it exists or not—we writers must concentrate on perfecting our craft to the point where editors can't possibly say no to our work for *any* reason.

Note: SPWAO

Small Press Writers and Artists Organization offers the greatest opportunity for publication, through market listings and up-to-date information, to new and noncommercial writers. Its roster carries the names of numerous women, both writers and editors. To contact SPWAO, write to small press fantasy-, science fiction-, or horror-oriented publications listed in your current WRITER'S MARKET and ask for the current president's name and address.

Chapter 20

"They Laughed when I Howled at the Moon"

Richard Christian Matheson

Okay, there's tons to cover, so let's crank.

But—if you don't mind, just one quick story before we start. You'll love it. It'll get us in the mood for this whole conversation.

You'll see.

Okay, there's this teeny farming town in Wisconsin called Plainfield, right? Can you picture it? Right. You got it. Well, in November '57 the local Wambaughs in this spot of *major* dull find that one Edward Gein, the fifty-one-year-old town pea-brain, had for a bunch of years been swiping female stiffs from fresh graves.

Yechhh. Sick, right?

I mean, aspirin isn't exactly going to make an impact on this guy, okay? Anyway, turns out he's also clipped a couple local babes on top of that. Stabbed them or opened them with a set of chopsticks or who knows what.

Let's not even speculate.

Now, does this *can of Spam* **stop** at that?

Huh-uh, not the *Ed*-man. He's just warming up his amp. Matter of fact, Eddie G. decides it would be like drinking imported beer from a clean glass to string these unhappy corpses up by their heels. And in his barn, no less. Very bad, Eddie. Sick, sick, sick.

Then Eddie pulls the ribbon and really unwraps the fun when he decides to . . . well, forgive my French . . . mutilate them. Slit, slash, saw, gash. And that's the *good* news! The ones he didn't like got dismembered. I mean, we all have bad days, Ed, but come *on*. . . .

So, anyway, here's the kicker: Jokes about this guy sprang up like black daffodils all over Wisconsin within *hours* of the news bullhorning all the gooshy, sqooshy details about Ed's bleed-as-you-are party.

You know, stuff like:

Eddie always liked nice skin on a girl. But he liked it even better *off*.

Or:

"Knock, knock."
"Who's there?"
"Eddie."
"Eddie who?"
"Hop up on this hook and I'll *tell* you."

Guess you could've figured it. The old death, deformity, and suffering material. Three-part harmony with slit throats. Strictly "B" stuff.

But you can see that tripe coming every time. Like families of ghouls in station wagons flocking to the half-mile smear on the highway that used to be a guy on a Harley named Nick.

The part I want to talk about is something else. And it's interesting because it nudges us closer to what's going on with horror and humor:

Nobody who lived in Plainfield got into the joking.

No one.

Not a single, grisly pun. A blood-splattered limerick. The profane imitation of a hacksaw dropping an arm onto a barn floor. None of it.

Evidently, amid the Plainfield population, the tension Eddie's little . . . *mood swing* . . . brought on created a literal epidemic of gastrointestinal problems. The traumatized townfolk suffered a collective nausea, which could find no punchline funny enough to quell the pain.

Tension.

That's the stuff that spikes the punch when you write scary or funny. But you have to do it just right or the words simply sun themselves on the paper like vapid blondes.

Tension.

Dr. Walter E. O'Connell, a psychologist for the Veterans' Administration in Houston, who has published articles and taught courses on the relationship between humor and death, says the big fact he's discovered in humor research is, ". . . too much tension—or no tension—and there's no laughter."

Think again about Plainfield.

The reason those shattered people, who so desperately needed to laugh, *couldn't*, was that they were too *close* to the horror. It was too overwhelming. The town was paralyzed.

Too much tension can kill everything.

And some carefully timed relief, whether a joke or a love scene, can buy a piece of horror fiction priceless *tempo*. And it's not that different writing humor. If the joke, the funny line, or the big scare is shoving from behind *at just the right moment of tension*, the moment bursts through the wall. If the moment is wrong—it's called a rejection letter.

Let's get into this a little more since the more carpeting you lift on this particular floor, the more you see odd patterns on the foundation.

I write both comedy and horror for a living.

What sort of person does such a thing?

A responsiholic.

Writing horror and comedy, unlike other forms of writing, isn't just about telling a story—even telling it well. Both forms are about making the reader's ganglion bubble to the surface and double over with amusement or dread. Getting folks to hang from the acoustical ceiling and wonder what the hell you're going to do to them next. Running that feather over the bottom of their psyche until they're screaming.

Getting the response.

The *rush*.

In comedy writing and horror writing, that's the name of the game. When you can give the "rush" to the reader, you stab a syringe full of broken glass or floppy shoes into his central nervous system. That's the tacit deal you make with the reader. They want the exquisite shudder. The unexpected laugh. The payoff. The *rush*.

It can be done. There are even a few writers who do it a lot. Roald Dahl, Kurt Vonnegut, Thomas Berger come to mind. You might have your own favorites. If you don't, try those guys and you'll get the idea. You'll be struck by how effortlessly they bridge comedy and horror, as if it weren't the intricate gene-splicing of ideas it actually is.

And though the premises of comedy or horror are often interchangeable, they must be approached *very* differently as writing experiences. Horror, after all, essentially deals with mortality and, by implication, spiritual concerns. Comedy can deal with nuances of the human condition, but it mostly walks away from the metaphysical needs of horror. You feel these components when writing in either form. And when you blend the two, you're really aware of them. Especially since they are both about exaggeration of reality, however slight; implantation of neon into the ordinary.

The *edge*.

When you are writing comedy or horror, the edge is everything. You must have it in your voice, and you must dangle readers off its side. And tension feeds off edge like it's red meat. The rush can't be far behind.

If it all goes well, you'll create the divine noise. The one people make when they're laughing or terrified. I've even thought at times that terror and laughter sounded like the same, shocked, emotive aria. And it's the one you live for as a writer.

You lull them, relax them, make them feel like all is well—and then you zap them. That's all there is to it.

Well, maybe not *all* . . .

But if I told you everything, that would mean I knew more than I actually do. None of us knows exactly how it's done beyond a certain point.

Just be glad Eddie never found you, and keep writing.

If it's going to happen, it will. And if it isn't, it still might if you hang-in.

I'll be looking for you.

Chapter 21

The Psychology of Horror and Fantasy Fiction

Katherine Ramsland, Ph.D.

Don't you laugh when the hearse goes by
Or you will be the next to die!
They wrap you up in bloody sheets
And then they bury you six feet deep!

One of my earliest memories of horror was hearing my childhood play-mates taunt each other with this chant. It was passed from the older to the younger children, who in turn grew up to pass it along to those coming after. And no one dared to laugh at a hearse! As much as I dreaded the ghoulish song, I always listened as it was repeated, chilled by the hideous images it raised in my childish mind, yet somehow attracted to the experience of being frightened. As I grew up, I continued to feed this attraction by reading about vampires and witches, by sneaking out at night to play in the graveyard, or by sitting alone in the basement late at night to watch hair-raising movies about psychopathic kill-ers. And as I cultivated the stimulation of horror in myself, I also developed a peculiar delight in drawing others into the net of horror with me. Before I grew up and left, all of the other kids in my neighborhood had heard about "the hook"—that ghastly, dismembered, artificial claw left on the car door of the oblivious couple who barely escaped a bloody death when they drove off.

From the enormous popularity of the horror genre, it is easy to conclude that I am not alone in my fascination with the raw experience of sheer terror.

Theaters overflow with people who want to scare themselves to the limit by watching a madman with an ax chase a little boy through a maze, or a murdered girl nursing vengeance over the years in her underwater casket. Best-seller lists inevitably seem to contain at least one horror novel. Why such widespread fascination?

The Scottish philosopher David Hume thinks it is part of our nature to subject ourselves to horror. He claims that if there were no real things to be afraid of, we would most certainly invent some. Although he attributes this phenomenon to the perverse human desire to make oneself as miserable as possible, I believe it derives from something more positive. Adi-Kent Thomas Jeffries, chronicler of numerous accounts of the supernatural, claims that she is fascinated by ghosts because "they are so unpredictable." Her statement reveals a clue to a more subtle function of dark fantasy than just that of scaring ourselves: horror fiction springs from the urge to preserve ourselves from the social dynamics of uniformity and security, which can eclipse who we are as individuals just as surely as can the vampire who visits us in the night to suck the life out of us. For many of us, horror is a means by which we can keep our fingers on the pulse of our own humanity.

So what is this *dread,* this attraction to what we most fear, that sends us back ever and again to read stories or watch movies that we swore off the last time we were terrified out of our wits? Why do some of us even go so far as to *create* the terror to which others succumb? I intend to address these questions, first by describing those aspects of human existence that create conditions of imbalance in our personal identity; then by showing how dark fantasy has an integral place in our efforts to regain that balance. The initial step, then, is to introduce us to ourselves.

Our most immediate experience, as human beings, is from the inside, from our own personal point of view. Our experience is unique, continuous, open-ended and reaches beyond our typical modes of moment-by-moment awareness. Much of the way we live out our lives is done at a prereflective level, and even when we attempt to subject our experience to self-conscious scrutiny, much of the immediacy eludes our attempts, like the scraps of dough left outside the cookie cutter. Our experiencing transcends itself even in the act of reflecting; it is already into the next moment by the time we have addressed it with intelligible concepts. So we live with a blur of ambiguity at the margins of our conscious awareness, an uncertain sense of things that clouds the choices we make with the fear of faulty decisions and weighs down our personal responsibility with self-doubt and guilt. The frustration of our existence is that there are no clear-cut absolutes by which we can measure our decisions.

To make matters worse, we find ourselves in a world of things that do not share our dilemma. A rock is a rock and will always be a rock. Its existence is stable and essentially defined. Lacking it ourselves, we are attracted to such categorical immutability. So we try to imitate our world by setting up artificial ways of avoiding ourselves and becoming *more* like things. Since we have the capacity to view ourselves from the outside, the way we view trees or beetles, we emphasize the external point-of-view and develop a basic approach to human existence that will allow us to extricate ourselves from the internal, experimental point of view as much as possible, and thus free us from the demanding and equivocal isolation of being individuals.

One of the ways that we step outside of ourselves is by promoting absolutes that rely on science and the precision of mathematics and technology. We see the world as something to be measured, categorized, predicted, and exhaustively explained in terms that we can understand within the limitations of language and logical concepts. According to this approach, nothing is, inherently, a mystery. And since we, ourselves, are part of this world, we, too, are categorized, analyzed, and put into a box. Aligned with this view, we convince ourselves that enough observation and calculation will eventually separate the ambiguities of our internal experience into the black-and-white results of external analysis.

However, this overreliance on science and technology blinds us to the fact that science and logic comprise only one way of interpreting the world—a way invented by humans and thus having no intrinsic truth value. It is an interpretation that has a valuable place in our quest for knowledge, but it forces us to abstract ourselves away from our unique personal identity. To avoid admitting that we have created a perspective on ourselves which diminishes us and which reminds us that it *is* a human invention, we shake off the "humanness" of our starting point as interpreters, then deceive ourselves into believing that the interpretation is just "out there" ready for us to utilize. The more we identify with the abstractions of science and modern intelligentsia, the more we detach ourselves from our own personal, concrete existence. Such an attitude, however, will eventually cancel us out altogether.

From an external point of view, each of us exists only by the merest chance, and an individual's death will be incidental, an anonymous number on a statistical chart. Personal qualities are diffused, and it no longer matters whether any of us, as individuals, ever even existed. No one is significant, and nothing personal really matters. The point-of-view on who we are is not influenced by our personal experience, but is rather a "view from nowhere." We are absorbed into the nebulous crowd, leveled out into anonymous nobodies.

In some ways, this absorption into the masses is comfortable for us. We are freed from the anxiety of personal guilt and decision. We just do what "they" do, think what "they" think, and wear what "they" wear—and "they" are responsible. We fade into the statistics. It frees us from the terrors of the extreme isolation of being an individual alone, where we see ourselves from within our own experience, a point-of-view which makes our own contingencies monumental and our eventual death a jarring issue demanding personal confrontation. In our attempt to escape individual isolation, then, we allow gross processes of self-obscuration to dominate our existence, and we allow ourselves to be seduced into believing that the partial lives we live when we are swallowed into the anonymous crowd make up the whole picture. We identify so strongly with a culture that seeks self-escape that we willfully ignore the marginal aspects of our experience that defy categorization and control, and we concentrate only on those aspects which can be viewed from an external, categorizing point of view. We subdivide, then truncate ourselves for the dubious benefits of the fleeting sense of security as nonentities.

But such security is a superficial comfort at best. We can never completely immerse ourselves in the crowd because we *do* have an internal point of view and can never really escape it through ideological reductions that leave out the personal, subjective perspective. We can never be made exhaustively transparent to ourselves, because we cannot completely grasp the most immediate, prereflective moments of our experiencing, and thus cannot effectively detach ourselves from the personal contingencies which are inherent in being human. We will always possess a marginal realm of experiencing that remains *unformed* in the ideas that result from attempting to calculate and control human personality. *How* we are will never be fully caught up in *what* we are. Thus, while the modern approach of technology and science views us astigmatically as one type of object in the world among many, we will never be as accessible to the dissecting boards of objective analysis as will roaches, fungus, and stalactites. If we fail to face who we truly are, and thus fail to develop ourselves fully as human beings, we leave ourselves defenseless to forces which threaten to annihilate our human integrity.

Our instinct for self-preservation is strong, however. While we attempt to escape the internal point-of-view, with its inherent ambiguity, discontinuities, and moment-by-moment self-transcendence, we begin to yearn—some consciously, others unconsciously—for something that will show us that we are not so easily analyzed, predicted, and controlled. We want something that will recall us to our primordial selves. When we inhabit only a partial existence, which can lead to self disintegration, we tend to create things, which will snap us back into our full human being. One of these means of self-restoration is fantasy.

Fantasy is a product of human imagination, which allows us mentally to experience things about which we have no real knowledge, which might or might not be "out there." It reminds us that we don't have all the answers, and it assures us of more possibilities than are granted by the philosophies of technology and modern civilization. It is an echo of our actual experience of ourselves, one that prevents the self-amputations of abstract categorical approaches. We might admit that *something* of our condition can be explained and externally analyzed—our physical parts, the chemicals in our brains, the stereotypical phobias we suffer—but the fact that we can create and get involved in fantasy functions to let us know that there is more to ourselves than that which can be held up to the sterility of public scrutiny. We retain and utilize the internal point-of-view, which is elusive but insistent, providing fertile ground for an imagination that interprets our subjective, individual, and private qualities into inventive visions that can promote self unification.

So where does horror fit in? Why do we create "things that go bump in the night"; the "something-I-know-not-what" under the bed or scratching at the door; werewolves and vampires and human flies? Dark fantasy serves the same function as ordinary fantasy but provides a more jolting, raw confrontation with ourselves.

We are effectively shocked by the various aberrations of human form, be they the gut-wrenching horror of *Friday the Thirteenth* or the less bloody but strongly suggestive terrors of situations like the babysitter who receives threatening phone calls from the psychotic murderer on the line upstairs. We are frightened of pain, dismemberment, and death, but we are also repulsed by self-transformations like psychosis or regeneration into animal form. Although some theorists claim that we tend to relate horror to our own mental and physical form because of an inherent limitation of the human imagination, I think we do so because we use horror as a means of reintegrating ourselves with those aspects of our subjective perspective that have been so often relegated to the shadows but which continue to make themselves felt on a subconscious level. Those psychological qualities that comprise our elusive individuality strive to make themselves known, and the imagination is an available channel for such activity. So we return to ourselves by exposing ourselves to things that touch on our humanity and that are comprehensible only where science and reflective analysis leave off. We create things to which we can humanly relate, but which bring us so close to our mysterious primal core that they also frighten us.

Horror stories force us to walk a tightrope between two kinds of self-annihilation: 1) the eclipse of the self, which hides in the false security of anonymity, and 2) the dreaded individual isolation in which we are vulnerable to physically and mentally destructive forces, which gang up on our weakness. When we read a story about a werewolf, or a creeping bone disease, or a chain-saw wielding midget, we are drawn away from the security of the crowd into the realm where we are exposed, isolated, and defenseless, to something we cannot comprehend in the normal world. Horror penetrates to our most individual secret fears, dredging up the bowels of the subconscious. We create monsters with unknown potential, an echo of the part of us that eludes predictability. It frightens us because of the view we get of our own souls, but it also prevents us from being swallowed up in the *they*. We step rather tentatively into this realm of body snatchers and tulpas, where little boys eat live puppies and grisly hands suddenly reach out at us from paintings, but we do step in, always keeping a cautious eye out for dangers. We waffle: Should we read/watch it? The risk we take is the risk of transformation or death or madness, self-annihilation in some form. But we step in because we cannot—try as we might to convince ourselves that we can—rest comfortably in anonymity, either. So we immerse ourselves in horror and thrill to the idea that there is something beyond artificially imposed boundaries. We subject ourselves to ghosts who lock us alone in dark rooms, to madmen who tie us under swinging, razor-sharp pendulums, to zombies, and banshees, and ravaging plagues brushing up against us in human form. We allow ourselves to enter an experience in which we have little control, and in which we are made to realize that control is an illusion anyway. Yes, we can slam the book shut, or turn off the television, or exit from the theater, but even if we do that, we go back to it, in one form or another. We can't really turn it off because it is an extension of ourselves.

The emotions of terror and horror keep us attuned to a full sense of ourselves, which includes a confrontation with personal vulnerability and death. If we avoid this confrontation, we reinforce the imbalance of unrealized autonomy and personal value, which is created by detached, external self-perception. However, neither can we wholly abandon ourselves to our fears on threat of self-destruction through death or madness. So horror fantasy acts like a valve that allows steam to escape when the buildup is too great. It invites us into a world where we can experience the possibilities suggested by ambiguity in their most extreme forms, yet the fictionality allows respite from a confrontation so strong that it would overwhelm us. It can provide a cathartic release without oppressing us with more than we are able to endure. Thus, while horror can be unpleasant, and even painfully shocking, it aids us to achieve the reassurance of momentary self-realization; we have access to the awareness that we are, essentially, one step beyond.

In this same light, those who move beyond reading and/or watching horror fantasy to creating it have achieved a stage in their self-development at which they accept the ambiguity of their existence and are prepared to face head-on the possibilities suggested. They are ready to so thoroughly engage with the terrifying unknown that they have freed their imagination to really explore what might be lurking out there. The boundaries between sanity and madness are titillating as well as frightening, and the storytellers are willing to risk the consequences should they go too far.

While the readers of horror are more adventurous and more willing to risk themselves than those who avoid reminders of their subjectivity, they are not as willing as those who create it. Despite being fully drawn into the material, the reader is at least subconsciously aware that the story has been created by another person, and dreamlike as it may be, it will end—most likely in a way that will relieve the reader of having the horror linger too strongly after he or she is finished with the story. The reader is in the comparatively safe position of taking fictional horror in hand and using it to experience strong emotions that can diffuse the real horrors of human existence.

On the other hand, the storytellers are often not in such a position, and might have no idea what they will find as they probe their minds and souls for the most original and terrifying ideas—ideas which might offer no cathartic resolutions for them. While it is true that a storyteller may have closure on a fantasy before he actually explores it, he is always at risk if he continues in this genre. So, for the storyteller, dark fantasy goes beyond just the function of contacting the primal self; it launches him across a spectrum where human existence shades into nothingness, closer and closer to the vulnerability of total individual isolation in the face of destructive forces. Thus, it is not only the call to self that motivates the storytellers; it is also the spirit that took David out to meet Goliath—the urge to issue a challenge to something beyond themselves, which may be more horrifying than they can bear, and then to return intact.

Horror fiction serves an important function in our attempt to achieve personal authenticity. While, superficially, it has entertainment value and may provide a cathartic release, its benefits reach far deeper into our psyches. When we allow ourselves to face the possibilities that are yet, and always will be, just beyond the realms of technology and scientific explanation, we alert ourselves to the ways in which we try to escape from the ambiguities of our internal point of view; we recognize how we try to bury ourselves by identifying with a culture that views us strictly from the outside. The exposure to horror and terror prevents us from moving too far away from ourselves toward the annihilation of objective abstraction, but the strength of fear prevents the total abandonment to individual isolation and vulnerability that horror invites us into.

While horror scares us on one level, you see, it preserves us on another.

Chapter 22

Fantasy and Faculty X

Colin Wilson

Early one morning in the spring of 1975, I was falling asleep on a friend's settee. I had traveled to London on the night train and was hoping to snatch a couple of hours' sleep before I set out for a long day of appointments. As I drifted on the verge of sleep, a strange image floated into my mind—an image of an enormous spaceship, battered and full of holes, drifting somewhere in the asteroid belt. It startled me into wakefulness, and I lay there and thought about it. A kind of Dracula's castle floating in the sky, looking derelict and abandoned, yet full of unseen dangers . . .

I began to try to imagine what it would be like inside. Would it be full of corridors and control rooms? If so, then why was it so huge? (I somehow knew that it was more than fifty miles long and twenty miles high.) I imagined floating through one of the gaping holes in its side, and finding myself in a vast emptiness, like the inside of a Gothic cathedral. The empty spaces are intersected by long catwalks that look like strands of spider web. And somewhere in the centre of the blackness, there is a faint glow that seems to be coming from below the endless metal plain that constitutes its floor.

In fewer than five minutes, I had sketched out the plot of a novel—my third attempt at science fiction. (It had been preceded by *The Mind Parasites* and *The Philosopher's Stone*.) At breakfast a couple of hours later, I outlined the book to my friend Bill Hopkins. In the bottom of the derelict spacecraft, the explorers find a number of human beings, apparently in a state of suspended animation. The craft was probably on its way to some distant star system when it was struck by a shower of meteors. So the explorers take three of these humanoids back to earth. They are not dead, yet they show no sign of life. All attempts to revive them are a failure until an enterprising young journalist succeeds in gaining access to the laboratory where they are being studied, and takes a photograph of the sleeping girl. Then, allured by her beauty, he leans over her, his hands brushing the cold flesh of the naked breasts. As his lips come close to hers, there is a sudden flash. He twists backwards, his face frozen with agony. As he sinks to the floor, the girl's eyes open and she slowly sits up in her coffinlike container. The man on the floor has becoms shriveled and grey, and the face is that of a man of ninety. . . .

Later that day, when I had attended an editorial meeting, I called on my publisher and told him the story of the novel. He told me he would send me a contract within the next few days. The work was to be called *The Space Vampires*.

Ten years later, the book reached the screen under the title *Lifeforce*. It had a brilliant production team—some of them had worked on *Star Wars* and *2001*—and cost twenty-five million dollars to make. The script was written by the man who wrote *Alien;* the music, by Henry Mancini. And it was a textbook example of how to make a bad movie.

To do the producers justice, the film's major shortcoming was not their fault, nor that of its director, Tobe Hooper. It was the distributor who decided that it was half-an-hour too long and that the excess half-hour should be cut out of the beginning. The result was that the film had no buildup. Within the first five minutes, it had launched into horror—when the spacecraft returns to earth, everyone on board is dead, and all of them are shriveled and decomposing. Then the young reporter tries to take his photograph of the girl, and she zaps him as well as the soldiers who are standing guard outside. Everyone she zaps turns into an energy vampire, and soon the streets of London are full of the living dead, all looking frantically for victims. . . .

I recalled my childhood favorite, *King Kong*—the old black-and-white version—and how it takes a good half-hour before Fay Wray gets chained to the stone pillars in the jungle and the great ape comes crashing out of the trees. By the time the distributors had removed that essential half-hour from *Lifeforce*, there was nowhere for it to go. Once you've seen one man sucked dry by a vampire, you've seen 'em all. In Japan, the complete version was shown, and it was an immense success. In Europe and America, the truncated version was a flop.

One Dublin critic—God forgive him—commented: "The film is nasty and cheap, like the Colin Wilson novel on which it is based." Now this, if I may say so, is untrue. It is a damn good novel. I am a good enough critic to know when I've written a bad book, or one that is only half good. (A few months ago, I read my novel *Necessary Doubt* to my son and realized that it needs cutting by a third.) And it *is* a good novel because I got fascinated by the basic question I set myself: If energy vampires can transfer themselves from body to body as they suck their victims dry, how could one possibly track them down? *Space*

Vampires is a kind of science-fiction detective story, and, as I wrote it, I began to feel like Watson when Sherlock Holmes shakes him and says: "The game's afoot!"

And here is Rule One about writing any kind of novel, science fiction or otherwise: When a writer says to himself, "I have an interesting problem . . .," he induces in himself the same state of mind that a child feels when his mother says, "Once upon a time . . ." *This* is the proper starting point of any novel. For once the writer had induced that feeling in himself, he has also induced it in the reader. His problem is to *visualize* what he is describing with such clarity that he feels as if he is actually present.

A few months ago, I decided that I would settle down to a novel I had always intended to read: *Buddenbrooks,* by Thomas Mann. I have always been familiar with certain chapters in the book but had never read it from the beginning, for *Buddenbrooks* has a particularly slow opening—a long description, which goes on for several chapters, of a family dinner party. This time, I persevered, reading slowly and carefully, with a sense of having all the time in the world. Soon I became totally absorbed, and saw why this novel, which Thomas Mann wrote in his early twenties, had been a best seller in the first years of the century. Mann *puts himself into* the scene he is describing, until he can feel it and see it and smell it. When a character speaks, you know that Mann could actually hear his voice as he spoke every word. He is *actually there,* and he wants you to be there, too. So although it is a first novel by a young man, it has an air of authority—the authority of a man who knows precisely what he wants to say.

In a book of mine called *The Occult,* I coined a name for this odd ability to put oneself into another time and place; I called it *Faculty X.* You might say that it is the ability to be in two places at the same time—to project your mind totally into some other time and place. I can cite an amusing example from my early days in London, when I was doing some research into the Jack the Ripper murders—which I used in a novel called *Ritual in the Dark.* I visited the back yard at 29 Hanbury Street, in London's Whitechapel area, where the Ripper disemboweled his third victim, a prostitute called Annie Chapman. In the corner of the back yard there was an outdoor toilet. The woman who took me into the yard—the wife of the owner of the house—told me how, a few months before, a female guest had asked for the lavatory, and she had accompanied her into the back yard and stook talking to her as she relieved her bladder. It was a dark, winter evening, and the visitor said she thought the yard was "spooky."

"As a matter of fact," said her hostess, "Jack the Ripper killed a woman in *this yard,* and her body lay right there" (pointing to a spot close to the lavatory door).

Her guest gave a loud shriek, jumped to her feet and ran clumsily—encumbered by her underwear—back into the house. She had *visualized* the body of the victim so clearly that she felt she had actually seen it. This is Faculty X at work.

Most of us can visualize something unpleasant when stimulated by the right kind of suggestion: an old house; the wind moaning through cracks in the door; the creaking branches of a tree. . . . There is a story about the poet Shelley, who was present at a house party in Italy when all the guests decided to tell one another horror stories. (One result was Mary Shelley's novel *Frankenstein.*) As they were talking about ghosts, Shelley suddenly shrieked and rushed out of the house. He explained later that he had been looking at his wife's nipples, which showed through her thin blouse, and that, suddenly, he had been seized by a fancy that she had *eyes* in the place of nipples—and that they were looking at him!

This story reminds me, in turn, of a remark Wordsworth made to some acquaintance—De Quincey, I think—to the effect that he was terrified of his imagination because it could carry him away into the depths of horror and despair. Poets often seem to have this odd power to supercharge the imagination to the point where they experience sensory delusions.

Every one of us can remember times in childhood when we have lain awake listening to the occasional creaking of the stair, convinced that some horrible fiend is creeping up on tiptoe. Most of us are glad to get rid of this disturbing faculty. Yet it is precisely *this* faculty, Faculty X, that can be trained and disciplined to produce a *Buddenbrooks* or *War and Peace.* The writer of horror fiction, who uses it in its simplest and most powerful form, could be compared to a bronco buster trying to break in a wild horse. He has taken the first step toward the development of Faculty X.

And what precisely *is* Faculty X? At the time I first wrote about it, in *The Occult,* I could not have answered that question, for I lacked the vital clue. At least, I possessed it without knowing I possessed it, since I had on my bookshelves bound copies of *Scientific American* dating from the early 1960s, including Michael Gazzaniga's article on the split brain. Most of my readers will be familiar with this research, but for the benefit of those who are not, I had better offer a brief summary: Although the brain consists of two identical halves, like a walnut, each seems to have completely different functions. In human beings, the left half deals with language and logic, and the right, with more 'intuitive' functions like pattern recognition. You could say that the left half is a scientist, and the right, an artist. The remarkable discovery made by Roger Sperry and Michael Gazzaniga was that the person you call *you* is the scientist; we are literally out of touch with the person in the other half. Sperry discovered that *split-brain* patients—patients whose hemispheres had been divided as a cure for epilepsy—turned into *two people.* When the patient answered a question, it was the left brain that replied. For example, a patient who was shown an indecent picture with the right brain (that is to say, with the left visual field, which, for some reason, is connected to the right brain) looked embarrassed. Asked "Why are you blushing?" she replied, "I don't know." That is to say, the *I* in the right brain did not know.

Mozart once remarked that tunes were always "walking into his head." What he meant, obviously, was that they walked *out* of the right—the *stranger*—and *into* the left. And when the image of the giant spaceship floated into my mind on the edge of sleep, it came from the right hemisphere of my brain.

But perhaps the most interesting discovery made by Sperry's team was that the right and left hemispheres operate at *different speeds:* the right is slow, the left is fast. And this explains why they are out of contact much of the time. They are like two men going for a walk, and one walks so much faster than the other that he is soon a hundred yards in front, and conversation is practically impossible. In primitive people, the hemispheres relate differently; the people *live* at a slower pace, so the left and right find it easier to stay in contact. The slower pace also makes them more intuitive; intuition is a function of the right hemisphere.

There are two basic methods for re-establishing contact between the two selves. One is to soothe yourself into a deep state of relaxation, so the left slows down. The other is to stimulate yourself into a state of intense excitement—the younger generation does it with loud music and strobe lights—so the right begins to move faster. Both these techniques have the same effect; the two halves are like two trains running on parallel tracks at exactly the same speed, so the passengers can lean out of the windows and talk. . . .

One of my favourite examples of Faculty X involves the former method. The historian, Arnold Toynbee, was sitting in the ruins of the citadel of Mistra, on Mount Taygetus in Greece, looking down on the plain of Sparta, and chewing a bar of chocolate. The thought entered his head: "Two centuries ago, barbarians scrambled over *those* walls and slaughtered the inhabitants, and ever since then, this place has been a ruin." And suddenly it was as if he could *see* the barbarians clambering over the walls; it was as real as if it had happened a half-hour ago. It happened, obviously, because Toynbee was relaxed and feeling contented, and the left half of the brain *slowed down* until it was walking beside the right.

But my other favourite example of Faculty X affords an even more important insight. It is Proust's description, from *Swann's Way,* of how he came home one day feeling tired and a little depressed, and his mother offered him a cup of herb tea and a small cake. As he tasted the cake dipped in tea, "an exquisite pleasure invaded my senses . . . I had ceased to feel mediocre, accidental, mortal. . . ." And by carefully studying this sensation, he is able to recall that it reminds him of his childhood—how he used to come in from his walk, and his aunt used to offer him some of her cake dipped in herb tea.

But why should this memory of his childhood fill him with "exquisite pleasure?" The answer is surely as follows: He is feeling tired and impatient (another way of saying the left brain is in its usual mad hurry). He is *trapped* in left-brain consciousness, which is as unsatisfying as a lukewarm bath. He tastes the cake dipped in tea, and the right brain sends a momentary surge of memory.

He is reminded that life can be delightful and full of richness. The effect is to *make* the left slow down—like a man in a hurry who suddenly remembers that he has left his train ticket at home. In other words, we can make the left slow down by *taking thought*. The left can *order itself* to slow down.

It is this latter realization that is of central importance in creative writing. Consider again Thomas Mann's *Buddenbrooks:* It is a long chronicle of a Hamburg family, describing four generations. Mann deliberately begins *slowly,* with a lengthy and precise re-creation of a family party. Everything is described: the room, the dress and the mannerisms of the characters—nothing is too small or too trivial to seize his attention. But once he has persuaded his right brain to conjure up the scene in detail, the right has begun to *understand* what is demanded of it, and, as the novel begins to move faster, it continues to conjure up each scene in rich detail.

We can see the same process at work in *War and Peace,* where Tolstoy spends a half-dozen boring chapters describing a party in the year 1805, then goes on to conjure up a panorama of Russia at the time of the Napoleonic wars. In those early chapters, he is 'teaching' the right brain what is demanded of it.

This is something that, as a writer, I have always understood instinctively. When I began writing stories—as a teenager—I was influenced by H. G. Wells and R. L. Stevenson. Because both are excellent storytellers, they were a bad influence on me. They *tell* a story: "Once upon a time there was a man called Kipps. . . ." And when I tried to imitate them, I became oddly self-conscious, like an inexperienced liar trying to convince someone he is telling the truth. Then I read Joyce's *Ulysses* and Dostoevsky's *Crime and Punishment,* and I began to see where I was going wrong. I had to try to put *myself* inside a scene and visualize it so clearly that I could describe it. Once I learned not to try to *tell* a story—that is, to *try* to make it interesting—but merely to try to visualize a scene until it was real, I had discovered the basic secret. That secret is to try to persuade the "stranger" to cooperate in the telling of a story: to try to induce a condition approximating to Faculty X. It was, admittedly, a long and painful business. When I began writing my first novel, *Ritual in the Dark,* I often wrote the same scene again and again, until I seemed to know it by heart. With each rewriting, it became more real. I walked around the Jack-the-Ripper murder sites in the East End of London, trying to soak myself in their atmosphere. I paid special attention to such details as the rubbish on a bomb site, the bric-a-brac in a junk-shop window, and the precise way that a cat stretches itself and extends its claws. (I had always been impressed by Joyce's rendition of the sound made by a cat: not "meow," as most of us would write it, but: "mrkrgnao!") Then, back in the British Museum Reading Room—where I kept my typewriter—I tried to visualize it as if I were still there.

This training paid unexpected dividends more than thirty years after I had written *Ritual in the Dark*. A couple of years ago, an old friend and fellow writer, Donald Seaman, told me he thought of writing a science-fiction novel about animals who had undergone genetic mutations as a result of radioactivity. But he was still trying to construct a plot. That same evening, I watched a television program about insect defense. The next day, when I met Don on our daily walk on the cliffs, I said, "I've worked out your novel. *Spider World*. It's about a future date when the earth is dominated by gigantic telepathic spiders who breed human beings for food, as we breed cattle. . . ." And I sketched out the plot, which I had worked out just before I fell asleep the night before.

When I'd finished, Don shook his head. "It doesn't sound the kind of thing I could write." But by this time, I had talked myself into a state of enthusiasm. "All right. We'll write it *together*," I said. (We had already written two encyclopedias in collaboration.) I wrote a ten-page outline of the book and sent it to my publisher, who immediately gave us a contract.

A few months later, we had both finished our current books and were prepared to begin work on *Spider World*. Don asked, "How do you want to work? Shall I write a chapter, then you write a chapter? Or would you like to start the book and I'll finish it?" I decided that I would get the book started, continue until I felt my invention flagging, then turn it over to Don.

I began in my usual way—by trying to visualize precisely, in this case, what it would be like for human beings to live in holes in the desert. For the purpose, I borrowed a dozen books about deserts from the library and learned all I could about their flora, their insect life, their climatic conditions. I had never before attempted to write fantasy, as distinct from science fiction. There is, of course, a basic similarity; but fantasy still carries the flavour of its origin in the fairy tale. For me, science fiction is a form of realism; fantasy is pure romance. The starting point for *Spider World* was a great deal of careful research into the habits of spiders and other insects. But the moment I began typing the first page, I realized that this experience was *totally* unlike the writing of science fiction. My imagination worked as precisely as ever; I visualized what it would be like to crouch in an underground cave while spiders floated across the desert in reconnaissance balloons, probing the ground with a beam of sheer willpower, trying to arouse a response of terror that would betray their prey. . . .

And suddenly, to my surprise, there was no question of flagging invention! It seemed as if the book was writing itself—which I knew to be a sure sign that my right brain was offering its full cooperation! The publishers had contracted for a novel of about three hundred pages; but I watched it expand to four hundred, five hundred, *six* hundred, with still no sign of the end. I knew better than to try to bring it to an end prematurely; it had to keep on growing, like a tree, until it had reached the limit of its natural development.

By this time, Don had grown tired of waiting and had started a spy novel, the genre in which he excels. And I continued to write, slightly astonished at what was happening, watching the book expand of its own accord. In the original outline, I had described the city of the spiders—a concrete city that had once belonged to human beings, in the old days when man was the master of the earth; but there were immense cobwebs stretching between the skyscrapers. Apart from this description, I had no idea of what the city would be like. As my hero was taken into the city, with the small band of human captives, I knew as little about its geography as any prospective reader. I learned about it exactly as the reader would: by imagining that I was "walking" into it and looking around. I am not, of course, claiming that I wrote in some kind of trance. But as I set the words down on paper, there was always an odd feeling, as if I were in a kind of waking dream. And a year later, when I submitted the thousand-page manuscript to my publisher, there was a slight sense of bewilderment, like waking up and finding yourself lying in your own bed after traveling through some remote landscape.

I was lucky; my British publisher decided to print it without cuts, even though it would have to be issued in two volumes. The American publisher who accepted it decided it would have to be brought out in four volumes. As to my patient and good-tempered collaborator, he had decided about halfway through to abandon all claim on the project and allow me to publish it under my own name. As I write this article, the first half of *Spider World* has just gone to the printers. And I still have a sensation of having been through an experience I do not fully understand. . . .

Why do animals *not* experience Faculty X, since they have not yet experienced that internal division that has turned man into a schizoid personality? The answer, I believe, is that the brain needs to *divide* before the reaction can occur. Unlike animals, human beings have learned to live in a world of abstractions: hence the feeling of unreality that haunts the modern mind. Faculty X involves the deliberate *and concerted* activity of the two selves inside the head. This means that we use the hidden powers of the brain to overrule the sense of unreality—to brush it aside as we brush it aside whenever we confront a serious crisis. Arnold Toynbee was able to experience Faculty X because he knew about the history of Sparta and the invasion of the citadel of Mistra; then, as he sat looking down on the plain of Sparta, some spontaneous process *raised* this abstract knowledge to the level of reality. The nature of the process can be compared to the deliberate bringing together of two small quantities of uranium 235 to form a critical mass. But this process is *not only* the basis of the atomic bomb; it can also be used to produce nuclear power in precisely controlled quantities. The same precise control can also be applied to Faculty X.

Of one thing I am certain: that creative writers—particularly those working in the realm of fantasy—are instinctively groping toward the development of Faculty X. My own experience of it convinces me that it is closely related to what Jung called "active imagination," but even *more* closely to what another psychologist, Pierre Janet, called "the reality function." And I suspect that, when professors of the twenty-fifth century come to write the history of the past thousand years, they will see the development of the fantasy novel as one of the turning points of human evolution.

Chapter 23

A "Do" List for Getting Your Literary Agent

Mary T. Williamson

"Get an agent? What do *I* need with an agent? Everyone who's read it says this book will sell itself! Why should I let somebody I don't even know have 10 percent of my money? Like I said, *this* novel is something everyone will want. I can do it myself."

And—you may be right.

But you're probably wrong. Why? There are many reasons, and here are some: Regardless of how good it is, novel or nonfiction, you must get some editor somewhere to read it before a publisher can buy it. And while this is not always true, most full-sized publishing houses still *prefer* to look at agency-represented manuscripts. If you think about that carefully, you'll see why: The agent already culls out the poor-quality material before sending out any manuscripts, and he sends out only those that may be worth his time.

This isn't to say that unagented manuscripts are never read. They are. But, as a rule, they don't get first consideration even by houses that do accept unagented material. Would you rather your manuscript be on the desk of the fourth reader or on the desk of an acquiring editor?

There's another excellent reason for taking the time and making the effort to acquire an agent. Do *you* know today's market, what publishers are paying, what terms are acceptable for a first book, what rights the author should be able to retain? No? Your agent will. And even if you can place a manuscript on your own, you may be better off having an agent handle the transaction. I know, personally, authors who have signed away a lot—more than they understood that they were doing! One well-published writer told a publisher, "I'm asking only two thousand for the book; no more. *If* you'll sign the contracts now!" Boy, did they ever! Because the "no more" meant, to them, *no royalties*!

Fortunately, the writer asked me to step in, try to get him something—*anything* else—and I succeeded in obtaining a flat 2 percent royalty. That's not much, but it's something. And the whole mess could have been avoided if the author had not tried to make the deal on his own.

Contracts can be very tricky, and you'd better know what you are signing before you sign one. Most publishers—like anyone else—try to get all they can. After all, they're in publishing *as a business*—to *make money*.

Briefly, I'd like to discuss the matter of short-fiction submissions. You've written a dynamite story and want it in the best possible magazine. Fine; please, do it. Most agents do *not* represent short stories for their writers, simply because it just isn't very profitable. Since a typical short story probably earns less than five cents per word and runs no more than three thousand words, an agent's 10 percent comes to possibly fifteen dollars. It takes a similar amount of time to place a story and winds up being as costly, for the agent, as placing a novel. The remuneration is simply not sufficient to warrant the time outlay. Besides, magazine editors, unlike book editors, really don't seem to have an across-the-board preference for agented manuscripts. And since most mags are buying only first North American rights, contracts aren't a gigantic problem.

So go ahead and submit your short fiction yourself—but please let me give you some advice on how to do so: First, check out the market to which you intend to send the story. Pick up a copy of the publication; make sure the story you wrote fits the format. A gentle fantasy may not go over too well at *Night Cry* but might be suitable for *Twilight Zone.*

Enclose a brief cover letter, listing credits, if any, and be sure to address it to the proper person. (The fiction editor of a magazine is usually listed in the masthead. If not, send it to the managing editor—by name, if available.)

And, if you want to have the story returned to you if it is not accepted, you *must* enclose a self-addressed stamped envelope (SASE) for that purpose. If you don't need to have it returned, tell the editor so in your letter. Sometimes it is cheaper to make a photocopy or a computer copy than to enclose an SASE. That decision is yours. Also: *never fold* a story. Use a 9"x12" envelope both for mailing and for SASE.

All longer manuscript submissions, without exception, whether to magazines, book publishing houses, or agents, *must* be accompanied by an SASE; without one, *you will not get your manuscript back.*

While most books on how to write will give you an example of a standard manuscript page, I believe there are no hard-and-fast rules.

However, there are some small things that *must* be followed, in my opinion. When submitting a manuscript either to an agent or to an editor, book *or* magazine, neatness does count. Once you have begun typing your pages a certain way, stick to that format. Keep your margins the same throughout; have the same number of lines on each page; don't change typewriters in the middle of a manuscript. Also: *Never* submit a dot-matrix copy. Most agents won't read dot matrix; I know no editors who will. It simply doesn't convey professionalism, and it is extremely hard to read over long stretches of time.

Handwritten manuscripts will absolutely never be accepted, by anyone. If you must pay to have your work typed, alas, so be it. That is the only way your work will be considered.

If you wish, you may add a copyright line to your first page of manuscript. Most professionals, however, do not do so. There is really no need since 99 percent of agents are honest; neither they nor editors will plagiarize your work. They won't jeopardize their own careers by stealing newcomers' writing.

Where can you find lists of literary agents? A fine source is *Literary Market Place,* which almost all large libraries have available. *Writer's Market* and *Fiction Writer's Market* also have agents' listings.

How do you choose an agent? You don't, really. Ultimately, starting out, they choose you. In order for this to happen, you must let an agent know that you exist. Most agents prefer, I believe, to be queried first regarding the possibility of reviewing a writer's work. Many will not accept a manuscript without a referral; when sent to them, unsolicited manuscripts tend to be returned, unread.

You need to learn how to write a clear, cogent query letter to the literary agent you wish to acquire, setting forth your writing credits of any kind and telling the agent succinctly the premise of your novel or nonfiction book. Enclose an SASE with your query. Always address the literary agent by his surname, not the first name; any other approach is rude and amateurish. You don't know the agent personally, and you are trying to establish a professional relationship. A query letter should be as brief as possible while still imparting the necessary information about you and your book.

If an agent is interested in seeing your manuscript, he will inform you as to the length of the material he wishes to review. In most cases, the length will probably be only a chapter or two, to begin with—probably no more than four, or around seventy-five to eighty pages plus an outline. However, *do* tell the prospective agent how much of the book is *available* for his consideration. If the book is completed, make it known that you will, upon request, send along the entire manuscript.

Once an agent has let you know how much of the work he would like to read, be sure to submit exactly that amount—no more, no less. Several people who have sought my own services have lost the chance because they insisted on sending me more than I was prepared to read. They were certain that I could not tell if the writing was any good unless I read an entire manuscript. Unfortunately, bad writing will evidence itself on the first page most of the time. Fortunately, good writing will usually do so, too. So, let the agent be the judge of how much of your manuscript he needs to review in order to determine whether or not he will represent you.

Like the manuscript, the query letter should never be handwritten; it will not be considered seriously if it is. I have received handwritten queries with the excuses "my typewriter is temporarily out of commission"; "I didn't have availability to a typewriter at the moment"; and even "I don't own a typewriter." *I* don't really care! If the author wanted badly enough to be published, he'd have found a typewriter to use for the twenty minutes it would take to write the query. Since he broke the first cardinal rule, I can be pretty certain he will break others.

Once you have been asked to submit a portion of your manuscript for consideration, send just what is asked for. An agent has only so much time to read. You will *delay* the reading of your work if you send the entire manuscript when what was requested was four chapters. Once, I had a "partial" come in for my consideration that proved to be an entire book—over 1,400 pages long! It went back very quickly.

Many agents will request for submission only a partial manuscript and an outline, instead of the completed book. They do this because most paperback houses will buy only from a partial and outline, and agents want the option to choose between hardcover and paperback houses. It also saves the writer a good deal of time. If the book sells, he can complete it then. And if it does *not* sell, he has tied up only a fraction of the time. Many hardcover houses, however, still prefer entire manuscripts; so do half or more of the publishers of mystery/thriller novels.

When you are asked to send only a few chapters and an outline, the agent, generally speaking, wants consecutive chapters (usually chapters one through whatever will comprise approximately 100 pages), not five chapters chosen randomly from an entire book.

Be sure that the work you mail to an agent is as professional in appearance as it can possibly be. Fresh typewriter ribbons, good quality paper, and adequate typing are essential. Before you send it along, proofread your own work, and clean up any typos you may find. Remember that an agent is not an editor, and he will not, under typical circumstances, edit your work for you. He must receive it the way you hope to see it submitted to an editor. And please, *please,* do not have your manuscript bound in any form. This is the hallmark of an amateur. Professionals send loose copy, not bound; a novel or story is not a screenplay. It is easier for editors to work with loose pages than bound, and that's the way they want them. All manuscripts must be double-spaced, typed on one side only, with sufficient margins at the top and bottom as well as on both sides. The agent is not a typist, either; he will not retype copy for you, so it must be presentable and properly typed when he receives it.

If you don't wish to mail your original manuscript to an agent, but prefer to send a copy, that is fine—so long as it is a good, quality photocopy or a letter-quality printout from your computer. Never send a carbon copy, a dot-matrix copy, or anything less than a letter-quality printout.

Here's a last look at the *why* of obtaining a literary agent:

While all your friends and family have "just loved" your book, can you really be sure that it is a *professionally written* manuscript? Your agent will know, and he will tell you. If he does not think it is quite ready for sale, he may be able to help you make it so. Whenever I think a work has merit, but it is not quite ready for submission, I try to make suggestions to help the writer upgrade his work. Not all agents do this, but many do. Not that any of us will actually *do* the work for you; we won't. Most of us are not writers, but we can and sometimes do make suggestions.

Next, having an agent to handle the more mundane aspects of writing (such as figuring out ways to make a living from it) enables a writer to devote the time to what he or she really does best: *writing*. Contacting editors and publishers is time-consuming, often emotionally draining work. And it is often difficult for a writer to properly "sell" himself, as a writer or a person.

It is a fact that most writers have no realistic idea of what the market is buying and what they are paying. Your agent will have much better insight into these trends and will, for your benefit and his own, endeavor (1) to make the best possible sale for your work and (2) to get you the most advantageous arrangements possible.

One word of warning: Once your literary agent has submitted your work, and it has been accepted by a given publishing house, be prepared to *accept* any reasonable offer he may bring to you. Remember: Your agent is really the best judge of what constitutes a reasonable offer. If you turn down the deal after an agent has worked for weeks or months to set it up, your agent will expect a very, *very* good reason; if you don't have one, be prepared to find another agency.

Some agents believe it is best for the author-agent relationship to develop into a friendship—a sort of big brother or big sister setup. They consider it necessary for the writer and agent to be closely matched in personality. In some ways, certainly, this would be ideal; some author-agent relationships do, in fact, become intimate.

While it's best for the two of you to get along, I don't personally feel that it is mandatory. It's definitely necessary to remain on speaking terms; but the relationship can be just as beneficial, in my experience, if the agent is able to retain an objective distance. For my tastes, I try not to allow friendship to get in the way of my doing my best work. Sometimes, this policy compels me to tell an author, "This is not quite good enough." If there's a close bond, that becomes excruciatingly difficult, if not impossible. The agent will subtly let you know how close the relationship is going to become. Then it's up to you to decide if what he offers is what you need, want, or expect.

Should your author-agent relationship not be satisfactory, you're free to try again. Usually, written contracts between agents and authors are not used, though a few very large agencies may have them. If there *is* a contract, it will stipulate how and when an author may sever the relationship. Without a formal contract, rule-of-thumb and sheer good manners dictate that the author give the agent thirty to ninety days' notice of the intent to withdraw his work from the agent and seek other representation.

In any case, you are not automatically bound together forever. You do not have to retain an agent with whom you are displeased; similarly, an agent does not have to continue with an author.

What obligations do you have to your agent? Mainly, to provide him with material that is professional, which he can probably sell for you. But beyond that, you are obligated to fulfill all contracts he may have negotiated for you, precisely as they are agreed to. Most houses will give a writer sufficient time to finish a book if it was purchased from a partial. If an author cannot do so for sound reasons, he should notify both the agent and publisher that he needs an extension of time. It is almost always given. But don't take this route too often! Houses do not like to deal with unreliable authors or the agents who represent them.

An agent earns a living only by handling the work of the author; most agents are appreciative. However, the author who produces one book every six or seven years is not usually worth taking on by most agents. Productivity is the key to your success—*and* the agent's. It is difficult enough in today's marketplace to establish yourself as a writer, then to make a living from it, without drifting into the habit of not producing as much good work as is reasonable and possible.

Remember that an agent cannot sell what you do not write. Most agents seek full-time, working pros. If you have five manuscripts circulating, you have five times the chance of making it than if you had written one, then sat back to wait for a sale. To be a writer, truly, you must write, and write, and write some more.

Then learn patience. Even with an agent, it can take months for a manuscript to be considered, then accepted or rejected, by a publishing house. While you're waiting, you might as well write something else—right?

Understand now that being an author is probably not going to set you on a road to riches. Many writers make a darned good living doing what they do, but they work at it full time; they produce an impressive body of work. It takes time to establish yourself, to earn the really big money that is always hypothetically available.

That big money, as everyone knows, is most readily made from films. Most literary agents do not directly sell to the movies. That's handled most frequently by movie agents, who deal exclusively in films. (They are present on both coasts.) Don't confuse books with movies. While most literary agents are capable of handling film sales, they tend not to seek them actively. In addition, sales of rights to the movie industry are often handled by the publishing houses themselves.

I believe that you *can* make it as a writer if you are talented and have both the desire and the willingness to devote the necessary amount of time and great effort to the task. While it may be discouraging to try to acquire an agent, remember that agents are out there—and they are looking for good, new talent.

If you choose not to have an agent, there *are* houses who will consider your work. They, too, are always on the lookout for particularly talented writers; they'd like nothing more than to build them into giants of the literary world. Consequently, whether you elect to be agented or not, hang in there and keep trying! Hone your skills incessantly; be as professional as you can be; and don't give up—ever! Because if you are a genuine fiction writer, you will write, and eventually—maybe not in the too-distant future—you *will* sell and be published.

And become the happiest person on earth.

Chapter 24

Putting It on
the Editor's Desk

Alan Rodgers

First of all, let me try to discourage you: Writing is not a practical avocation. It does not pay very well—or at least not well enough often enough—and a lot of awfully bright and talented people want to do it. I'm in a position to know: I edit *Night Cry,* the digest-sized horror magazine, and I'm also the associate editor of *Twilight Zone* magazine. No one should seriously plan to write short fiction for a living; it just doesn't pay very well—not by the hour, nor, for most of us, in cumulative dollars. Writing in general isn't very lucrative, and writing short fiction pays even less well: even established professionals often write stories that no one wants to buy. And an unsold story amounts to hours of work with no pay.

There's worse, too: It takes a *long* time to learn how to write. Most of the writers I deal with spent somewhere between ten and fifteen years learning to write and establishing themselves before their work even began to sell. At the World Science Fiction Convention this year (1986), I looked around and realized that all the hot young writers were at least thirty-five years old.

There are *lots* of good reasons not to try to become a writer, even in a field like this one (which has always been open to new talent). Unless you're fairly sure that you have an unstoppable need to write, you're probably better off putting this book down and going about your business.

But chances are that if you're picking it up in the first place, you can't be discouraged that easily. And the news isn't *all* bad, either; there's always a need in the fiction magazines for new talent. And as fiction magazines go, *Night Cry* and *Twilight Zone* are especially open to unpublished writers. Both magazines almost always have at least one story in each issue from someone who had never been published before.

Even if your need to write is strong enough, be aware that the competition is tough and you're going to need whatever edge you can get. So let me start at the *real* beginning of the story-selling process—the story itself. One of the first things you're bound to read about in a book like this one is the importance of having a good *hook*—a catchy opening, something that catches the reader's interest right away and rivets him to the story. Well, getting the reader's interest right away *is* important, but the idea that a story's first sentence should somehow have all the properties of good ad copy has led to more garishly stupid openings than I want to think about. Don't open your story by using a cheap shocker for a lead and expect it to scare me. It's my observation that cheap gross-outs are funny, not frightening, and while I'm not positively averse to humorous horror, unintentional humor is always obvious and usually not very amusing.

On the other hand, a story *does* have to work clearly and well from the very first word. How important is it? Let me put it this way: As an editor, my rule of thumb is that I read three times as much as I need to, to be absolutely certain that I don't want to buy a story. Sometimes that's *very* little. But the solution isn't to do something loud and obnoxious; the way to get an editor's attention is to have a *story* to tell and to *tell the story* from the very first word. Use as many words as you need to tell it, but every one of them should *tell* the *story*.

What should your manuscript look like? It should have wide margins—you should leave at least an inch on each side and about the same amount at the top and bottom. It should be double-spaced—that is, it should have an extra line of space between each line of text. (Believe it or not, I've actually seen manuscripts come in with extra spaces between the words, and one poor soul wrote in to ask if I wanted an extra space between each letter.)

Your first page should begin with your name and address in the upper left (or right) corner. The story's title should appear about a third of the way down, and a couple of lines below that, your byline—not necessarily your name; if you want to use a pseudonym, then this is where you should put it. It's also a useful place to distinguish between the form of your name you use for business and the one you want to be published under—if, for instance, you ordinarily do business as Joe Smithe but you'd like to be published as Joseph W. Smithe, then put *Joe* in the top corner and *Joseph W.* underneath the title.

Should you write a cover letter? When I was in school, the going advice was that if you didn't have anything particular relevant to say to an editor—such as, for instance, "I've sold three stories to *Awesome Stories,* your sister publication," or "We met last month at the writer's conference," or "My aunt Ellen, who you've been dating for six months, says that I should send you my story"—then you shouldn't waste his time by making him read a cover letter as well as a story. Michael Blaine, a man who used to edit *Twilight Zone,* was of exactly the opposite opinion; he felt that it was something of a cardinal sin *not* to send a cover letter.

My own impression is still developing, and it's mixed: God knows I've read enough *awful* cover letters to know that many people do their stories harm by being smug or pompous or obviously ignorant.

But I've also seen stories from semiprofessional and professional writers end up in the slush pile because the writer didn't send a cover letter and the person who opened the mail that day was the woman who works up at the front desk. One thing you *shouldn't* do is begin your cover letter in an echo of an old Rod Serling monologue. At least a third of the stories in *Twilight Zone's* slush pile have cover letters that begin something like this: "Submitted for your approval—one story, the work of a very hopeful man. Its whereabouts: unknown. Its chances: unknowable. Its status: lost somewhere in the slush pile, lost somewhere between here . . . and the Twilight Zone." Trust me: The joke wasn't all that funny when the first one of you tried it; it's just too obvious.

Regardless, if you *do* send a cover letter it should be simple and straightforward and to the point; it probably shouldn't be chatty unless we are personally acquainted.

The Xerox machine has had a deep and abiding effect on the publishing industry. Thirty years ago a manuscript really couldn't be in more than one place at a time, unless it was a carbon. And who wants to read a carbon copy? No one. I don't generally object to photocopied submissions, although I'm never eager to read a badly photocopied story. In fact, if you take your story down to a good copy shop and have it photocopied onto high-quality bond, it'll be just as readable as if you'd sent the original, and you won't have to worry about losing your manuscript in the mail or retyping it after it's been through a few rejections and has begun to get a little mangy.

But the fact about photocopying that has real bearing on the editorial process is that it allows a story to be on more than one editor's desk at a time—it's called simultaneous submitting, and it's a practice that's often frowned upon. I personally don't mind simultaneous submissions, but not many editors are open to the practice. If you want to submit your stories simultaneously, you should probably send for each magazine's writers' guidelines, and/or check the magazines' listings in *Writer's Market,* and make sure that no one objects. Simultaneous submitting can lead to some awfully sticky situations.

The last thing I have to offer you—and perhaps it's the most important—is an observation: I've been watching the slush pile here at *Twilight Zone* and *Night Cry* for three years now, and the people I've seen climbing out of it aren't always the most talented—they're sometimes the ones who keep trying. Mind you, they're talented people, and the ones who seemed at first hopeless have somehow *grown* talented. But talent isn't the common factor among them; each of them seems to have a different talent, in measure and in type. What they all share is persistence. God knows, I've gotten rejection slips myself, and *I* know how it hurts and how hard it can be to get up in the morning and write after you've been rejected. But the ones who make it are the ones who lift themselves up and keep trying after they've been knocked down.

And that's a valuable thing to know.

Chapter 25

The Mechanics and Mystique of Submitting Your Novel

Patrick LoBrutto

You're asking my advice? Just remember, this is only the opinion of one editor—a really knowledgeable and hip editor. Better people than I have given you all sorts of advice and instruction about the actual writing of your novel. So, assuming you've got the easy . . . satisfying . . . *fulfilling* part—writing the novel—all taken care of, now comes the hard work and nasty business.

Okay, you've got a really fine piece of fiction here (or there), that you want to sell to a deserving publisher. You will be paid *big bucks*—you hope. (You'll settle for bucks.)

There are two ways to do this: The Hard Way (Writer of the Past) and The Easy Way (Writer of the Future).

I know, dear reader, that this book applies to speculative fiction only, but much of what is said in this essay—and indeed, in this whole volume—will apply to all genre lit—westerns, romances, mysteries as well.

WRITER OF THE PAST

The Hard Way. You live in Tahlequah, Prescott, Eureka, Yazoo City, or Newark. You go to the library and ask how to find the addresses of publishers.

If you're lucky, this particular librarian will steer you to the LMP (*Literary Market Place*), which will give you addresses, phone numbers, editors' names and positions, and the kind of fiction a house generally does. A handy tool, this LMP.

Two asides: First, if you've written spec fic (or SF, fantasy, or horror), you probably know which publishers you're going to (you should excuse the expression) submit to. Spec fic is a small town and, like all small, incestuous towns, everybody knows everybody else and what they're up to. (That's the second sentence I've ended with a preposition, and it's something I'm sorry for.) If you don't read much SF, then it's easy to do some market research: march your *tohkes* to some bookstores and study the racks. Second aside. Agents: detestable, scrofulous bloodsuckers . . . oops! (Sorry, that's from my speech to the Association of Publishing Executives.) Seriously, if you really mean what you say about writing a novel and can convince an agent to represent you, *do it* as soon as possible. Agents specialize in the *business* of writing. If you let an agent do the business, you can spend more time writing.

How do you get an agent? There's a bit about that under "Writer of the Future." If you already have an agent, skip the rest of this except the part about conventions and conferences. If you already attend those, go to your typewriter and do magic.

Okay, you've got a list of editors and publishers, and a manuscript to show them. You don't have an agent. Say you've never been published before (sorry, not being published includes your stuff appearing in newspapers, scholarly journals, college yearbooks, and the like: if you haven't been paid for fiction by a publisher, you haven't been published.)

You can send your full manuscript in, blind (*Please* make copies of your work before you send it—have you ever been in the back of a Post Office?). You can just take your months of sweat and toil, the creative result of your talent and imagination, and fling it onto a steaming heap of other slush-pile manuscripts next to some myopic, lonely, neurotic (read: underpaid and overworked) genre editor's desk. It will be read, and you should count yourself lucky: outside the genre, nobody's flying the plane when it comes to "slush," or unsolicited manuscripts. Square business—manuscripts will be returned unopened. Try it and see; maybe then you'll believe me.

If you must submit in this outmoded and inefficient fashion, then the rules are simple. Submit to a particular editor—get his name. Call ahead, tell whoever answers the phone that you are sending a manuscript—don't ask if you can send it, act like its a constitutional right—and inquire whether the house prefers the full manuscript or a partial. If the person hangs up or if you'd rather not be ignorant and pushy on the phone, you can check the listing in *Writer's Market* for the publisher's submission preferences. If the editor is like me, he'll want a partial and an outline. A *partial* means a readable chunk, usually the first fifty pages. Now, listen—I mean this—if they want fifty pages, it's the first fifty, *not* the first ten, then 200-220, and the nice chunk around 302. You'd be surprised at how many otherwise-intelligent people are guilty of this hooter. Submit a cleanly typed, double-spaced copy with a stamped, self-addressed return envelope. If you possibly can avoid it, don't grovel, beg, threaten, cajole, or try to shame your potential editor in your cover letter. (Bribing? Well, I've never been successfully bribed. But no one's tried hard enough.)

Finally, be patient. Wait at least six weeks before sending a polite follow-up query. (Generally, in their *Writer's Market* listing, they'll tell you how long they wish it took for them to get to a submission, if the world were run properly. Add maybe four weeks to that, *then* write or phone.)

Oh yeah, simultaneous submissions. Some editors don't care, some do. I personally don't care so long as I'm told that other people are looking at it. *Writer's Market* listings will tell you policies on simultaneous submissions and such things as dot-matrix printouts, too.

All right, your manuscript *will* be read, but consider the conditions under which it will be read: The editor will be hoping to reduce the Olympian piles on the floor next to his desk; the time used to read slush is *snatched, stolen* from time supposedly spent on the important tasks—phone calls, meetings, and writing memos to those insensitive bastards in every other division of the company. He, she, or it won't even have time to read *all* your manuscript before rejecting it. I probably do more publishing from the slush pile on a regular basis than any other science-fiction publisher (if you want to know why, get somebody to pay me to write about it) and I only take one or two a year, at best, from the slush. I won't ever tell you the number I get. There aren't enough zeros.

It's a sad fact that the odds are better in Las Vegas; America's a tough town. Why should publishing, even genre publishing, be different from the rest of life?

Discouraged? Don't be. Read on and find relief.

WRITER OF THE FUTURE

Okay, same manuscript. Same author. Same universe and dimension. But you're armed with the information in this essay. The writing is done, you send your manuscript to your agent in New York, he has lunch with the editor and hands it over to him, and (zip! zip!) the editor recognizes your name and puts it on the shelf (not on the floor). This means that it will be taken home and read or read in the office on a Saturday or read on the train to or from the office. (You can be sure it won't be read in the office during working hours—if you want to know why, get somebody to pay me to write about it.)

Even if you don't have an agent yet—Putz! hurry up and get one—you send your manuscript to the editor and (zip! zip!) he recognizes your name and puts it on the shelf (not the floor), etc., etc. What happened? You did your homework and laid some groundwork, that's what.

What happened is that you got personal contact, you got off the slush pile before you sent your manuscript. When you've done that, you've gotten an editor to read, not skim, your work. (I'm assuming all along that you *can* write, of course.) Don't for a minute think that editors are arrogant—they're overworked. They're generally people who love books, with too many clamoring for their attention. Getting them to know your work is getting them to *commit time* to your work. Remember how lucky you are—yes, lucky: spec fic is the only field in which professionals—established writers, agents, and editors— are so accessible to beginning writers.

It's *true!* Did you know that there are SF conventions and writers' conferences going on all over the country just about every weekend? Did you know that varying numbers of agents and editors and writers and seriously involved fans attend them? Did you know that these SF conventions (cons) range in size from small cons of fewer than 100 to an annual World Con of 6,000 to 9,000 people? These cons are held at universities and hotels and motels and resorts. If you know where to look, I betcha you could find several a year within driving distance of your home.

Writer's conferences are different. They're usually not confined to just spec fic, they cost more money, and they are more formally run. Some are college courses, for Pete's sake, and are pretty intensive. They are valuable because there are several editors and agents who attend, speak, and meet with participants. But the expense can be prohibitive. Most colleges and universities have some kind of writers' program, and writers' magazines (I know you'll be able to think of at least one) will have listings. If you've got the time and the bread and the wherewithal, this is a great way to *meet* editors and discuss your projects with them. When you send your manuscript to them, believe me, you'll get a much better reception—it doesn't hurt to remind somebody in your cover letter that you met at the writers' course at, for example, Oklahoma University (a very good writers' conference, by the way).

Back to science-fiction cons. They combine many of the best and worst elements of writers' conferences, parties, Shriners' conventions, minimum-security mental institutions, orgies, and roadside taverns. They are great, exhausting fun and are great ways to meet other people involved in spec fic—especially those pros (authors, agents, and editors) you'll need to know. There is a problem, of course. Most people in the little pond that is SF prodom and fandom (oh, they *are* different: the pros get paid and have expense accounts and mucho prestige) are pretty cliquey. And SF conventions can be really lonely if you don't know anyone. Hey, I could be wrong and I'll hear from people who walked in off the street and were welcomed like brothers; but my observation is that unless you are a pro or know a lot of people, it could appear to be a very large party that you're only allowed to watch. Which is why I suggest that if you're going to write spec fic and are dumb enough to follow my advice and go to cons, you should probably bite the whole wienie and become a fan by joining your local SF club, society, or group. This way, you have somebody to go with to these cons.

Is this my third or fourth aside? Whatever. Romance, mystery, and western pros and fans have conventions, too. But they are neither as large, frequent, nor frantic as those in SF. They're still valuable, however, as a way to make personal contact with the people who will be judging your work for publication, who will be advising you on how to do better work in an increasingly competitive world.

But beware: Fandom and prodom can take you over. FIAWOL: Fandom Is a Way of Life. It's fun, it's instructive, you'll get adopted by a new family structure, and it will help increase your ability to sell your writing, which is the original point—remember? If you don't want a new lifestyle but still want to know about the cons, subscribe to *Locus* or *Science Fiction Chronicle*.

Well, there you are. The modern way to submit your manuscript and finesse the mystique is to get yourself off the slush pile. You'll still have to write a good novel, you know, and you or your agent will still have to make enough of a pitch to get your editor to get the rest of his publishing house behind the book so they can get booksellers to order it so they can get readers to *buy* it.

I know you have one more question. If I know so much about getting a manuscript published, why don't I do it myself? Good question: Get somebody to pay me to write about it and find out why.

Chapter 26

Darkness Absolute: The Standards of Excellence in Horror Fiction

Douglas E. Winter

What makes great horror fiction?

This question has weighed heavily on my mind these past few years. As a critic, I am called upon regularly to pass judgment on the writing of horror fiction's leading talents. I've probed the phenomenal success of Stephen King in a book-length study, and I've also written a history of modern horror, as told through the lives of seventeen of its brightest and best-selling talents. As a compulsive reader and filmgoer, I've experienced nearly everything the field of horror has to offer. My own fiction returns with regularity to themes of violence and fear.

Still, I'm tempted to answer this rather ultimate question with the same alacrity as Supreme Court Justice Potter Stewart, who once offered as his definition of obscenity that he knew it when he saw it.

The temptation stems, in no small part, from an utter abhorrence of rules for writers. This book offers a wealth of practical advice to the fledgling writer, and certain insights into the business of writing that most of us learn only by experience. But recipes for success? There are no such things when we talk about quality fiction. Indeed, the best horror fiction is often that which breaks the perceived rules.

What follows, then, is a series of principles intended to offer general guidance to the developing writer. As generalizations, they are subject to inevitable exceptions; and they must not, under any circumstances, be considered hard-and-fast rules. They deserve your attention, but not slavish devotion. These principles also have little, if anything, to do with bestsellerdom, a phenomenon that may (as in the case of Stephen King) concern talent, but that is more often the result of extrinsic factors. If your sole ambition is commercial success, look elsewhere for guidance; you probably lack the courage to write great horror fiction.

Originality. Perhaps the most difficult lesson for would-be horror writers is to learn that their stories rarely offer anything new. Few plots in this field are fresh and exciting; indeed, most editors lament how easily horror stories can be pigeonholed into recognizable types. (T. E. D. Klein, the original editor of *Twilight Zone Magazine,* once told me that he could fit 90 percent of the submissions to his magazine into ten clichéd categories.)

The problem, simply stated, is that most horror writers are, first and foremost, horror fans. Their stories naturally tend to emulate, in style and subject, the film or fiction that they like best. In rare cases, such as Klein's own *The Ceremonies* (an intentional *homage* to Arthur Machen), the result transcends its source material. But for each such book, there are hundreds that read like rote imitations of best-selling novels or popular films, replete with such well-worn icons as Indian burial grounds, small towns besieged by evil, and ghastly presences that are revealed as the spearhead of an alien invasion.

Familiarity has its benefits. Imitation is a time-honored method of learning the fundamentals of writing. Moreover, to judge by the bookracks, an audience exists for the paperback equivalent of leftovers—writing intended to remind us of someone else's success. But, as the saying goes, familiarity also breeds contempt; and it certainly does not make for memorable horror fiction.

If you would excel in this field, remember that a fundamental mistake is to strive to emulate the commercial horror novel or story. The bulk of this fiction is poorly written and itself imitative; you will risk learning your craft at the feet of mediocrity. And even if you choose the field's most original voices to guide your efforts, the dangers of pastiche should be obvious.

If you admire Stephen King or Peter Straub or Dennis Etchison, fine; but save that admiration for party conversation. When it comes to committing words to paper, *you* are the writer, and it must be your ambition to better those you admire. If not, you are condemning yourself to be second-rate before you have even started.

Originality cannot be taught. But the task of finding your own voice will be eased if you stop reading what the marketplace calls horror fiction and join me in an important bit of heresy:

Horror is not a genre. It is an emotion.

It can be found in all of great literature, not simply that with lurid dust jackets. Read Conrad. Read Faulkner. Read Kozinski. Read Ballard, Cormier, Fuentes, McGuane, Stone, Whittemore. Read and read and read of the ways in which writers relate horrors without the strictures of genre.

Then return to your writing with a new perspective, unguided by the publishers who package their products for mass consumption with labels such as "horror." Recognize that the fiction that we hold dearest, the fiction that you are seeking to write, is not a *kind* of fiction, meant to be confined to the ghetto of a special bookstore shelf like science fiction or the western.

It is any and all kinds of fiction.

Characterization. A common mistake of beginning writers is to assume that horror alone is sufficient; but horror, as an emotion, is measured by its context—its time, its place, its characters. Anyone who has sat through a body-count film like those of the *Friday the 13th* series will understand that we care about the outcome of a story only if we have some emotional stake in its context.

For this reason, an essential element of great horror fiction is character. "You have got to love the people," says Stephen King. "There has got to be love involved, because the more you love—kids like Tad Trenton in *Cujo* or Danny Torrance in *The Shining*—then that allows horror to be possible."

One clue to developing effective characterizations is to recognize that stories do not proceed from events, but from the perception of events. Your story will be colored in its telling by your personality; similarly, the acts and words of its characters should, in turn, be colored by their personalities. Unfortunately, most beginning writers focus upon character types (tough-guy cops, dizzy blondes, gays, misunderstood Vietnam veterans) rather than personalities. Worry less about what types of people should be your characters, and more about investing them with everyday humanity. If the reader can identify with the hopes, fears, flaws, and foibles of your characters, then love—and thus horror—is possible.

Reality. The emotion that is horror contrasts violently with our understanding of all the things that are good and normal. There is thus no effective horror without a context of normality. Indeed, the best horror fiction effectively counterfeits reality, placing the reader firmly within the worldly even as it invokes the otherworldly.

For this reason, Richard Matheson is the most influential horror writer of this generation. In novels like *I Am Legend* (1954) and *The Shrinking Man* (1956), as well as his teleplays for *The Twilight Zone,* he helped wrest the fiction of fear from such traditional locales as mist-laden moors and gothic castles, and invited it into our shopping malls and peaceful neighborhoods—into the house next door.

An effective horror writer acknowledges Matheson's legacy, embracing the ordinary so that the extraordinary events he depicts will be heightened when played out against its context. Eschew exotic locales and the lifestyles of the rich and famous—rock stars, best-selling novelists, world travelers—in favor of all that is mundane in your world. Not only will your horrors work better; you will be writing about the people and places that you know best, and your fiction, as a result, will live.

Mystery. The workaday world is indeed mundane when compared with the prospect of vampires, ghouls, demonic possession; but it is a world whose ultimate meaning is shrouded by unanswered and unanswerable questions.

Where did we come from? Where are we going when we die? Does evil exist beyond the mind of man?

It is not the purpose of horror fiction to answer such questions. Indeed, nothing could be less frightening than most stories of so-called black magic, which suggest that the chaos of our world is nothing but a form of science, capable of invocation by formulaic chants. Or Wes Craven's overrated motion picture *A Nightmare on Elm Street,* whose mysterious dream-invader, once explained, becomes little more than another mad slasher, reduced to a pathetic comic-book figure by the film's closing scenes.

When the printed tale of terror was young—in those days of "penny dreadfuls" and Gothic novels—a rigid dichotomy was observed between supernatural fiction and fiction based in rational explanation. The latter form, exemplified by Ann Radcliffe's *The Mysteries of Udolpho* (1794) and reprised briefly in the "Baby Jane" maniac films of the 1960s, proposed apparently supernatural events that were explained away at the story's end, usually as the nefarious deeds of another.

But today, explanation, whether supernatural or rational, is simply not the business of horror fiction. One source of horror's popularity is that its questions are unanswerable. At its heart is a single certainty—that, in Hamlet's words, "all that live must die"—and a single question: What then?

We're not looking for answers to that mystery—we know, if only instinctively, that these are matters of faith. What we are looking for is a way to confess our doubts, our disbeliefs, our fears. The effective horror writer cultivates our existential dilemma rather than arrogating the power to resolve it.

Bad Taste. Horror fiction is rarely in good taste. Indeed, most conventional horror stories proceed from the archetype of Pandora's Box: the tense conflict between pleasure and fear that is latent when we face the forbidden and the unknown. In horror's pages, we open the Box, exposing what is taboo in our ordinary lives and witnessing both its dangers and its possibilities.

Not surprisingly, the best horror fiction tests the boundaries of acceptable behavior—consider, for example, the undercurrent of lesbianism in Shirley Jackson's *The Haunting of Hill House* (1959); the cruel violence of Iain Banks's *The Wasp Factory* (1983); the obsessive sexuality of Thomas Tessier's *Finishing Touches* (1986). A would-be horror writer should thus be prepared not only to indulge in bad taste, but also to grapple with the taboo, dragging our terrors from the shadows and forcing readers to look upon them and despair—or laugh with relief.

The risks of bad taste are obvious; but in the words of James Herbert, "You can forgive virtually anything—any perversion, any nastiness—if it's really done with style." Most great horror fiction is informed with a keen aesthetic sense. The writer must know when the boundary has been reached, and when he is stepping over the line into the no-man's land of taboo. Those without this sense are doomed to purvey cheap thrills, confirming the worst doubts of the Meese Commission.

Suggestion. Although bad taste is intrinsic to great horror fiction, a "show-and-tell" mentality is not your key to success. While a current trend in horror fiction is toward explicit imagery of sex and violence, few writers seem to recognize that such explicitness is often anathema to horror.

How many times have you been disappointed by a motion-picture adaptation of a favorite horror novel? The reason is usually simple: the pictures were those of the director's choosing, not those you had seen with your mind's eye while reading the book.

Reading is an intimate act, a sharing of imagination by writer and reader. Its power is undoubtedly heightened when the subject involves our deepest and darkest fears. When a writer chooses explicit images, spelling out his horrors, he (like a film director) provides the picture, depriving the reader of the opportunity to share in the act of creation. Reading explicit fiction is thus a passive act, a take-it-or-leave-it proposition that may soon cause the reader to lose interest in you and your story.

But there is a more fundamental objection to explicitness. Too many purveyors of the "gross-out" are working from the proposition that the purpose of horror fiction is to shock the reader into submission. They indulge in the cheap tactic that motion-picture directors call "pop ups": the hand thrusting into view, the sudden close-up of a ravaged corpse. But shock is a visceral experience, a sensory overload from which most of us recover quickly, with a laugh or with a scream.

Great horror fiction is rarely about shock, but rather more lasting emotions; it digs beneath our skin and stays with us. It is proof that an image is only as powerful as its context. Stylists such as Ramsey Campbell and Charles L.

Grant can invoke more terror through a lingering shadow, a fugitive stain, than most "splatter" films can produce with gallons of spilled blood. That power—not only to scare, but also to disturb, a reader, to invoke a memory that will linger long after the pages of the book are closed—is the true goal of every writer of horror fiction.

This should not suggest that the gross-out lacks effectiveness as a tool of the horror writer. There are moments when a vivid image is the only means by which the heights (or depths) of horror may be expressed. Special effects are also useful to open the readers' minds to possibilities; indeed, the outlandish violence of Clive Barker's *Books of Blood* (1984-85) or Lucio Fulci's zombie films can be seen as acts of liberation, freeing the viewer's mind to resonances of mythic proportions.

Subtext. D. H. Lawrence wrote of Edgar Allan Poe's horror fiction: "It is lurid and melodramatic, but it is true." Great horror fiction provides the shocks, the scares, all the entertainments of the carnival funhouse; but it also offers something more: a lasting impression, one both disturbing and oddly uplifting.

The best horror stories move beyond entertainment to serve, consciously or not, as imperfect mirrors of the real fears of their time. The masterpieces of "yellow Gothic," such as Oscar Wilde's *The Picture of Dorian Gray* (1891) and H. G. Wells's *The Island of Dr. Moreau* (1896), echoed the fears of an age of imperial decline. The big-bug horrors of the 1950s were analogs of the cold war mentality and the sudden shadow of the atomic bomb. More recent examples are discussed below.

Subtext is not simply the source of much cognitive power in horror fiction; it is also the means by which the traditional imagery of horror may be reenacted, updated, elevated. *Dracula's Children* (1974), by Richard Lortz, and *'Salem's Lot* (1975), by Stephen King, are ready examples, infusing fresh blood into vampire mythology by imprinting it with sociopolitical themes.

Subversion. The best horror fiction is intrinsically subversive, striking against the pasteboard masks of fantasy to seek the true face of reality. Indeed, the great horror fiction being written today runs consistently against the grain of conventional horror, as if intent on forging something that might well be called the *antihorror* story.

American horror, particularly in film, has always been rich with Puritan subtext: if there is a single certainty, it is that teenagers who have sex in cars or in the woods will die. Most books and films of the eighties offer a message as conservative as their morality: Conform. The bogymen of the *Halloween* and *Friday the 13th* films are the hitmen of homogeneity. Don't do it, they tell us, or you will pay an awful price. Don't talk to strangers. Don't party. Don't make love. Don't dare to be different.

Their victims, lost in the peccadilloes of the "me generation," waltz again and again into their waiting arms. Their sole nemesis is usually a monogamous (if not virginal) heroine—a middle-class madonna who has listened to her parents, and thus behaves. And it is proper behavior, not crucifixes or silver bullets, that tends to ward off the monsters of our times.

But the antihorror story tells us that conformity is the ultimate horror—and that monsters are, perhaps, passé.

Monsters. The monster is the paramount image of horror fiction and film, a trademark as enduring as the spaceship of science fiction, the hard-boiled detective of mystery fiction—and, no doubt, as inescapable. But those monsters have changed; indeed, the great horror fiction being written today is rarely about monsters.

The vampire is an anachronism in the wake of the sexual revolution. The bite of Bram Stoker's *Dracula* (1897), sharpened in the repression of Victorian times, has been blunted by the likes of Dr. Ruth Westheimer. The bloodthirsty Count and his kin survive today because of sentiment rather than sensuality— and as a fantasy of upper-class decadence, the commoner's forbidden dream of languorous *chic* (replayed most recently by Catherine Deneuve and David Bowie in the film adaptation of Whitley Strieber's *The Hunger*).

The werewolf, too, has grown long in the tooth; its archetypal story, Robert Louis Stevenson's *The Strange Case of Dr. Jekyll and Mr. Hyde* (1886), also hinged on the Victorian mentality, with its marked duality of civilized gentleman and low-brow brute. As class distinctions wane in our populist times, the duality blurs. The werewolf will live so long as we struggle with the beast within, but its modern incarnations—from Whitley Strieber's *The Wolfen* (1979) and Thomas Tessier's *The Nightwalker* (1979)—suggest that the savage has already won and is loose on the streets of the urban jungle.

The invader from outer space, that prominent bugaboo of the Eisenhower era, regained a brief vogue with *Alien* and John Carpenter's remake of *The Thing,* but was transformed by the wishful fantasies of Steven Spielberg into a cuddly savior from the skies. The instant legacy of *Close Encounters of the Third Kind* and *E.T.* has been a series of lovable aliens, from the mermaid of *Splash* to the cozy extraterrestrials of *Starman* and *Cocoon,* that may not be overcome by the "bug-hunt" mentality of *Aliens.*

Gone, too, are the survivals of past cultures—the mummies, the golems, the creatures from black lagoons; they cannot survive in a no-deposit, no-return society whose concept of ancient history is, more often than not, the 1950s.

The monsters of our time are less exotic and more symptomatic than their predecessors. A soulless insanity sparks the finest horror novel of the eighties, Thomas Harris's *Red Dragon* (1981). Child abuse is the relentless theme of the best-selling novels of V. C. Andrews, while the dissolution of family and marriage haunts the fiction of Charles L. Grant. The curse of socialization—notably, venereal disease—infects the films of David Cronenberg and the fiction of Clive Barker. Urban decay is the relentless background of Ramsey Campbell's short stories. Stephen King glories in the malfunction of the mundane, giving life to the petty tyrannies of our consumer culture—our household goods, our cars and trucks, our neighbor's dog.

And the true monsters of the eighties look even more familiar. We may call them zombies, but as a character in George A. Romero's *Day of the Dead* pronounces, "They're us."

Endgame. Whether your story involves traditional monsters or more progressive forms of horror, there must come a time when it draws to a close. Ending a horror story—particularly one of novel length—is probably the writer's greatest challenge. Its success often distinguishes the best horror fiction from the merely competent.

In the final trumps, the quality of horror is proportionate to its cost. Most horror fiction is about payback: the restoration of order, normally by destruction of the agent of chaos. In the archetypal horror story, some malevolent phenomenon is loosed upon an unsuspecting world, claiming stock victims from central casting as appetizers for the main course, a virginal heroine or an innocent child. At the last moment, the phenomenon is understood and destroyed, order is restored, and all is well with the world . . . until next time.

This hackneyed formula—which nevertheless serves as the basis for most horror novels published today—works passably until its ending. But when a writer imagines a horror of overwhelming proportion, the reader will normally feel cheated by the last-minute intervention of God or nature or manmade solutions. This strategy may have worked for H. G. Wells's *The War of the Worlds* (1897-98), which saw its invincible Martian invaders felled at the last moment by microbes; but today's readers are wiser—and, perhaps, more cynical.

After all, we know that horror exists in our world; indeed, we need look no further than the daily newspaper. We know, if only implicitly, that consummate evil cannot be overcome, cast out of our world completely.

We also know that the good in this world is not free—that there must be payout as well as payback.

The conclusion of a novel is not merely the stopping point of your plot; it is the vehicle by which the reader is awakened from your nightmare and returned to his workaday world. Writers who recognize the importance of this reintegration to the reader will tend to craft the most satisfying conclusions. Those who do not are doomed to such devices as the infamous "It was all just a dream," or the false ending, exercised brilliantly by Brian DePalma in his film adaptation of *Carrie* and trivialized by ham-fisted writers and directors ever since.

A final note: The standards of excellence in horror fiction are constantly shifting, growing, expanding—certain evidence of a thriving art form. Despite its rich traditions, horror fiction should not look back; its best writers constantly push at its limits, redefining the boundaries even as they are established.

In the end, it is writers, not principles, that make great horror fiction. Writers with persistence. Writers with a vision that extends beyond marketing categories.

Writers who care.

Chapter 27

Overview of Horror, SF and Fantasy: A Long-range Market Study

Janet Fox

If you're reading this in printed form, we have just traveled through time in the only way humans are yet enabled to. And between the time I compiled this market overview and the time you read it, no doubt many interesting changes have taken place. Publishing houses and magazines have burgeoned or fallen by the wayside or changed their addresses, their editors, or their policies. The intent of this chapter is only to make clear the idea that all market listings are only jumping-off points. From here you must devise and keep current your own files, your own strategies.

Listings are necessary and useful because you can't submit manuscripts to markets you've never heard of, yet in most cases, for a short story submission, you should look through a copy and send for guidelines if they're available. I won't lie and say I've never submitted material *blind*, without the preliminaries (and sometimes it resulted in a sale), but doing so often only led to wasted postage and lost manuscripts. Most editors will urge you to see a sample copy because this will tell you even more than a guidelines sheet. It also lets you see the format and the way your work would be presented.

Since I've made you responsible for a certain amount of follow up on market listings, it seems a good idea to provide a few suggestions as to where to find markets, outside of formal listings, such as this chapter. It's said that "classifieds sell"; they're also a dead giveaway to new presses, which must advertise their product. I always check the classifieds in the genre publications and writers' magazines.

You may be aware that speculative fiction fans organize and hold conventions in all parts of the country (and overseas). While these conventions are organized chiefly for the enjoyment of fans and the promotion of name writers, a lot can be learned by circulating, communicating, and gathering the literature that's available there. Writers' conferences can also serve this purpose, with a more sedate and educational atmosphere, although these don't usually offer the same genre orientation.

"Networking" is a trendy new term for what writers have been doing for years. Contact other writers in your area or beyond it and share market news as well as the vicissitudes of the writing life.

If you're lucky enough to have a large library nearby, you can avail yourself of the wealth of leads it offers, since libraries regularly subscribe to many publications. A bookstore can also let you know what's currently available or what sort of books a publisher specializes in. A certain awareness is developed after a while that will let you pick up on leads from even the most unlikely sources.

When producing genre fiction, it's easy to have tunnel vision and to think only in terms of the professional science fiction/fantasy magazines, but speculative fiction *of the proper type* can find a home in almost any magazine that will look at fiction. For example, men's magazines have long been ready markets for speculative fiction, from *Playboy,* which has published work by masters in the field, to lesser-known magazines at the other end of the scale, which want their stories heavily laced with sleaze no matter what sort of fiction it is. Still, I can't stress enough the idea that you must do your homework here and try to decide whether the stories you write are close enough to the average story published by a certain magazine. I know horror writers who have had success in selling fiction to biker magazines, but of course this presupposes a knowledge of bikers. You have to work from your own strengths.

Regional magazines have lately become popular. It might be possible to do a fantasy story with a folktale flavor representing what you know about your own particular region. Arts and entertainment magazines as well as some Sunday supplements will occasionally use a piece of fiction. There is also a whole range of little magazines and *literaries,* which may not be interested in typical genre fiction; but science fiction, fantasy, or weird horror at the *experimental end* of the spectrum may fit in very well. After all, the whole idea of speculative fiction is seeing things with a fresh, if not a bizarre, point of view.

Children's publications are usually looking for good fiction that will fit the ages and interests of their readers, and children are avid consumers of science fiction/fantasy, to judge from what appears on Saturday-morning television. There is also the possibility of adapting an idea to fit the formula of womens' magazines, but, to be honest, I think this category is least likely to be open to speculative fiction.

I'm sure I've missed some possibilities along the way, but you get the idea. You'll have to let your own inclinations, interests, and skills guide you. Not everyone can do a literary story or a formula men's magazine tale, and I don't recommend warping your writing talents out of shape to fit some particular type of magazine. In my view, marketing should always be done *after* the piece is completed; but I wanted you to be aware of the possibilities.

Rather than an exhaustive list of all markets and outlets, I've attempted to put together a solid core of listings from which you can begin your own exploration of the field. I based my choices on the presumption that if a market has existed for some time in the past, it will continue to be around for awhile; however, that didn't preclude my listing a few newcomers. In my experience, a magazine or publishing house is always in greater need of material at its inception than when it has become established. While I've stayed pretty much with those markets that make some sort of cash payment, I'm nonjudgmental about writers who publish their work for contributor's copies, probably because I've done it so much myself.

Editors and publishers were invited to comment on future directions for their publications or their genres, and understandably, not everyone wanted to venture an opinion, but those who did comment present a varied and exciting picture for the fields of science fiction, fantasy, and horror.

As compared to other genres, the number of professional magazines devoted to some form of speculative fiction is relatively large, and most of those on the list have had long and successful runs. The professional magazines have traditionally leaned more toward science fiction, but a few offer fantasy or horror.

Three continuing anthologies have been placed at the end of the list. A number of anthologies are published each year, but since they appear sporadically, popping up like ducks in a shooting gallery, it can be difficult to make a sale here, although it's well worth your while if you happen to hit one.

Aboriginal SF
Charles C. Ryan
P. O. Box 2449
Woburn MA 01888-0849

A new bimonthly SF magazine, which debuted in '86. Looking for SF stories 2,500-4,500 words and will respond in 2-4 weeks. Editor Charles C. Ryan says he hopes to hear from new writers and from those he worked with while editing *Galileo*. He prefers true SF to fantasy or science fantasy but will consider an exceptional story from any speculative-fiction category. Not interested in sword and sorcery. Payment $200 flat rate, upon publication.

Amazing Stories
Patrick L. Price
TSR, Inc.
P. O. Box 110
Lake Geneva WI 53147-0110

A bimonthly magazine of SF and fantasy with a long history. Looking for SF and heroic fantasy stories 500-25,000 words (no serials) for an adult readership. Seeking primarily hard, speculative, militaristic or anthropological SF. Not interested in horror or supernatural fiction. Payment 4¢-7¢/word, on acceptance. "As for future trends, we've determined next year's trends by what we've bought this year. Current needs are for shorter lengths, 9,000 words and under. We're overstocked on fantasy and won't be buying any for some time."

Analog
Stanley Schmidt
380 Lexington Ave.
New York NY 10017
(212) 557-9100

A well-established monthly magazine of science fiction and science fact. "Basically we publish *science* fiction stories, in which some aspect of future science or technology is so integral to the plot that, if that aspect were removed, the story would collapse. Try to picture Mary Shelley's *Frankenstein* without the science and you'll see what I mean. No story. *Analog* will consider material by any writer, and consider it solely on the basis of merit. We are definitely anxious to find and develop new, capable writers." Payment varies—from 3.5¢-7¢/word, depending on length. Preferred lengths: 2,000-7,000 for shorts; 10,000-20,000 for novelettes, and 40,000-80,000 for serials. Payment is on acceptance.

Dragon Magazine
Patrick L. Price
TSR, Inc.
P. O. Box 110
Lake Geneva WI 53147
(414) 248-8044

A monthly magazine which contains material of interest to the fantasy-role-playing gamer, as well as fantasy and adventure fiction. Possible themes might be problem solving, adventure and survival tales, quests, battles, and magical warfare and challenging missions. Fiction should be written for an older-adolescent and adult audience; no obscene language or sexually explicit detail. Fiction should be under 10,000 words; query for anything longer. Pays 4¢-6¢/word, on acceptance.

Isaac Asimov's SF Magazine
Gardner Dozois
380 Lexington Ave.
New York NY 10017

A monthly magazine of SF and fantasy. Looking for literate, well-crafted stories, character oriented, some "hard" science. No sword and sorcery, cute elves, trolls, or dragons. Not interested in explicit sex or violence. Pays 4¢-7¢/word, on acceptance. Replies within 1-3 months.

The Magazine of Fantasy and Science Fiction
Edward L. Ferman
P.O. Box 56
Cornwall CT 06753
(203) 672-6376

A long-established, monthly magazine using both SF and fantasy. "There is no formula, but you should be familiar with the magazine before submitting." In general no sword-and-sorcery fiction is used, and not much horror is used. No stories over 25,000 words. Best lengths: under 10,000 words. Pays 4¢-6¢/word, on acceptance.

Night Cry
Alan Rodgers
800 2nd Ave.
New York NY 10017
(212) 986-9600

A magazine whose focus is primarily horror fiction. "We're looking for fiction that can scare us (no easy task; we read a lot of horror stories); not averse to fantasy, SF, or even an occasional mystery." Pays 5¢-7¢/word; responds in 2-6 months. Uses all lengths from short-shorts to novels (serializations). "For the future, we intend to continue in basically the same way as far as bringing the readers the best in horror fiction with possibly a slight turn toward less-graphic horror and a more sophisticated type of story. Possibly a letter column and book review column will be added."

Omni
Ellen Datlow, Fiction Editor
1965 Broadway
New York NY 10023-5965
(212) 496-6100

The only glossy magazine to publish science *and* science fiction. Looking for strong, well-written SF stories. *Omni's* readers are, for the most part, new to SF. They're interested in the subject but have little understanding of technical jargon. The stories must be written in clear, understandable prose. Not looking for fantasy but will consider contemporary, hard-edged stories. No sword and sorcery or space opera. Lengths: 2,000-10,000 words. Pays $1,250-$2,000. "We have a reputation for weirdness (in fact and fiction), and I believe that will continue."

Rod Serling's Twilight Zone Magazine
Tappan King
401 Park Ave. 3rd Floor
New York NY 10016-8802

A monthly using fiction similar to the type made popular by Rod Serling on the original "Twilight Zone" television show. "*TZ* should not be thought of as a magazine of horror fiction only. We are interested in other types of fantasy as well as 'non-hardware' SF." Pays 6¢-10¢/word, half on acceptance, half on publication.

Shadows
Charles L. Grant
28 Linwood Ave.
Newton NJ 07860

An annual hardcover anthology of quiet horror with a contemporary setting. Nothing Lovecraftian, and no splatter stories. They should all have a hint of the supernatural, and most of all, they should be people-oriented. "I particularly dislike stories that have main characters that are mean and rotten; who cares what happens to them? For the future, I hope to continue as long as there are good stories, and I'd like to continue to see new writers among those who are more established. The trends I see I don't much like—too much film influence. I especially see and hate the slice-and-dice stuff. That's not horror, that's shock, and a fair amount of writers don't seem able to tell the difference." Pays 3¢/word, on acceptance, plus a share of royalties.

Sword and Sorceress
Marion Zimmer Bradley
Box 245-A
Berkeley CA 94701

A yearly anthology of sword and sorcery with a strong female protagonist or central character. Reads from about February 1 to June 15 each year; write for current guidelines before submitting anything. Volumes 1-4 of *Sword and Sorceress* are good guides to what is wanted. Long stories are bought first, so send anything over 7,500 words in early. "Best chance for a beginner to sell to me is something short and slightly humorous. I work with new writers and don't hesitate to ask for rewrites. No science or space fiction, no rewritten fairy tales, nothing cutesy, no strident or separatist feminism. For the future—to create new ideas in women's adventures, rather than replicating old elements." Pays 2¢-6¢/word plus a share of royalties.

Synergy: The New Review of Science Fiction
George Zebrowski
Box 486
Johnson City NY 13790

An anthology to be published twice a year by Harcourt Brace Jovanovich. Ambitious, realistic SF written with great attention to writerly virtues and mature themes. No genre clichés; no fantasy. Pays 6¢-10¢/word, depending on length. No restrictions on length; no taboos of any kind. Replies in 6-8 weeks. Query for opening and closing dates.

Selling a novel is different from selling short fiction—more lucrative to begin with, but understandably so, since the commitment of time and effort to a novel is much greater. The following publishing houses either specialize in or have strong lines in speculative fiction:

Baen Books
Elizabeth Mitchell, Senior Editor
260 5th Ave. Suite 3S
New York NY 10001
(212) 532-4111

Looking for strongly plotted SF by authors willing to research their subject matter, and interesting new fantasy stories "set against convincing backgrounds that aren't rehashes of past best sellers. All is judged primarily by plot, as we consider plot more critically than style. This does not mean we're willing to read outright first-draft material." Payment rates are very competitive. Submit sample chapters and synopsis. Responds in 3-5 weeks, longer for full manuscripts. Does 60 mass-market and 8 trade paper/hardbound titles a year.

Bantam Books
Lou Aronica, Publishing Director, Bantam Spectra Books
Shawna McCarthy, Senior Editor
Amy Stout, Associate Editor
666 5th Ave.
New York NY 10103

"We are open to all types of SF, fantasy, and horror, as long as a submission exhibits good storytelling values and strong characterization. A query letter is preferred for submissions. Manuscripts from unpublished writers are read." Responds in 6-8 weeks. Payment and rights bound are negotiable. Publishes 50-60 SF/fantasy books a year.

DAW Books
Betsy Wolheim, Editor-in-Chief
Sheila Gilbert, Senior Editor
1633 Broadway
New York NY 10019

Looking for serious, hard-core SF with strong characterization and story line, and also for serious, deeply detailed fantasy, with no fluff. "Our policy is not to publish work that is basically pessimistic—a vision of the future may be bleak but not devoid of hope." Enthusiastically reads manuscripts from newer writers. Responds in 8-12 weeks. All terms negotiable. Prefers to see entire manuscript.

Del Rey Books
201 E. 50th St.
New York NY 10022
(212) 572-2677

"Del Rey publishes SF and fantasy—we won't read anything else. Our SF runs the gamut from the technological wonder of Clarke, Niven, and Forward to the rousing space adventures of Asimov, McCaffrey, and Foster. For our fantasy, we insist that magic or the supernatural be so basic to the plot that the story could not happen without it. You do not need an agent; we will look at all material submitted in the proper form. It can take several months to respond, as we employ no outside readers. We will read complete novels. If you wish to submit a partial, include a detailed outline and the first three chapters." Lengths: 60,000-120,000 words. Contracts negotiated on an individual basis. Advances and royalties are competitive.

The Donning Company/Publishers
Starblaze/Starblaze Graphics
Mary E. Gray, Assistant Editor
5659 Virginia Beach Blvd.
Norfolk VA 23502

Publishes SF/fantasy novels and graphic novels. Not particularly interested in postapocalyptic literature or near-future thrillers. Dark fantasy OK, but no "cut-and-slash." Prefers to see outline/synopsis with three consecutive chapters. Include brief cover letter with writing history and/or credits. Will read manuscripts from unpublished writers. Response time varies. Pays $2,000-7,500. Publishes 10-12 SF/fantasy books a year.

Leisure Books
Tracey Lubben
Dorchester Publishing
6 E. 39th St.
New York NY 10016

Leisure specializes in horror fiction; no hard SF or fantasy. "Horror/occult novels that are really scary, à la Stephen King, but not disgusting—or not *too* disgusting, anyway. We prefer an element of the occult in our horror novels but will consider straight horror if it's well written. Prefer manuscripts of approximately 100,000 words. Query with SASE; no manuscripts, please." Reads work by unpublished writers. Responds in 6 weeks. Payment negotiable. Buys all rights. Publishes 24 horror titles a year.

Tor Books
Beth Meacham, Editor-in-Chief
49 W. 24th St.
New York NY 10010

(Send horror to Melissa Ann Singer, Editor, same address.) Tor publishes a full spectrum of speculative fiction, producing 7 SF and fantasy, and 3 horror titles, each month. Looking for all types of fiction within these genres. Welcomes manuscripts from previously unpublished writers. Send 3 sample chapters and an outline. Responds in 8 weeks on SF/fantasy, 10-12 weeks on horror. Rate of payment, rights acquired are industry standard. Publishes 80-85 SF books a year, 36-40 horror.

Small press, in general, is just what its name denotes—smaller in circulation, more modest in format, and lower in payments to its contributors. Some pay only in copies. In many cases, a small-press magazine is only a sideline or hobby to its editor and response time can be slow. In my experience, small-press magazines don't start small and grow up to become professional magazines. (David Silva may just be proving me wrong with *The Horror Show,* and I'd be delighted if he did.) As in any activity that depends upon the enthusiasm and work of one or two people, there is ample room for rise and fall. Despite all the seeming drawbacks, the greatest strength I've found in the small press is that it offers participation for writers at all levels of achievement, whether you consider it a training ground or a discrete world of its own.

I'm listing only a few of the small-press outlets currently active, but it's unnecessary to list them all, since small press tends to be a network. You can often find lists of other publications in the magazines, or, when submitting, you can ask the editor to suggest other small-press editors who might be interested in the story if he is not. For the future, I can reasonably predict more small-press activity, since it's based on technological advances in computers, copiers, laser printers, and the like.

The last two entries are admittedly overstocked for some time to come, but their editors are knowledgeable about small press, and the magazines provide a quality example of what can be produced:

Fantasy Book
Dennis Mallonee, Nick Smith, Editors
Box 60126
Pasadena CA 91106

A quarterly magazine devoted to illustrated fantasy fiction across a wide variety of genres. In the past, *Fantasy Book* has featured high fantasy, light fantasy, contemporary fantasy, horror stories, fairy tales, heroic fantasy, science fiction, and fables. Pays 3¢-5¢/word for stories in the 2,000- to 10,000-word range, payable prior to publication.

Fantasy Macabre
Jessica Amanda Salmonson, Editor
Box 20610
Seattle WA 98102
Richard Fawcett, Publisher
61 Teecomwas Drive
Uncasville CT 06382

Submissions go to Jessica Salmonson; business matters, to Richard Fawcett. A fantasy magazine using stories to 3,000 words "with a focus on charnal romanticism; ghost stories; and modern horror with psychological, rather than child-ishly gross, underpinnings. We also use translations of European and South American fantastic tales and love to hear from experienced translators." Pays an honorarium of 1¢/word.

Grue
Peggy Nadramia
Box 370
Times Square Station
New York NY 10108

A relatively new small-press horror magazine that is attempting to break new ground, to establish itself as the one that dares to be different, that pulls no punches, honors no taboos. "I see too many writers approach horror as if it's *in-herently* funny, not taking it seriously—if you don't respect the genre, write something else. I enjoy stories that involve sexuality; we're sensitive about this subject, don't like to talk about it—precisely *why* situations involving our sexu-ality are the more disturbing and unsettling." Future plans include more pages, color covers—dependent, of course, on reader support. Pays ½¢ a word on publication.

The Horror Show
David B. Silva
14848 Misty Springs Lane
Oak Run CA 96069

A quarterly looking for horror fiction in a contemporary setting. No SF, sword and sorcery. Length: a firm 4,000 words. Pays 1¢/word. Generally responds in 3-4 weeks. "For the future, I'd like to meld the written and visual aspects of the horror field a little more. And if I'd have to guess, I'd say that short horror fic-tion will become a little nastier in some respects, a little more complex in oth-ers. The most fascinating delight I find in the field is its unlimited potential. Nothing is untouchable. What more could a writer want?"

Pandora
Meg MacDonald, Editor
609 E. 11 Mile, #12
Royal Oak MI 48067

"*Pandora* is an SF and speculative-fantasy magazine published twice a year. She is role-expanding. This means she is nonsexist, nonracist and nonstereo-typed. She does not print stories that exist only for the sake of a pun, X-rated material, or retellings of the Adam-and-Eve story." Works with new writers as well as with established authors trying experimental stories. Length: under 5,000 words. Pays 1¢/word, on acceptance.

Space and Time
Gordon Linzner
138 W. 70th St. Apt. 4-B
New York NY 10023

A "little" magazine devoted to publishing fantasy and SF stories. Material used includes supernatural horror, sword and sorcery, high-tech SF, etc. Length: no more than 10,000 words. "Competition for space in *S&T* is fierce. We can buy only one or two stories per month, about 1 percent of all those received. As to the future, horror will more and more establish itself as a separate category, so that there will be separate horror sections in most bookstores. This ghettoization will work to the advantage of lesser-known writers, but it will make it more difficult for them to break through into big bucks and fame. Swords and sorcery, currently moribund, will experience a revival in the next five years, when the modern barbarian popularity fades (you know, Rambo and company)." Pays ¼¢/word, on acceptance. Responds in 6-8 weeks.

Space and Time Books
Jani Anderson; address same as for *Space and Time*

A relatively new operation with a small backlist, 2½ years and 4 books. "Looking for short (200- to 240-page), fast-paced, tightly plotted fantasy novels of any genre in the fantasy realm. Contracts signed on complete manuscripts. Advances, if any, are modest. The books are published in a trade paperback format." Query first.

Eldritch Tales
Crispin Burnham
1051 Wellington Road
Lawrence KS 66044

Weirdbook
W. Paul Ganley
Box 149, Amherst Branch
Buffalo NY 14226-0149

Both these magazines offer dark fantasy/horror, and while both are currently overstocked, plans are that the magazines will continue; possibly at some point they will become open markets again.

Contributors to This Book

Robert Bloch

Bloch, a native Chicagoan whose success with motion-picture and TV scripts made him a Los Angeles resident, sold his first short story in 1934. He was seventeen. Renowned as a suspense writer who authored such mystery and horror tales as *Psycho,* "Yours Truly, Jack the Ripper," *Firebug,* and *Night of the Ripper,* Bloch has also delved successfully into the SF and fantasy genres ("The Old College Try"; *Twilight Zone: The Motion Picture*).

He holds to a regular work schedule, five days a week—never at night or at home. He distinguishes between, in his words, "actual writing duties and research. Writing is writing—research is what I do all the time I'm *not* writing." No writer has proved himself in more fictional forms than Robert Bloch.

Ray Bradbury

Bradbury (born August 22, 1920), still wrote a short story a week—or the equivalent of it—in the autumn of 1986. "I'm an emotional person," he said, "and I must write regularly. To express my emotions." The author of immortal short stories ("Small Assassin," "The Fog Horn," "There Will Come Soft Rains") and novels (*Something Wicked This Way Comes, October Country,* and above all, *The Martian Chronicles*) turned to the "mystery suspense novel" in 1984 with *Death is a Lonely Business,* to which a sequel is planned. Indeed, he has "seven or eight things going simultaneously."

Bradbury's essential Knopf collection, *The Stories of Ray Bradbury* (1981), remains available through many bookstores and clubs.

Mort Castle

Castle, forty, is that rare, sought-after writer who describes himself first as a teacher. A long-time instructor for the Writer's Digest School, he is also constantly in demand in the Chicago-Chicago Heights area as a freelance creative-writing teacher. His story "And of Gideon" appeared in the 1986 limited anthology *Nukes* (Maclay & Associates), of which one critic commented: "Four extraordinary scenarios (which) just might succeed in bringing sanity to the concept of nuclear freeze."

Other short fiction by Castle has appeared in the anthologies *Masques* and

Masques II; his 1984 novel, *The Strangers* (Leisure), drew critical raves; and the imminent release of *Diakka* is apt to do the same.

Steve Rasnic Tem

Tem, a native Virginian but current resident of Colorado, has written and published over eighty horror, fantasy, and SF short stories, as well as nearly one hundred poems. His distinguished fiction has appeared in *Twilight Zone, Whispers,* the *Shadows* series, *Isaac Asimov's Science Fiction Magazine, Masques II,* and *Weirdbook.* In addition, Tem, who recently wrote his first novel, published no fewer than seven of his short stories in the widely regarded *Night Visions* anthology (Dark Harvest) edited by Alan Ryan. The bearded computer expert has also edited the *Umbral Anthology of Science Fiction Poetry.*

Thomas Millstead

Millstead, yet another Midwesterner (a Chicago resident, from Milwaukee originally), has published three quite different novels: A western, *Comanche Stallion; Cave of the Moving Shadows,* a vividly researched fantasy voted into this volume's recommended library; and a new mystery novel, *Behind You,* from Dell.

When he was fresh out of Marquette, he was one of the founders of the Upper Berkley Mews Haloes (UBMH), which honored Leslie Charteris's debonair antihero, The Saint. Millstead has crafted many scholarly essays and fine short stories for magazines such as *Fate, Manhunt,* and *Ellery Queen's Mystery Magazine.*

William F. Nolan

Nolan, coauthor with George Clayton Johnson of the famed *Logan's Run,* has also scripted many screenplays, including *Burnt Offerings* and *Bridge Across Time.* New short fiction by him appeared in the *Masques* and *Masques II* anthologies and—with most of his famous tales—the story collection *Things Beyond Midnight* (Scream Press, 1984).

"I write at the far corner of counters . . . on a stool at all-night coffee shops in the San Fernando Valley," Nolan said. "Just some white paper and the land inside my head."

Nolan submitted his first short story to editors in 1953, and sold it. Since then, he has submitted ninety others. And *sold* ninety others. He's written seven novels. And *sold* seven. He figures he must be doing something right.

James Kisner

Kisner, writer of sardonic "Southern Indiana" stories, moved from Evansville to Indianapolis following the publication of his hardcover novel, *Nero's Vice*. He was that rare author who'd freelanced his first book; "a learning experience," Kisner says wryly. His Zebra novel, *Slice of Life*, and boldly individualistic short stories in *Grue, Dementia,* and the *Masques II* anthology have made him an artist of the macabre, one of the quick-rising innovators of both horror and science fiction. It will be impossible to overlook his work in the future, including *Strands*, recently acquired for publication in 1988.

Ardath Mayhar

Ms. Mayhar is the one to mention when the next superannuated soul asks if there are "any women" who write horror. Or fantasy. Or mysteries; or children's fiction. Or science fiction. Or all kinds of poetry—in all three genres. And not in genres at all. Her current novel is *The Wall*.

This unpretentious Texan's novels and short fiction are cited all over the library. With her husband, she operates a bookstore; she teaches for Writer's Digest School and manages to be more prolific as a writer than almost anyone else. Her prizewinning work should become a reading habit of yours.

Dean R. Koontz

Koontz, closer to forty than fifty years of age, owns a literary track record that almost defines the term *popular fiction*. Whether with dozens of novels (*Phantoms; Whispers; Strangers; Twilight Eyes; Shattered; The Vision*), informative books for Writer's Digest, or recent short stories in *Night Cry, The Horror Show*, and *The Twilight Zone*, the dapper first president of Horror Writers of America *sells*—and turns the most idle readers into devoted fans. What makes him more special is that (1) many Koontz novels were written under other names (Leigh Nichols, for example) and (2) he was a writer of both science-fiction and so-called mainstream novels before achieving his immense popularity in horror/terror fiction. Categories cannot define him; Dean Koontz, simply and accurately, is a gifted *writer*. His newest novel is *Watchers*.

Charles L. Grant

Grant is known almost equally well as the author of unsettling novels of dark fantasy set in the mythical Oxrun Station and as the editor of such award-winning anthologies as the Shadows series. For the latter—he recently finished the *tenth* volume in the series—Grant has found or developed many skilled craftsmen of disquieting, psychological horror.

The New Jersey-based, forty-five-year-old husband of talented writer Katherine Ptacek won a World Fantasy Award for his own story collection, *Nightmare Seasons*.

Robert R. McCammon

McCammon, well short of forty summers, is southern-born and -bred, inheritor of many literary mantles worn by beloved authors of the region. His fast rise in the ranks of those novelists known mainly for horror included such best sellers as *Baal, Bethany's Sin,* the immense success called *Mystery Walk,* and the acclaimed *Usher's Passing.* It was a rare McCammon short story, "Nightcrawlers" (in the 1984 *Masques* anthology), that won the courtly Alabaman a World Fantasy nomination plus its dramatization on the revived, TV *Twilight Zone*. Horror Writers of America was his idea; he served as the first editor of its publication, *Our Glass*. His newest novel is entitled *Swan Song*.

Marion Zimmer Bradley

Ms. Bradley, a favorite in science-fiction and fantasy voting for this volume's recommended reading library, is the author of such watershed novels as *The Bloody Sun, City of Sorcery, The Inheritors, The Shattered Chain,* and *The Heritage of Hastur.* Still young, still stretching her considerable talents, Ms. Bradley is an author whose legends create legions of devoted readers. She has served on the grievance committees of both Science Fiction Writers and Horror Writers of America.

Darrell Schweitzer

Schweitzer is a many-sided writer of almost untrackable versatility, who does all things well. His seventy-plus science-fiction, fantasy, and horror tales have graced magazines from Asimov's and *Amazing* (for each of which he served as assistant editor) to *Weirdbook* and *Twilight Zone*, while many of his finest yarns are found in *Tom O'Bedlam's Night Out and Other Strange Excursions*.

A poet, Schweitzer has also published novels and books comprising Stephen King "higher criticism." His reviews appear frequently in leading newspapers, and he's written columns for *Science Fiction Review, Fantasy Re-*

view, and *Aboriginal SF.* Recently, Schweitzer—with George Scithers and John Betancourt—founded Owlswick Literary Agency.

Michael A. Banks

Banks, a young, former instructor for Writer's Digest School, is a sought-after guest for science-fiction conventions surrounding his Cincinnati home base. He is unstintingly building an impressive reputation as the possessor of one of the most versatile and knowledgeable minds in the science-fiction community. Editor and anthologist, Banks co-wrote the recent, generally acclaimed science-fiction novel, *The Odysseus Solution,* and makes his mark wherever he goes or whatever new enterprises fire his imagination.

Sharon Baker

Ms. Baker is one of the scholarly new science-fiction and fantasy writers who produces steadily and sells steadily. Avon was the publisher of her first novel, *Quarreling, They Met the Dragon,* as well as of her *Journey to Membliar* and *The Burning Tears of Sassurum.* Her articles have been accepted by *SF & Fantasy Workshop Newsletter, Northwest Review of Books,* and the present volume; her poetry, for a major anthology of children's horror poems, *Now We Are Sick.* For Sharon Baker, the cosmos—not the sky—is the limit.

Ramsey Campbell

Campbell—both as novelist and as short story writer—is one of the world's favorite writers of horror. Equally admired in the United Kingdom and the United States, he is also a generous supporter of the small press; his short fiction is as likely to appear in *The Horror Show* as in *Night Cry,* in small-press collections such as *Medusa* (Footsteps Press) as in major anthologies such as *Masques II.* Editor himself of the highly regarded anthology *New Terrors,* Campbell is a world traveler from Merseyside, the author of such unforgettable novels as *Parasite, The Doll that Ate its Mother, Incarnate,* and *The Rage.*

Jeannette M. Hopper

Ms. Hopper, a straight-A grad of Writer's Digest School only a few brief years ago, is swiftly gaining a reputation in horror and in humor as one of those many

Women to Watch; her first novel is widely anticipated. Already published in most small-press magazines, Ms. Hopper's work will first be seen in permanent form—apart from this book—in a limited-editions collection with the working title *Expiration Dates* (Dark Regions Press). It's due out soon, with an introduction by the present editor. (She's presently editing *Gas*.)

Richard Christian Matheson

Matheson was the writing mind behind such TV programs as *The Incredible Hulk, The A-Team,* and *Quincy.* He's also appeared as a vividly inventive short-storyist in the leading horror magazines including *Twilight Zone,* in both *Masques* anthologies, and—with father Richard Matheson—in the famed *Dark Forces* collection. What's in the works: a film for Amblin Entertainment and Steven Speilberg from his original screenplay, with a summer 1987 release date; two feature movies for United Artists (comedy *and* drama); two others for Disney (drama *and* comedy); an original screenplay for another Speilberg feature (in development); five pilot scripts for networks and studios; another original screenplay being written in collaboration with his father; his first story collection; and his first novel—due within the year. He won't be thirty-four until October.

Katherine Ramsland

Ms. Ramsland has a B.A. in experimental psychology, an M.A. in clinical psychology, a Ph.D. in philosophy, and a diploma from Writer's Digest School. She has also published dissertations on Kierkegaard and is the author of a truly psychological horror tale included in *Masques II.* She views the genre as "an exciting arena for new discoveries." So is Ms. Ramsland's work. Recently she completed her first novel of horror.

Colin Wilson

Wilson, while still in his twenties, became world famous as one of Britain's "Angry Young Men" after writing *The Outsider,* an incomparable and unique creation. Self-taught, this Cornwall dynamo could argue that his writing has been more diverse than that of any other living writer. His work ranges from science-fiction and fantasy novels (*The Space Vampires; God of the Labyrinth; The Mind Parasites*) to mystery novels (*The Schoolgirl Murder Case;*

Lingard); encyclopedias on crime to theological study (*Religion and the Rebel*). He has also written biographies, ranging in subject from Bernard Shaw and Wilhelm Reich to Uri Geller and Rasputin; literary how-to (*The Craft of the Novel*); comprehensive studies of metaphysics and the supernatural (*Mysteries; Poltergeist*); social concern (*Order of Assassins*); and psychology (*Origins of the Sexual Impulse; Access to Inner Worlds; New Pathways in Psychology*). Wilson is not yet out of his middle years.

Mary T. Williamson

Ms. Williamson founded Midwest Literary Agency after mothering and rearing six children. Within three years, she'd placed approximately a dozen novels, including her husband, J. N. Williamson's (the well-reviewed *The Longest Night*); James Kisner's *Slice of Life;* and Mort Castle's much-praised horror novels. She also placed the prestigious *Masques* anthologies. Her "stable" includes some half-dozen other novelists.

Alan Rodgers

Rodgers, editor of *Night Cry* since its inception, and associate editor of *Twilight Zone* since the days of T. E. D. Klein, is on the brink of a brilliant writing career. Deep into his first novel—a work of horror, as befitting his editorial involvement with *Night Cry*—his first published fiction is a well-regarded novelette in the hardcover anthology *Masques II,* and his second is a short story in the *Scare Care* anthology from Graham Masterton. Rodgers is a few years short of his thirtieth birthday.

Pat LoBrutto

Born and bred in Brooklyn, New York, LoBrutto is the sociable and accessible senior editor for Doubleday and Company, Inc., heading up their western and science-fiction departments. He has a keen personal interest in horror fiction, too, and is currently working on projects with not only Walter Tevis and Isaac Asimov, but also Dennis Etchison and Robert Bloch.

Married and the father of two, LoBrutto is not yet forty. He won, in 1986, a World Fantasy Award for his many contributions.

Douglas E. Winter

Winter, a Washington, D.C. attorney, is the author of *Stephen King: The Art of Darkness, Faces of Fear,* and other critical writings in the *Washington Post, Philadelphia Inquirer, Cleveland Plain-Dealer,* and magazines as diverse as *Gallery, Harper's Bazaar, Fantasy Review, Saturday Review,* and *Twilight Zone.* He has also edited a story collection, *Black Wine,* and written several short stories—he calls them "legal Gothics"—which have appeared in the anthologies of Charles L. Grant and J. N. Williamson. The hilarious 1986 master of ceremonies for the World Fantasy Convention, Winter has been called "the conscience of horror and dark fantasy."

Janet Fox

Ms. Fox is a widely published writer of always-underivative short story gems of horror and SF which have appeared in the majority of commercial and small-press magazines, and she may well know more about how and where to market fiction in the genres analyzed within this book than anybody else. Also an award-winning poet and stout supporter of the Small Press Writers and Artists Organization, she shares her expertise in a monthly publication entitled, with characteristic modesty and wry wit, *Scavenger's Newsletter.* An Osage, Kansas, resident, Ms. Fox has also served with distinction as the small-press representative for Science Fiction Writers of America.

J. N. Williamson

Williamson's *Houngan* won a Best Fantasy Novel award (*West Coast Review of Books*); his *Ghost* was nominated for the 1984 Balrog Best Novel; *Masques,* an anthology he edited, won the Balrog for Best Professional Achievement of that year and was runner-up for a World Fantasy Award. His novella, *Night Seasons,* became the first such serialized in *Night Cry* and was nominated for a 1987 World Fantasy Award. An original Baker Street Irregular, Williamson is also a Writer's Digest School instructor; columnist (*2AM*); former recording artist as a singer; author of twenty-eight published novels, since 1979; editor of the 1987 anthology *Masques II* (Maclay) and the '88 anthology *The Best of Masques* (Berkley). He was the first secretary of Horror Writers of America. His next, new novels are *Dead to the World* and *The Black School.*

The Top Ten
"Favorites" List—
in Horror, Fantasy,
& SF—(Novels and
Short Stories)

For a professional writer, the challenge of identifying and publicly naming all-time favorite books and shorter works is not taken lightly—nor was it by the dozens of well-known people who were invited to name their choices for the present book. *Weirdbook* publisher W. Paul Ganley may have summed up the collective sense of frustration in a letter accompanying his nominations: "You are a vile person," he began. "You have stolen six whole hours out of my life—that's how long it took to make up these lists—and now that I'm finished, I'm not entirely happy with the choices I've made."

Second thoughts were the rule. Gene Wolfe went so far as to suggest, "These are not *really* Top Tens," adding, "They are lists of my own favorites." That was when I decided to title this list precisely that.

Stephen King, like Ganley, called me a name: *slyboots,* a clever word his "mum" coined. King declared that if I had asked him to name one hundred great novels and short stories, he'd have replied, "Ah, shit, I don't have time to do that." And he'd have yelled that it was unfair if I'd asked him "to name [his] *single* favorite in each of these categories . . . or top three . . . or even [his] top five." But I'd sought a Top Ten. King's comment: "So here I am, slipping the noose around my neck, and I suspect I'll not be the only one to do so. Oh, what a slyboots you are! My admiration is unbounded!"

Still, the compilation of what Cheryl Curry Sayre termed a *basic bookshelf* didn't meet with universal cooperation or approval. Arthur C. Clarke wrote from Sri Lanka that he wished he'd had the time. Jack Williamson (no kin) observed candidly that "Too many of the titles I wanted to list were published before 1940." (I had stipulated to all invited participants that their chosen titles be published after 1940.)

I had reasons for my seemingly arbitrary editorial fiat. Least of all, I believed it was very likely that SF people would begin by listing the marvelous inventions of Jules Verne or H. G. Wells and soon find themselves out of room to cite any contemporary authors' work. Enthusiasts of horror, arguably as much from reflex as admiration (or recent reading), would begin with Bram Stoker's *Dracula* or Mary Shelley's *Frankenstein*, choose others by Poe or Robert Louis Stevenson or H. P. Lovecraft, and have no alternative to filling up the remaining spaces in their lists with titles by King and Ray Bradbury.

Everyone knows about the gifted writers I've just mentioned, or their major works. Anybody who wants to read them can locate this remarkable fiction at any book shop or library.

The far more important reasons for including only *post*-1940 titles were as follows: I wanted aspiring writers of all speculative fiction to have the chance to grow aware of and to read the incredibly well-crafted, brilliantly imaginative tales by Stephen King or Ray Bradbury that aren't ordinarily reprinted—and to know the satisfying novels and stories by less-renowned writers whom King, Bradbury, and speculative fiction writing professionals in the diverse fields respect just as much. *That* is one of my major reasons.

The other one is the biggie: I doubt with all my heart and knowledge that Verne, Stoker, Lovecraft, Wells, Shelley or Stevenson—or Edgar Allan Poe—starting in writing today would write even *one* novel or story exactly as he wrote it for his contemporary audience. And, as an instructor for Writer's Digest School, I've had upwards of five hundred students whose chances of breaking into print are retarded or ruined at those times when, consciously or unconsciously, they are writing under the influence of the great-but-long-dead.

New writers who do so, I think, are intoxicated by the masters—out on a literary highway without a license for a time machine that would return them to a world in which such influence might (or might not) make their own work better. New writers who emulate such past masters write for an audience, and worse, editors, who have been dead for decades or centuries. Would-be Lovecrafts, Burroughses, Machens, and Jameses of any variety are probably never going to be published until they can find their own, contemporary voices.

It's not so much that the ideas of the classic authors are necessarily outdated as it is their writing styles. Yet even in terms of their imaginative concepts and plotting, as a close reading of this book should have instructed you, the long-gone and the once-great influenced so many other writers that much of what was once marvelously fresh and original had been *fully explored* before you and I enrolled in high school.

In short, if reincarnation theories are correct and Eddie Poe is hard at work today, he's very probably *in print*—but he himself would never see a connection between "The Tell-Tale Heart" or "The Fall of the House of Usher" and the yarn he just sold to *Night Cry* or *The Horror Show*. Suggesting anything to the contrary would, I believe, be actively bad advice.

Participants in this survey were often faced with problems of the kind that, to twist a familiar quote, fry one's soul. Gene Wolfe listed "as fantasy what [*he* thought was] fantasy, and as science fiction what [he considered] science fiction. To hell with anybody else—let him write his own list."

There are "entirely too many wonderful stories and books out there [so] my list was chosen to reflect purely personal tastes," wrote Melissa Mia Hall. (Personal preferences were precisely what I sought.) "The most difficult category to define," she added, "was *fantasy.*" SF's Barry Malzberg called his story list "a gambler's compilation, a system, an approximation."

Editor J. R. McHone confessed ruefully that he "did not *intend* for 50 percent of the fantasy short stories" to be by Harlan Ellison; "it just came out that way." Ms. Sayre admitted that she "could have filled the short story category with Bradbury," adding, "He gave me my love of prose, of the way words work, to evoke images and moods."

Horror-and-SF writer James Kisner said that his "criteria for choosing a story or novel [was] that it be memorable and well-written, and ultimately, of course, entertaining." McHone spoke for many in pointing out that "Trying to separate SF, fantasy, and horror *re*-reminded me how *thin* the line is between genres, in many cases."

Fantasist Suzy McKee Charnas nominated a story that was part of a *larger* story and submitted not one but *two* lists for what was essentially the same genre! All were counted in, partly because Ms. Charnas is a wonderful writer, partly because she proposed that the two Top Tens were divided into "classics" and "works of newer date." (Ingenuity still counts!)

Some of the "Bests" lists, particularly those that brought work to my attention that was unfamiliar, contained informed and interesting comments. British author Simon Clark said of William Golding's relatively unknown *Pincher Martin,* "Nominal mainstream literature . . . it foreshadows modern-style horror, then takes another step forward." But if I started including, for genre fiction, all the things the writers in the genre want to claim cousinship with, the resulting list would have been as long as this whole book. So, with regret, I've had to let you discover this borderline not-quite-fantasy, sort-of-SF and scary-therefore-nearly-horror on your own.

The problem of deducing the correct genre was echoed by author Ron Wolfe, who, nominating *Sandkings* by George R. R. Martin, wrote: "The fear of strange insects, of strange places, of dangerous people, of entrapment: all of this is a science fiction/horror gem with a beautifully mean twist at the end." A. R. Morlan, who seems to be in almost every issue of *Night Cry,* said of a recommended John Wyndham novel: "While *Re-Birth* is usually classified as sci-fi, I find it works better on the psychological horror level; likewise *A Clockwork Orange* [by Anthony Burgess]." The blurring of genre lines is unavoidable. Don't argue with the categories: go read the stories and novels and decide for yourself.

A man who can write anything and frequently does, Mort Castle, whose idea became this book, will have the last word preceding the presentation of certain "broken-out-and-bylined" Top Ten lists. Of Charles Beaumont's "The Hunger," Castle writes: "Every one of Beaumont's stories had a fine inventive premise—but not every one fully explored the concept. This one does. *Beaumont*—another one of those masters to whom all of us reading/writing folk owe ever so much." Of Wolfe's *The Island of Dr. Death and Other Stories* Castle observed: "What Bradbury does to you when you're thirteen, this Wolfe story does when you're an adult." Of his own "Altenmoor, Where the Dogs Dance": "Not a fantasy, but *about* fantasy." Of my own "They Never Even See Me". "A look at the generation gap—and as that, the story is every bit as poignant as anything written by J. D. Salinger." Of Richard Matheson's "The Jazz Machine": "A prose-poem. . . . Had a black man written it, [it] would today be a part of every important 'black pride' anthology. As it is, I think it's not even in print anymore."

There's one last reason that the bylined "favorites" lists and the recommended fantasy "library" were painstakingly provided by a remarkable array of talented pros, to whom we should all be grateful: To recall, at least one more time, those fine but not necessarily famous speculative yarns of every length in the hope that you'll seek many of them out and do the easy, pleasant thing that writers of all statures continually and for all times seek: *Read* them.

ROGER ZELAZNY

The Novels: SF

Alfred Bester, *The Demolished Man*
Ray Bradbury, *The Martian Chronicles*
Arthur C. Clarke, *Childhood's End*
L. Sprague De Camp, *Lest Darkness Fall*
Philip Jose Farmer, *To Your Scattered Bodies Go*
Frank Herbert, *Dune*
Fritz Leiber, *The Big Time*
Clifford Simak, *Time Quarry*
Theodore Sturgeon, *More Than Human*
Jack Williamson, *The Humanoids*

The Stories: SF

Isaac Asimov, "Nightfall"
James Blish, "Surface Tension"
Arthur C. Clarke, "The Nine Billion Names of God"
Philip Jose Farmer, "The Lovers"
Tom Godwin, "The Cold Equations"
Robert A. Heinlein, "The Roads Must Roll"
Daniel Keyes, "Flowers for Algernon"
Murray Leinster, "First Contact"
Cordwainer Smith, "The Game of Rat and Dragon"
Theodore Sturgeon, "Microcosmic God"

STANLEY SCHMIDT

The editor of *Analog,* Mr. Schmidt said his contribution is "a list of ten things I recommend highly. The list is not intended to be definitive, exhaustive, or in order; and I have tried to include some things I especially like which you probably won't hear about too often."

A Combined Novel and Story Top Ten

Robert Heinlein, *The Moon Is a Harsh Mistress*
Daniel Keyes, "Flowers for Algernon"
Chad Oliver, "Transformer"
David R. Palmer, *Emergence*
Ted Reynolds, "Can These Bones Live?"
Bob Shaw, "Light of Other Days"
Mark Stiegler, "Petals of Rose"

Theodore Sturgeon, *More than Human*
S. C. Sykes, "Rockabye Baby"
A. E. van Vogt, *The World of Null-A*

ROLAND J. GREEN & FRIEDA A. MURRAY   SF

Roland Green is a well-known Chicago-based reviewer of SF and the author of such novels as the Peacekeeper stories, *Sherran,* and—with Jerry Pournelle—*Storms of Victory*. Frieda A. Murray is also Mrs. Green and his collaborator on the fine novel *The Book of Kantela*.

The Novels

Isaac Asimov, *The Caves of Steel*
Arthur C. Clarke, *Rendezvous with Rama*
Gordon R. Dickson, *The Alien Way*
William Gibson, *Neuromancer*
Robert A. Heinlein, *The Moon Is a Harsh Mistress*
Tanith Lee, *Sung in Shadow*
Ursula K. Le Guin, *The Left Hand of Darkness*
Andre Norton, *Star Man's Son*
Frederik Pohl and C. M. Kornbluth, *The Space Merchants*
J. R. R. Tolkien, *The Lord of the Rings*

ORSON SCOTT CARD   SF and Fantasy

Orson Scott Card is one of SF's new shooting stars whose *Speaker for the Dead* and *Songmaster* provided portents for what was to lie ahead—including a four-star review of his compelling novel, *Ender's Game*, in *West Coast Review of Books*.

Card, who also compiled the Nebula Awards nominations for Science Fiction Writers of America, herein presents *six* specific lists of the very best in his genre. Each is defined and introduced by him.

Ten Great Novels of Human Science Fiction

SF began with roots in the romantic tradition—with an overlay of fascination with the ideas and gadgets of modern technology. For me, however, science fiction came of age when it began to do all that, and yet deal realistically with human beings in society. Here are the novels that I think represent the finest extrapolations of human society transformed by the stress of fictional futures.

1. John Hersey, *White Lotus*
2. James Blish, *A Case of Conscience*
3. Ursula K. Le Guin, *The Left Hand of Darkness*
4. Anthony Burgess, *A Clockwork Orange*
5. Joe Haldeman, *The Forever War*
6. Michael Bishop, *Ancient of Days*
7. George Orwell, *1984*
8. Walter M. Miller, Jr., *A Canticle for Leibowitz*
9. John Crowley, *Engine Summer*
10. Samuel R. Delany, *Babel-17*

Ten Great Novels of Cosmic SF

Jules Verne laid the foundation of *sense of wonder* science fiction; E. E. "Doc" Smith set it among the stars with his Lensman and Skylark series; and some of the best of it has been in film, from Flash Gordon to *Star Wars*. Its silliest manifestations are sometimes tagged "space opera," but at its best, cosmic science fiction creates a sense of awe and grandeur as it shows the vast movements of human, natural, and physical history. The authors dare to declare the meaning of life, the struggle of good and evil, the beginning and end of the universe; godlike, they create and destroy communities, nations, and species with the irresistible logic of science—not to mention poetic justice and biting irony.

If the same author earned the right to have two or more entries on this list, I've cheated and put the others in parentheses on the same line. Also, I've tended to put the most recent works last, since I haven't yet got the perspective to judge fairly where their work belongs in this list.

1. Larry Niven, *Ringworld* (also *Protector*, and with Jerry Pournelle, *The Mote in God's Eye*)
2. Robert A. Heinlein, *The Moon Is a Harsh Mistress* (also *Stranger in a Strange Land*)
3. Arthur C. Clarke, *The City and the Stars* (also *Childhood's End* and *2001: A Space Odyssey*)
4. Frank Herbert, *Dune*
5. Kurt Vonnegut, *Slaughterhouse-Five* (also *Cat's Cradle*)
6. Philip Jose Farmer, *To Your Scattered Bodies Go*
7. Ray Bradbury, *The Martian Chronicles*
8. Mike Resnick, *Santiago*
9. Richard Lupoff, *Countersolar!* (also *Circumpolar!*)
10. Stephen King, *The Stand* (also *The Dead Zone*)

Seven Great SF and Fantasy Series

SF and fantasy are rife with series—books or stories set in the same world, often using continuing characters. Off the top of my head, I can think of Zelazny's *Amber*, Bradley's *Darkover*, Herbert's *Dune*, Le Guin's *Earthsea*, Leiber's *Fafhrd and the Gray Mouser*, Norman's *Gor*, Adams's *Horseclans*, Walton's *Mabinogion*, McKillip's *Riddlemaster*, Donaldson's *Chronicles of Thomas Covenant*, Kube-McDowell's *Trigon Disunity*, Tepper's *True Game*, Anthony's *Xanth*.

What makes a *great* series, beyond the normal requirements of excellent storytelling and aesthetically pleasing language? The books or stories should be nonrepetitious—each succeeding volume should have something new to say. They should be unified—there should be more binding them together than a shared geography. Almost invariably, the great series are conceived as a whole from the beginning, not endlessly built up in a ramshackle structure of sequels. And the series as a whole must be ambitious: the authors should attempt magnificence and achieve it. These seven series are science fiction and fantasy at their grandest.

1. Brian W. Aldiss, Helliconia: *Helliconia Spring, Helliconia Summer, Helliconia Winter*
2. Gene R. Wolfe, Book of the New Sun: *The Shadow of the Torturer, The Claw of the Conciliator, The Sword of the Lictor, The Citadel of the Autarch*
3. J. R. R. Tolkien, Lord of the Rings: *The Fellowship of the Ring, The Two Towers, The Return of the King;* with the "prequel," *The Hobbit*

4. C. S. Lewis, The Chronicles of Narnia: *The Lion, the Witch, and the Wardrobe, Prince Caspian, The Voyage of the "Dawn Treader," The Silver Chair, The Horse and His Boy, The Magician's Nephew, The Last Battle*
5. Mervyn Peake, Gormenghast: *Titus Groan, Gormenghast, Titus Alone*
6. Isaac Asimov, Foundation: *Foundation, Foundation and Empire, Second Foundation, Foundation's Edge*
7. Evangeline Walton, The Mabinogion: *Prince of Annwin, The Children of Llyr, The Song of Rhiannon, The Island of the Mighty*

Ten Great SF and Fantasy Books for Young People

The only people fit to judge books for young people are young people. I belonged in that category during the 1950s and early 1960s, so the first part of my list comes from that time. Since then, I have found other books marketed as young adult books that nevertheless appealed to me as an adult. Those make up the *second* part of this list. I can't decide if it's mere coincidence that the first part is entirely SF and the second part, fantasy. (Note that most of the recent books are the first volume of a *series*.)

1. Robert A. Heinlein, *Citizen of the Galaxy*
2. Andre Norton, *The Stars Are Ours*
3. Robert A. Heinlein, *Tunnel in the Sky*
4. Andre Norton, *Galactic Derelict*
5. Andre Norton, *Catseye*
6. Patricia McKillip, *The Throne of the Erril of Sherril*
7. Ursula K. Le Guin, *A Wizard of Earthsea* (sequels: *The Tomb of Atuan, The Farthest Shore*)
8. Lloyd Alexander, *The Black Cauldron* (sequels: *The Book of Three, The Castle of Llyr, Taran Wanderer, The High King,* also known as the Prydain series)
9. Lloyd Alexander, *Westmark* (sequels: *The Kestrel, The Beggar Queen*)
10. Patricia McKillip, *The Riddlemaster of Hed* (sequels: *The Heir of Sea and Fire, Harpist in the Wind*)

Fifteen Best Contemporary Novels of SF and Fantasy

It's impossible to guess which of the works of the last few years will endure and which will fade. But here is a list of the novels of the mid-1980s that, I believe, represent the best of each genre. (Novels from this period that appear on other lists are omitted.)

Science Fiction

1. George Alec Effinger, *When Gravity Fails*
2. Rudy Rucker, *The Secret of Life*
3. Howard Waldrop, *Them Bones*
4. Christopher Priest, *The Glamour*
5. Michael P. Kube-McDowell, *Enigma*
6. William Gibson, *Neuromancer*
7. Richard Grant, *The Saraband of Lost Time*
8. Jim Aikin, *Walk the Moons Road*
9. James Patrick Kelly & John Kessel, *Freedom Beach*

Fantasy

1. Leigh Kennedy, *The Journal of Nicholas the American*
2. Robert Silverberg, *Gilgamesh the King*
3. Steven R. Boyett, *The Architect of Sleep / The Geography of Dreams* (multi-volume novel)
4. John Maddox Roberts, *King of the Wood*
5. Tim Powers, *The Anubis Gate*
6. Stephen Brust, *Brokedown Palace*

Ten Great Novels of Fantasy

When J. R. R. Tolkien's *Lord of the Rings* caught on with American college students in the 1960's, it spawned a host of imitators— and made fantasy a viable commercial category for booksellers. Those who know the romantic tradition, however, recognize that this is merely the latest burst in an unbroken literary line that extends back to the Hellenistic era. Choosing the best of these since 1940 is *not* easy—but here's my attempt.

1. C. S. Lewis, *Till We Have Faces*
2. T. H. White, *The Once and Future King*
3. William Goldman, *The Princess Bride*
4. Peter S. Beagle, *The Last Unicorn* (also *A Fine and Private Place*)
5. Robert Holdstock, *Mythago Wood*
6. John Myers Myers, *Silverlock*
7. George Orwell, *Animal Farm*
8. John Crowley, *The Deep*
9. Patricia McKillip, *The Forgotten Beasts of Eld*
10. Megan Lindholm, *Wizard of the Pigeons*

HARLAN ELLISON

The answering machine was set so that my wife, Mary, and I could hear the caller's incoming voice before electing to pick up the receiver. Rude, perhaps, but that's how it was. I ought to have recognized Harlan Ellison's mercurial speaking patterns at once, but we'd chatted just last week about his work habits—I was doing a piece for Horror Writers of America's *Our Glass*—and hadn't discussed this book for months. Consequently, I thought for a moment Harlan was John Silbersack of NAL and, when I snatched up the phone to shout "Hullo," the author of "Jefty Is Five," "Shatterday," and "Paladin of the Lost Hour" was promptly deafened by the phone device's echoing loudspeaker. And, of course, bewildered by being called John.

Details like that don't throw Harlan Ellison; he knew who *he* was calling, and why. Undaunted, raising his voice to be heard above the electronic din, the man who's won virtually every award the fantasy umbrella has to shed upon him proceeded to make his recommendations. If they were hard to add or didn't add up to ten, if they seemed to have forgotten my post-1940 edict in some instances, this was Ellison—and his opinions mattered.

He started with the novel *Song of Kali* by Dan Simmons, "which is probably the most brilliant novel in the last decade." By now I'd hung up in order to let Harlan's exact words be duly recorded—and so he wouldn't be permanently deafened. I remembered, hearing that recommendation, that Dean R. Koontz also spoke highly of the Simmons novel.

"No collection of fantasy is complete," Harlan continued, "without mentioning the novels of Dr. Seuss." I recalled the delight of my own children and nodded. "Lovecraft's 'Rats in the Walls'—probably the most perfect piece of fantasy ever written."

I gestured to Mary, who at once understood what I meant: I'm not in my office now and we need a pen and pad to transcribe this. She found them as we listened.

"Frederick Prokosch," Ellison machine-gunned on, spelling the name without being asked, mentioning the Prokosch title: *Seven Who Fled*. "It has a surreal quality about it—even though it's not really a fantasy—that has informed much of my writing." That said something special to me; I imagine it does to you, as well. Then Ellison was winding up in a rush, anxious to speed on to the next item on his day's agenda. He recommended Clark Ashton Smith's *City of the Singing Flame*, then added, without taking a discernible breath, Fritz Leiber's *Our Lady of Darkness*.

I was back on the phone again, quickly—the laid-back, lethargic, or leisurely find Harlan Ellison long gone, streaking off to other projects, other friends—to express my appreciation for the long-distance call. "Thanks, buddy," I told him. "I owe you one."

"To hell with that," he replied. Clearly his mind was already miles—or galaxies—away. "You don't either."

And in Harlan Ellison's universe, that was precisely how he felt about it.

RAMSEY CAMPBELL

Ten Best Postwar Horror Novels

Peter Ackroyd, *Hawksmoor*
James Herbert, *The Fog*
Shirley Jackson, *The Haunting of Hill House*
Stephen King, *It*
T. E. D. Klein, *The Ceremonies*
Fritz Leiber, *Conjure Wife*
Richard Matheson, *I Am Legend*
David Morrell, *Testament*
Peter Straub, *Ghost Story*
Thomas Tessier, *Phantom*

Ten Best Postwar Horror Stories

Robert Aickman, "The Hospice"
Clive Barker, "In the Hills, the Cities"
Jerome Bixby, "It's a *Good* Life"
David Case, "Among the Wolves"
Philip K. Dick, "Upon the Dull Earth"
Dennis Etchison, "It Only Comes Out at Night"
M. John Harrison, "Running Down"
Fritz Leiber, "A Bit of the Dark World"
Thomas Ligotti, "Dream of a Mannikin, or the Third Person"
John Metcalfe, "The Feasting Dead"

Ten Best Postwar Fantasy Novels

Peter S. Beagle, *The Last Unicorn*
John Crowley, *Little, Big*
Alan Garner, *Elidor*
Alan Garner, *Red Shift*
M. John Harrison, *In Viriconium*
Ursula K. Le Guin, the Earthsea trilogy
Mervyn Peake, the Gormenghast trilogy
Jack Vance, *The Dying Earth*
Karl Edward Wagner, *Bloodstone*
Manly Wade Wellman, *Who Fears the Devil?*

Ten Best Postwar Science Fiction Novels

Brian Aldiss, *Hothouse*
Alfred Bester, *The Demolished Man*
J. G. Ballard, *The Drowned World*
Ray Bradbury, *The Martian Chronicles*
Algis Budrys, *Rogue Moon*
Philip K. Dick, *Flow My Tears, The Policeman Said*
Ursula K. Le Guin, *The Lathe of Heaven*
Bob Shaw, *The Palace of Eternity*
John Sladek, *The Muller-Fokker Effect*
Theodore Sturgeon, *More than Human*

JOHN SILBERSACK (of NAL)   SF

Pierre Boullé, *Planet of the Apes*
Arthur C. Clarke, *Childhood's End*
Susan Cooper, *The Dark is Rising*
Paul Gallico, *The Abandoned*
Frank Herbert, *Dune*
C. S. Lewis, *The Voyage of the "Dawn Treader"*
William Mayne, *Earthfasts*
Robert Nathan, *Portrait of Jenny*
J. R. R. Tolkien, *The Fellowship of the Ring*
T. H. White, *The Once and Future King*

ARDATH MAYHAR

Science Fiction

Poul Anderson, *The High Crusade*
Alfred Bester, *The Demolished Man*
Ray Bradbury, *The Martian Chronicles*
Orson Scott Card, *Speaker for the Dead*
Pat Frank, *Alas, Babylon*
Robert A. Heinlein, *The Green Hills of Earth*

Andre Norton, *The Beast Master*
Chad Oliver, *Mists of the Dawn*
Theodore Sturgeon, *More than Human*
A. E. van Vogt, *The World of Null-A*

The SF short stories that Ms. Mayhar chose are "Black Destroyer" by van Vogt; and "Tight Little Stitches in a Dead Man's Back" by Joe R. Lansdale.

Fantasy

Poul Anderson, *Three Hearts and Three Lions*
Ray Bradbury, *The October Country*
Joy Chant, *Red Moon, Black Mountain*
Susan Cooper, *The Dark is Rising*
Ursula K. Le Guin, the Earthsea trilogy
A. Merritt, *The Face in the Abyss*
Andre Norton, the Witch World series
Mervyn Peake, the Gormenghast trilogy
L. Sprague de Camp & Fletcher Pratt, *The Incomplete Enchanter*
J. R. R. Tolkien, *The Lord of the Rings*

Ms. Mayhar recommended one fantasy short story—"Fish Night" by Joe R. Lansdale.

Horror

William Peter Blatty, *The Exorcist*
Stephen King, *The Shining*
Stephen King, *Pet Sematary*
Robert R. McCammon, *Mystery Walk*
Anne Rice, *Interview with the Vampire*
Whitley Strieber, *Night Church*
Whitley Strieber, *The Wolfen*
J. N. Williamson, *Ghost*
Thomas Tryon, *Harvest Home*
Thomas Tryon, *The Other*

Ms. Mayhar's horror short story nominations are "The Autopsy" by Shea; "Seventh Sister" by Mary Elizabeth Counselman; and "The Desrick on Yandro" by Manly Wade Wellman.

JANE YOLEN   Fantasy

The Novels

Lloyd Alexander, the Prydain series
Peter S. Beagle, *The Last Unicorn*
Randall Jarrell, *The Animal Family*
Ursula K. Le Guin, the Earthsea trilogy
C. S. Lewis, *The Chronicles of Narnia*
Patricia McKillip, the Riddlemaster of Hed trilogy
James Thurber, *The Thirteen Clocks*
J. R. R. Tolkien, *The Hobbit*

J. R. R. Tolkien, *The Lord of the Rings*
E. B. White, *Charlotte's Web*
T. H. White, *The Once and Future King*

The Stories

Peter S. Beagle, "Come, Lady Death"
Ray Bradbury, "The Invisible Boy"
Angela Carter, "The Courtship of Mr. Lyon"
Shirley Jackson, "The Lottery"
Richard Kennedy, "Come Again in the Spring"
Ursula K. Le Guin, "The Ones Who Walk Away from Omelas"
Tanith Lee, "Red as Blood"
Gabriel Garcia Marquez, "Very Old Man with Enormous Wings"
Theodore Sturgeon, "The Silken Swift"
Jane Yolen, "The Lady and the Merman"

Ms. Yolen's honorable mention fantasy novel list includes "McKinley's *Beauty,* Babbit's *Tuck Everlasting,* Jones's *The Spellcoats,* something of Patricia Wrightson, Wolfe's 'Torturer' books [*Book of the New Sun*], Stewart's Arthurian trilogy." Among shorter works, Ms. Yolen also cites "anything by Isak Dinesen, Jarrell's 'The Bat Poet,' which is published as a children's book but is really the size of a short story . . . any Isaac Bashevis Singer *shetle magic* stories," and her own splendid "Evian Steel."

DOUGLAS E. WINTER   Horror

J. G. Ballard, *The Atrocity Exhibition*
J. G. Ballard, *Crash*
William Peter Blatty, *The Exorcist*
Thomas Harris, *Red Dragon*
Shirley Jackson, *The Haunting of Hill House*
Stephen King, *The Body*
Stephen King, *The Dead Zone*
Stephen King, *'Salem's Lot*
Richard Matheson, *I Am Legend*
Peter Straub, *Ghost Story*

STEPHEN KING

My Ten Favorite Fantasy-Horror Novels

Ray Bradbury, *Something Wicked This Way Comes*
Ramsey Campbell, *The Doll Who Ate His Mother*
Jack Finney, *The Body Snatchers*
Shirley Jackson, *The Haunting of Hill House*
T. E. D. Klein, *The Ceremonies*
Robert Marasco, *Burnt Offerings*
Richard Matheson, *I Am Legend*
Anne Rice, *Interview With the Vampire*

Curt Siodmak, *Donovan's Brain*
Peter Straub, *Ghost Story*

My Ten Favorite Fantasy-Horror Short Stories or Novellas

Clive Barker, "In the Hills, the Cities"
Robert Bloch, "Sweets to the Sweet"
Ray Bradbury, "Small Assassin"
Joseph Payne Brennan, "Slime"
Ramsey Campbell, "The Companion"
Shirley Jackson, "The Lottery"
T. E. D. Klein, "Children of the Kingdom"
Fritz Leiber, "The Pale Brown Thing"
Richard Matheson, "Prey"
Robert R. McCammon, "Nightcrawlers"

Mr. King requested, "be clear on one thing: I've picked no best or worst within either list; I've listed my picks on the basis of alphabetical order, and have of course excluded H. P. Lovecraft on the basis of your chronological cutoff point." Adding that his selections leave out "what seems like a billion good stories and novels—three more Leibers I can think of offhand (including that weird exercise in paranoia, 'You're All Alone'); five more shorts by Bradbury, including 'The Crowd,' 'The Jar,' and 'Heavy-Set'; Matheson's 'Duel' and that eerie tale about the drive-in succubus; four or five Bloch tales (including 'That Hell-Bound Train'); two more from Clive Barker's *Books of Blood;* William Sloane's *The Edge of Running Water; The Shrinking Man* by Richard Matheson; Whitley Strieber's vampire novel *The Hunger; The Totem* by David Morrell; novels by Les Daniels and Les Whitten; Leiber's *Conjure Wife; The House Next Door* by Anne Rivers Siddons . . . and so on. But I'll stand by these . . . and probably hang by them."

THE EDITOR'S CHOICES

The following selections for all three genres of the fantasy umbrella are as eclectic and subjective as I can make them. I exerted special effort to recall, and when necessary, to track down, those imaginative works that are either lodged in memory, or more recently read, seem sure to follow their predecessors into that mental vault where fascination, awe, surprise or shock, hope and caution, and *wonder* are retained—involuntarily.

I didn't choose tales because their writers were famous, or worse, critically acclaimed. Each choice is here because to conceive of a world without it is to picture a lesser world. I seized the chance to think and rethink selections as well as the opportunity editorship affords to cite Honorable Mention works—with greater glee than I've known since Mother believed I was really too ill for school.

No list here is better than another. But if you would care to form a splendid, new ambition . . . *try* to read them all. Doing so can only improve your chance of installing a yarn of *yours* in a list of the future.

HORROR

The Novels

Robert Bloch, *Psycho*
Mort Castle, *Diakka*

Stephen King, *Pet Sematary*
Dean R. Koontz, *Phantoms*
Ira Levin, *Rosemary's Baby*
Richard Matheson, *I Am Legend*
Dan Simmons, *Song of Kali*
Peter Straub, *Ghost Story*
F. Paul Wilson, *The Keep*

The Stories

Charles Beaumont, "In His Image"
Charles Beaumont, "Miss Gentilbelle"
Ray Bradbury, "The Crowd"
Fredric Brown, "The Geezenstacks"
Mort Castle, "And of Gideon"
Stephen King, "The Mist"
James Kisner, "The Litter"
Richard Matheson, "Duel"
Robert R. McCammon, "Nightcrawlers"
Thomas Sullivan, "The Man Who Drowned Puppies"

Honorable Mention: Novels

Robert Bloch, *The Scarf;* Mort Castle, *The Strangers;* C. Terry Cline, *Damon;* George Ernsberger, *The Mountain King;* James Herbert, *The Fog;* Stephen King, *Carrie;* James Kisner, *Slice of Life, Strands;* Dean R. Koontz, *Darkfall, Strangers, Watchers;* Joe R. Lansdale, *Act of Love;* Robert Marasco, *Burnt Offering;* Robert R. McCammon, *Baal, Bethany's Sin, Usher's Passing;* Ray Russell, *The Case Against Satan;* Sol Stein, *The Resort;* Bernard Taylor, *The Godsend;* J. N. Williamson, *The Longest Night*

Honorable Mention: Stories

Mona B. Clee, "Dinosaurs"; Charles Beaumont, "The Howling Man"; Robert Bloch, "Yours Truly, Jack the Ripper"; Ray Bradbury, "The Town Where No One Got Off"; Ramsey Campbell, "Second Sight"; Roald Dahl, "Ratcatcher"; Harlan Ellison, "I Have No Mouth and I Must Scream"; Dennis Etchison, "Daughter of the Golden West"; Dennis Hamilton, "The Alteration"; Jeanette Hopper, "Final Notice"; John Keefauver, "Kill For Me"; Stephen King, "Children of the Corn," "The Mangler"; Joe R. Lansdale, "The Pit"; Richard Matheson, "Prey," "Being"; G. Wayne Miller, "Wiping the Slate Clean"; William F. Nolan, "Dead Call," "Lonely Train A' Comin'," "The Yard"; Paul Olson, "Valley of the Shadow"; Ray Russell, "Sardonicus"; David B. Silva, "Ice Crystals"; Steve Rasnic Tem, "Motherson"; J. N. Williamson, "The Book of Webster's," "The Night Seasons"

SCIENCE FICTION

I'm not an authority on SF. Two "howevers": Most of it that I read, I read for the reasons anyone else reads. However II: I know what constitutes a good story, and, if it's stuck with me over the years, we may be sure it's a book or story worth reading. Consequently, my SF choices serve a small, strange function: They're works a professional writer and editor loved and admired, but unlike my horror selections, and to a lesser extent, my fantasy picks, they've been chosen more the way a typical reader of this book might select them. I make no apologies for them.

The Novels

Ray Bradbury, *Fahrenheit 451*
Ray Bradbury, *The Martian Chronicles*
Fredric Brown, *The Mind-Thing*
Fredric Brown, *What Mad Universe*
Orson Scott Card, *Ender's Game*
Richard Matheson, *The Shrinking Man*
William F. Nolan & George Clayton Johnson, *Logan's Run*
George Orwell, *1984*
Gene Wolfe, *Free Live Free*
Roger Zelazny, *The Dream Master*

The Stories

Charles Beaumont, "The Crooked Man"
Ray Bradbury, "The Veldt"
Fredric Brown, "Arena"
Harlan Ellison, "A Boy and His Dog"
Daniel Keyes, "Flowers for Algernon"
Richard Matheson, "Mute"
Richard Matheson, "The Test"
Robert R. McCammon, "I Scream Man"
Ray Russell, "Xong of Xuxan"
F. Paul Wilson, "Soft"

Honorable Mention: Novels

Michael A. Banks & Dean R. Lambe, *The Odysseus Solution;* A. Bester, *The Demol-ished Man;* Hal Clement, *Needle;* Michael Crichton, *The Andromeda Strain;* L. P. Da-vies, *The Artificial Man;* Michael P. Kube-McDowell, *Enigma;* Stephen King, *The Stand;* James Kisner, *Nero's Vice;* Robert Sheckley, *Mind Swap;* Theodore Sturgeon, *More than Human;* Colin Wilson, *The Space Vampires;* Jack Williamson, *The Human-oids*

Honorable Mention: Stories

Charles Beaumont, "Elegy"; Robert Bloch, "The Old College Try"; Ray Bradbury, "A Sound of Thunder"; Fredric Brown, "Knock"; Harlan Ellison, "Jefty Is Five"; Jerry Eubank & Parke Godwin, "An Unmarked Grave"; Joe R. Lansdale, "Tight Little Stitches in a Dead Man's Back"; George R. R. Martin, "SandKings"; Gene Wolfe, "Westwind"; Roger Zelazny, "Graveyard Heart"

FANTASY

It may be noticed that I've made certain citations as a lifelong Sherlockian—one of the original sixty Baker Street Irregulars—that may be unfamiliar to you. I implore you to remedy the situation by seeking such selections out and reading them—soon.

The Novels

Ray Bradbury, *Dandelion Wine*
Ray Bradbury, *Something Wicked This Way Comes*

Richard Matheson, *Bid Time Return*
Richard Matheson, *What Dreams May Come*
Ardath Mayhar, *Khi to Freedom*
Thomas E. Millstead, *Cave of the Moving Shadows*
Vincent Starrett, *Private Life of Sherlock Holmes*
J. N. Williamson, *Ghost*
Colin Wilson, *God of the Labyrinth*
Bari Wood, *The Tribe*

The Stories

Charles Beaumont, "My Grandmother's Japonicas"
Anthony Boucher, "The Greatest Tertian"
Ray Bradbury, "I Sing the Body Electric!"
Fredric Brown, "Imagine"
Richard Matheson, "Deathbed"
Richard Matheson, "Little Girl Lost"
Alan Rogers, "The Boy Who Came Back from the Dead"
Ray Russell, "The Charm"
Ray Russell, "Czadek"
J. D. Salinger, "A Perfect Day for Bananafish"

Honorable Mention: Novels

Ray Bradbury, *October Country;* Marion Zimmer Bradley, *The Bloody Sun;* Suzy McKee Charnas, *Motherlines;* Roland J. Green & Frieda A. Murray, *Book of Kantela;* Robert Holdstock, *Mythago Wood;* Herbert Leiberman, *The Eighth Square;* Barry N. Malzberg, *Beyond Apollo;* Ardath Mayhar, *Golden Dream;* Ellery Queen, *A Study in Terror (Sherlock Holmes vs. Jack the Ripper);* Herman Richter, *Maynard's House;* James Thurber, *The Thirteen Clocks;* Kurt Vonnegut, *Cat's Cradle, Galapagos;* J. N. Williamson, *Ghost Mansion;* Roger Zelazny, *Nine Princes in Amber*

Honorable Mention: Stories

Charles Beaumont, "Last Rites," "Place of Meeting"; Ray Bradbury, "The Foghorn," "The Million Year Picnic"; Fredric Brown, "Armageddon," "Letter to a Phoenix"; Anthony Boucher, "The Bogle-Wolf"; Mort Castle, "Altenmoor, Where the Dogs Danced"; August Derleth, "The Adventure of the Perfect Husband"; Jessica Amanda Salmonson, "View from Mt. Futaba"; Janet Fox, "The Bug Boy"; Stephen King, "Popsy"; Richard Matheson, "Children of Noah"; Ray Russell, "Comet Wine"; Vincent Starrett, "The Unique 'Hamlet' "; J. N. Williamson, "Bopping in Bohemia, or, Sheerbach Tones in Basin Street," "The House of Life," "Wordsong"; Jane Yolen, "The Lady and the Merman," "White Seal Maid"

THE 238[1] EXPERTS WHO CHOSE
THE BEST-REMEMBERED AND MOST RESPECTED NOVELS
& STORIES OF HORROR, FANTASY, AND SCIENCE FICTION

One of the more mysterious things on the planet: the source of the view too many potentially publishable new writers hold that they need not familiarize themselves with the

---

[1]The total includes eighteen experts whose versatility required more than a single vocational identification.

well-known, published work of other authors.

Apart from the need to learn what the competition is doing—and, despite the fact that most writers are among the truly approachable people on earth, not even professional basketball is as competitive as fiction writing—there are persuasive reasons that *all* writers need to know what has already been done.

First and foremost is this: If you are not widely acquainted with what has been printed, how can you know if your ideas are fresh and original—or hackneyed? Or if they demand some new twist, a just-born, scintillating variation?

Further, most professional wordworkers become familiar with the fine writing that has preceded them out of a sense of deep, abiding respect—even love—naturally felt for that fiction that's forever embedded in memory. In a frequently rude, nose-thumbing sort of era, it's a question of deference, courtesy, homage. Some newcomers find it difficult to recall who wrote *Dune*, say, "Flowers for Algernon," *Fahrenheit 451*, or "Duel"; professionals rarely forget. Such convocations as this are kin to the gathering of actors who watch admiringly as silent movies are shown. Among creative people, if among no other kind on earth, those who paved the way are venerated. More importantly, their creations are long remembered.

Businesspersons, particularly those who are driven to get ahead, somehow manage to read the publications appertaining to their industries, and they are swift to celebrate and salute those giants who paved the ground for their individual ascensions. Can we writers afford to do otherwise?

Throughout the spring and summer of 1986, more than 200 members of the fantasy writing community worldwide—not writers alone, but reviewers, editors, illustrators, etc.—were asked to supply their lists of favorite fiction in the genre or genres of their individual expertise. More than 60 percent of them found the time for this relatively thankless task. It was one that sometimes became frustrating, since no more than ten choices were allowed for either books or short fiction. Some voted in a single genre, others in two or all three genres; some submitted only novel Top Tens or only story lists. None received payment, including those particular craftsmen whose lists have been "broken out" and bylined in the preceding segment.

Yet in a deeper sense, each participant in this vast survey was rewarded—handsomely. More than a few informed me that the procedure of remembering a certain yarn resulted in another rereading of it or of other tales by that favorite writer—and old delights and thrills were regenerated. Other gifted contributors to these lists reminisced about the way that a Marion Zimmer Bradley, a Ray Bradbury, a Ted Sturgeon, an Ursula Le Guin, or a Charles Beaumont had influenced them to begin writing. As well, ideas for brand-new yarns were sparked in that wondrous way that a Leiber, Mayhar, Koontz, King, Bloch, or Zelazny has of evoking magical ideas, sometimes by the whisper of his or her name . . . and the reverberating echo of luminous ideas was summoned from storylines that were invented up to *forty* or *more* years ago.

That, you see, is the quality of *all* the horror, fantasy, and SF that you have seen celebrated in the winning tabulations—and that, just importantly, you'll find in the more comprehensive, all-inclusive recommended library that follows. It is the quality of unforgettability.

An important matter to bear in mind as you look up your own favorite novels and shorter tales to be certain they are included is this: Fame is not always fickle, but she is also not blessed with an infallible memory. Despite the fact that I've added my own further choices, oversights and mistakes are—ruefully—likely.

While there should be no quarrel with any of the fiction you've seen singled out for praise, keep in mind, please, that *all* the books and short stories hall-of-famed in the library that lies ahead—save for those bearing my own initials (*JNW*)—were similarly honored by participating voters. Each novel or tale received *at least one* Top Ten vote, except my added selections. You may be certain that each and every fictive work, therefore, is well worth reading; you have the word of the following:

Participants in the "Favorites" Top Ten Lists:

The complete list of contributors is published with the editor's lasting gratitude to all who so wished to honor their predecessors or distinguished peers:

Agents: John Betancourt, Sharon Jarvis, Darrell Schweitzer, and Mary T. Williamson

Artists: James Garrison, Jeannette M. Hopper, James Kisner, Allen Koszowski, Harry O. Morris, and Alan Jude Suma

Editors & Academics: Gretta M. Anderson, *2 AM;* Marleen Barr, Virginia Polytechnic Institute Dept. of English; Mort Castle, Writer's Digest School; Nan Dibble, Writer's Digest Books; Joey Froehlich, *Violent Legends;* W. Paul Ganley, *Weirdbook;* Bob Hadji, *Borderland;* Gordon Linzner, *Space & Time;* John Maclay, *Nukes;* J. R. McHone, *SPWAO Showcase 5;* Joe Morey, *Dark Regions;* Peggy Nadramia, *Grue;* John S. Postovit, *Alpha Adventures;* Leland Sapiro, *Riverside Quarterly;* Stanley Schmidt, *Analog;* John Silbersack, New American Library; David B. Silva, *The Horror Show;* Keil Stuart, SPWAO *Newsletter;* D. W. Taylor, *Horrorstruck;* Wiewslaw Tumulka, *SF Spectrum* and *Macabre* (UK); J. N. Williamson, *Masques, Masques II,* and current book; Kathleen Woodbury, *F & SF Workshop* newsletter; and George Zebrowski, SFWA *Bulletin*

Reviewers: John G. Betancourt, *Amazing;* Michael Arthur Betts and William J. Grabowski, *The Horror Show;* Roland J. Green, *Chicago Sun-Times;* Stuart Napier, *Scavenger's Newsletter;* Harold Lee Prosser, *Fantasy Review;* Darrell Schweitzer, *Aboriginal SF;* Somtow Sucharitkul, National Book Critics' Circle, *Fantasy Review;* Stanley Wiater, *Fangoria;* J. N. Williamson, "The Dark Corner," *2 AM;* and Douglas E. Winter, *Fantasy Review, Shadowings*

Poets: Bruce Boston, Joey Froehlich, Maria Jacketti, John Maclay, Ardath Mayhar, Jim Neal, Mary Oliver, Steve Rasnic Tem, and T. Winter-Damon

Writers: Kevin Anderson, Paul Dale Anderson, Arlen Andrews, M. J. Bennett, Nancy Varian Berberick, John Gregory Betancourt, Bruce Boston, Stan Brooks, Ron Cain, Mort Castle, Ramsey Campbell, Orson Scott Card, Hugh B. Cave, Darwin Chismar, Suzy McKee Charnas, Simon Clark, Les Daniels, Ansen Dibell, Colleen Drippé, Denise Dumars, Phyllis Eisenstein, Joey Froehlich, Gregory Frost, William J. Grabowski, Roland J. Green, Stephen Gresham, Melissa Mia Hall, Dennis Hamilton, Philip C. Heath, Stephanie T. Hoppe, Jeannette M. Hopper, Gerard Houarner, Sharon Jarvis, Chris H. Kapral, Stephen King, James Kisner, Joe R. Lansdale, Kevin "Doc" Lee, Ron Leming, Michael Leonard, Gordon Linzner, Chris Liotta, Vincent McHardy, John Maclay, Barry N. Malzberg, Richard Christian Matheson, Ardath Mayhar, Thomas F. Monteleone, G. Wayne Miller, A. R. Morlan, Freida A. Murray, Stuart Napier, Jim Neal, Mary L. Oliver, Audrey Parente, Peter D. Pautz, Claudia Peck, Harold Lee Prosser, William Relling, Jr., Charles R. Saunders, Cheryl Curry Sayre, Darrell Schweitzer, David B. Silva, Steve Sneyd, Kiel Stuart, Somtow Sucharitkul, Thomas Sullivan,

David W. Taylor, Steve Rasnic Tem, Joan Vander Putten, Carolyn H. Vesser, Stanley
Wiater, Susan Lilas Wiggs, F. Paul Wilson, Chet Williamson, J. N. Williamson,
Douglas E. Winter, Gene Wolfe, Ron Wolfe, Jane Yolen, George Zebrowski, and Roger
Zelazny

The Best-Remembered Novels of Horror and the Supernatural

1. Shirley Jackson, *The Haunting of Hill House*   28 votes
2. (tie) Stephen King, *'Salem's Lot*   23
         Stephen King, *The Shining*   23
4. (tie) William Peter Blatty, *The Exorcist*   20
         Peter Straub, *Ghost Story*   20
         Robert Bloch, *Psycho*   20
7. (tie) Richard Matheson, *I Am Legend*   18
         Ira Levin, *Rosemary's Baby*   18
9. Ray Bradbury, *Something Wicked This Way Comes*   17
10. Anne Rice, *Interview with the Vampire*   12

The Best-Remembered Short Fiction of Horror and the Supernatural

1. Robert R. McCammon, "Nightcrawlers"   22 votes
2. Shirley Jackson, "The Lottery"   17
3. Stephen King, "The Mist"   13
4. Richard Matheson, "Born of Man and Woman"   11
5. (tie) Harlan Ellison, "I Have No Mouth and I Must Scream"   10
         Robert Bloch, "Yours Truly, Jack the Ripper"   10
7. J. N. Williamson, "The Book of Webster's"   9
8. (tie) Ramsey Campbell, "The Companion"   8
         Ray Bradbury, "Small Assassin"   8
         Karl Edward Wagner, "Sticks"   8

The Best-Remembered Novels of Fantasy

1. J. R. R. Tolkien, *Lord of the Rings*   21 votes
2. (tie) T. H. White, *The Once and Future King*   10
         Ursula K. Le Guin, *A Wizard of Earthsea*   10
4. Peter S. Beagle, *The Last Unicorn*   9
5. C. S. Lewis, *The Chronicles of Narnia*   7
6. (tie) Mervyn Peake, the Gormenghast trilogy   6
         Richard Adams, *Watership Down*   6
         Evangeline Walton, the Mabinogion series   6
9. (tie) J. R. R. Tolkien, *The Hobbit*   5
         Robert Holdstock, *Mythago Wood*   5
         Patricia A. McKillip, *The Riddlemaster of Hed*   5

The Best-Remembered Short Fiction of Fantasy

1. Ray Bradbury, "The Foghorn"   4 votes
2. (tie) Fritz Leiber, "Bazaar of the Bizarre"   3
         Ray Bradbury, "I Sing the Body Electric!"   3
4. (tie) Fritz Leiber, "Adept's Gambit"   2
         Thomas Disch, "Brave Little Toaster"   2
         Richard Kennedy, "Come Again in the Spring"   2

Charles deLint, "The Fair at Emain Macha" 2
Jerome Bixby, "It's a *Good* Life" 2
Jane Yolen, "The Lady and the Merman" 2
Peter S. Beagle, "Come, Lady Death" 2
Shirley Jackson, "The Lottery" 2
Roger Zelazny, "The Last Defender of Camelot" 2
Harlan Ellison, "Paladin of the Lost Hour" 2

Editor's Afterthoughts

The paucity of votes for the short story leaders and the hairbreadth closeness of tabulation might, at a glance, indicate some lack of interest in fantasy short fiction (in comparison to balloting for SF and horror). However, the reality is to the contrary. I believe that two factors emerge: First, the freewheeling independence of mind and spirit exemplified by fantasy enthusiasts, who aren't so much fickle or forgetful as adamant about making their *own* choices; second, the obviously robust health of the fantasy story, its far-flung and varied charms appealing, on uncountable levels, to every sort of reading taste.

The Best-Remembered Novels of SF

1. (tie) Arthur C. Clarke, *Childhood's End* — 17 votes
   Frank Herbert, *Dune* — 17
3. Ursula K. Le Guin, *The Left Hand of Darkness* — 15
4. Ray Bradbury, *The Martian Chronicles* — 13
5. (tie) Alfred Bester, *The Demolished Man* — 10
   Theodore Sturgeon, *More than Human* — 10
7. Walter M. Miller, Jr., *A Canticle for Leibowitz* — 9
8. (tie) Isaac Asimov, *The Foundation Trilogy* — 8
   Robert A. Heinlein, *The Moon Is a Harsh Mistress* — 8
10. (tie) Gene Wolfe, *Book of the New Sun* (series) — 7
   Alfred Bester, *The Stars My Destination* — 7
   Robert A. Heinlein, *Stranger in a Strange Land* — 7

The Best-Remembered Short Fiction of SF

1. Daniel Keyes, "Flowers for Algernon" — 12 votes
2. (tie) Cordwainer Smith, "The Game of Rat and Dragon" — 5
   Arthur C. Clarke, "The Star" — 5
4. (tie) Harlan Ellison, "A Boy and His Dog" — 4
   Isaac Asimov, "Nightfall" — 4
   John W. Campbell, "Who Goes There?" — 4
7. (tie) Tom Godwin, "The Cold Equations" — 3
   Eric Frank Russell, "Dear Devil" — 3
   Murray Leinster, "First Contact" — 3
   James Tiptree, Jr., "Houston, Houston, Do You Read?" — 3
   Jerome Bixby, "It's a *Good* Life" — 3
   Harlan Ellison, "Jefty Is Five" — 3
   Harlan Ellison, " 'Repent, Harlequin!' Said the
      Ticktockman" — 3
   George R. R. Martin, "SandKings" — 3
   Ray Bradbury, "There Will Come Soft Rains" — 3

Recommended Reading Library of Horror, Fantasy, and Science Fiction

Compiled and enhanced by J. N. Williamson

Although it is perhaps true that no library of recommended novels and stories for three genres can accurately be called complete, it's hard to imagine a more knowledgeably selected or comprehensive one than that which follows. It represents the favorite fiction of over 120 active professional and semiprofessional writers, reviewers, illustrators, editors, agents, publishers, and—above all—admiring readers with long memories.

A simple coding system has been added to enable you to identify quickly the genre of the given book or short story: H = Horror; F = Fantasy; SF = Science Fiction; CG = either a mainstream work with strong speculative fiction elements or a work with wide appeal, one that won't comfortably be shoehorned into just one category. The initials JNW identify your editor's arbitrary addition of fiction he felt deserved inclusion. Any duly nominated or otherwise entitled work that has been inadvertently omitted is the fault of the same editor, who humbly apologizes for the oversight.

NOVELS

A

Adams, Douglas, *Hitchhiker's Guide to the Galaxy*   SF
Adams, Richard, *The Plague Dogs*   CG/F
   Shardik   F
   Watership Down   F
   Girl in a Swing   F
Adams, Robert, the Horseclans series   F
Aiken, Jim, *Walk the Moons Road*   SF
Alexander, Lloyd, *The Beggar Queen*   F
   The Book of Three (one of the Prydain series)   F
   The Kestrel   F
   Westmark   F
Anderson, Poul, *Brain Wave*   SF
   The High Crusade   F
   The Merman's Children   F
   Orion Shall Rise   SF
   Three Hearts and Three Lions   F
Aldiss, Brian W., *Cryptozoic*   SF
   Frankenstein Unbound   F
   the Helliconia series   SF
   Report on Probability A   SF
Anson, Jay, *The Amityville Horror*   H
Anthony, Piers, *Cluster*   SF
   Macroscope   SF
   On a Pale Horse   F

Orn   SF
Xanth   F
Asimov, Isaac, *The Caves of Steel*   SF
   the Foundation trilogy   SF
   The Gods Themselves   SF
   I, Robot   SF
   The Naked Sun   SF
   The Robots of Dawn   SF
   Robots and Empire   SF

B

Bailey, Paul, *Deliver Us from Eva*   CG/F
Baker, Sharon, *Quarreling, They Met the Dragon*   F
Ballard, J. G., *The Atrocity Exhibition*   CG
   The Crystal World   SF
   The Drowned World   SF
Banks, Ian, *The Wasp Factory*   H
Banks, Michael A. & Dean R. Lambe, *The Odysseus Solution*   SF
Barker, Clive, *Damnation Game*   H
Beagle, Peter S., *A Fine and Private Place*   F
   The Last Unicorn   F
Bellair, John, *The Face in the Frost*   F
Benford, Gregory, *Timescape*   SF
Bester, Alfred, *The Demolished Man*   SF
   The Stars My Destination   SF
Bishop, Michael, *Ancient of Days*   SF
   No Enemy But Time   SF
Blatty, William Peter, *The Exorcist*   CG/H
   Legion   H
Blish, James, *A Case of Conscience*   SF
   Black Easter   SF
Bloch, Robert, *Pleasant Dreams*   H
   Psycho   H
   Psycho II   H
   The Scarf   H/JNW
Boulle, Pierre, *Planet of the Apes*   CG/SF
Bower, Brock, *The Late Great Creature*   H
Boucher, Anthony, *The Case of the Baker Street Irregulars*   F/JNW
Boyett, Stephen R., *The Architect of Sleep, The Geography of Dreams*   F
Brackett, Leigh, *People of the Talisman*   SF
   Sword of Rhiannon   SF
Bradbury, Ray, *Dandelion Wine*   F
   Fahrenheit 451   CG/SF
   The Martian Chronicles   CG/SF
   October Country   F
   Something Wicked This Way Comes   CG/H
Bradley, Marion Zimmer, *The Heritage of Hastur* (one of the Darkover series)   F
   The Shattered Chain (also a Darkover book)   SF
Brandner, Gary, *The Howling*   H

Brown, Fredric, *The Mind Thing*   CG/H
   What Mad Universe   CG/SF
Brunner, John, *Jagged Orbit*   SF
   The Sheep Look Up   SF
   Squares of the City   SF
   Stand on Zanzibar   SF
   The Traveler in Black   F
   The Whole Man   SF
Brust, Stephen, *Brokedown Palace*   F
Budrys, Algis, *Michelmas*   SF
Burger, Thomas, *Neighbors*   F
Burgess, Anthony, *A Clockwork Orange*   CG/SF
Butler, Octavia, *Wild Seed*   SF

C

Cabell, James Branch, *Jurgen*   CG/F
Campbell, Ramsey, *The Doll Who Ate His Mother*   H
   The Face that Must Die   H
   Incarnate   H
   The Rage   H
Capote, Truman, *Handcarved Coffins*   CG
   In Cold Blood   CG
Card, Orson Scott, *Ender's Game*   SF/JNW
   Hart's Hope   F
   Songmaster   SF
   Speaker for the Dead   SF
Carrington, Leonora, *The Hearing Trumpet*   H
Castle, Mort, *Diakka*   H
   The Strangers   H
Cave, Hugh B., *The Evil*   H
   Legion of the Dead   CG/H
   Shades of Evil   H
Chant, Joy, *Red Moon, Black Mountain*   F
Charnas, Suzy McKee, *Motherlines*   SF
   Vampire Tapestry   CG/F
Cherryh, C. J., *The Cuckoo's Egg*   CG/SF
   the Faded Sun trilogy   SF
Clarke, Arthur C., *Against the Fall of Night*   SF
   Childhood's End   SF
   The City and the Stars   SF
   The Deep Range   SF
   Prelude to Space   SF
   Rendezvous with Rama   SF
   The Sands of Mars   SF
   2001: A Space Odyssey   SF
   Tyger, Tyger   SF
Clement, Hal, *Mission of Gravity*   SF
   Needle   SF
Cline Jr., C. Terry, *Death Knell*   C/JNW
Compton, David G., *The Unsleeping Eye*   SF

Cook, Glen, the Dread Empire series   F
Cooper, Susan, *The Dark is Rising*   F
Coyne, John, *The Legacy*   H
   The Piercing   H
Crews, Harry, *Karate is a Thing of the Spirit*   F
Crichton, Michael, *The Andromeda Strain*   SF
   The Terminal Man   SF/JNW
Crowley, John, *Engine Summer*   SF
Cowper, Richard, *The Road to Corlay*   F

D

Daniels, Les, *The Black Castle*   H
   The Silver Skull   H
Davidson, Avram, *The Phoenix and the Mirror*   F
de Camp, L. Sprague, *The Fallible Fiend*   F
   The Goblin Tower   F
   Lest Darkness Fall   SF
de Camp, L. Sprague & H. L. Gold, *None but Lucifer*   F
de Camp, L. Sprague & Fletcher Pratt, *The Incomplete Enchanter*   F
de Felitta, Frank, *Audrey Rose*   H
de Larrabeiti, Michael, *The Borribles*   F
Delany, Samuel R., *Babel-17*   SF
   City of a Thousand Suns   SF/JNW
   Dhalgren   CG/SF
   The Einstein Intersection   SF
   The Falling Towers   SF
   Nova   SF
Delbo, Charlotte, *None of Us Will Return*   H
DeLint, Charles, *Moonheart*   F
   Mulengro   CG/F
Dick, Philip K., *Do Androids Dream of Electric Sheep?*   SF
   The Man in the High Castle   SF
   Time Out of Joint   SF
   Ubik   SF
Dickson, Gordon R., *The Alien Way*   SF
   The Childe Cycle   SF
   Dorsai!   SF
   Soldier, Ask Not   SF
Disch, Thomas, *Camp Concentration*   CG/SF
   334   SF
Donaldson, Stephen R., *The Chronicles of Thomas Covenant*   F
Drury, Alan, *Advise and Consent*   CG/SF

E

Eddings, David, the Belgariad series   F
Eddison, E. R., *Fish Dinner in Memison*   F
   The Mezentian Gate   F
   The Worm Ouroboros   F
Effinger, George Alec, *When Gravity Fails*   SF

Ely, David, *Seconds*   F
Endore, Guy, *The Werewolf of Paris*   H
Ends, Michael, *The Neverending Story*   S
Estey, Dale, *A Lost Tale*   F

F

Farmer, Philip José, *Image of the Beast*   SF
   Lord Tyger   F
   To Your Scattered Bodies Go (one of the Riverworld series)   SF
Farris, John, *All Heads Turn as the Hunt Goes By*   H
   When Michael Calls   F
Finney, Jack, *Invasion of the Body Snatchers*   SF
   The Circus of Dr. Lao   F
   Time and Again   F
Ford, John, *The Dragon Waiting*   F
Forsythe, Richard, *The Bishop's Landing*   CG
Forward, Robert, *Dragon Egg*   SF
Foster, Alan Dean, *Alien*   SF
   For Love of Mother-Not   SF
Fowles, John, *The Collector*   CG/H
Frank, Pat, *Alas, Babylon*   SF
Friesner, Esther M., *Harlot's Ruse*   F
   Spells of Mortal Weaving   F

G

Gallico, Paul, *The Abandoned*   SF
Gardner, John, *Grendel*   CG/F
Garner, Alan, *The Weirdstone of Brisingamen*   F
Garrett, Randall, *Too Many Magicians*   F
Gerrold, David, *Neptune's Cauldron*   SF
   When Harlie was One   SF
Gibson, William, *Neuromancer*   SF
Gilber, Stephen, *Ratman's Notebooks*   CG
Godwin, Parke, *Beloved Exile*   F
   Firelord   F
Golding, William, *The Inheritors*   F
   Lord of the Flies   CG
   Pincher Martin   CG/F
Goldman, William, *Magic*   CG
   The Princess Bride   F
Goldstein, Lisa, *The Red Magician*   F
Gordon, James, *The Stone Boy*   CG
Grant, Charles L., *The Nestling*   H
   Night Songs   H
   The Pet   SF
Green, Roland J., the Peacekeeper series   SF
   Sherran   SF/JNW
Green, Roland J. & Frieda A. Murray, *The Book of Kantela*   SF/JNW
Greenhough, Terry, *Time and Timothy Grenville*   SF

Gresham, Stephen, *Moon Lake*   H
Goulart, Ron, *Galaxy Jane*   SF
Grubb, Davis, *Night of the Hunter*   CG
Gunn, James, *The Magicians*   CG/H

H

Haldeman, Joe, *The Forever War*   SF
Halkin, John, *Slither*   H
Hallahan, William H., *The Search for Joseph Tully*   H
Harris, Thomas, *Red Dragon*   CG/H
Harrison, Harry, *Deathworld*   SF
    The Technicolor Time Machine   SF
Harrison, M. Joan, *The Pastel Lady*   F
Hebert, Anne, *Children of the Black Sabbath*   H
Hedeyat, Sadegn, *The Blind Owl*   F
Heinlein, Robert A., *Citizen of the Galaxy*   SF
    The Door into Summer   SF
    Double Star   SF
    Friday   SF
    Glory Road   F
    The Green Hills of Earth (short story collection)   SF
    The Moon Is a Harsh Mistress   SF
    The Past through Tomorrow   SF
    The Puppet Masters   SF
    Starship Troopers   SF
    Stranger in a Strange Land   SF
    Time Enough for Love   SF
    Time for the Stars   SF
    Tunnel in the Sky   SF
    Universe   SF
Heinlein, Robert A. (as "John Riverside"), *The Unpleasant Profession of Jonathan
    Hoag*   CG/F
Herbert, Frank, *Dune*   SF
    Hellstrom's Hive   SF
Herbert, James, *Domain*   H/JNW
    The Fog   H
    The Rats   H/JNW
    Shrine   H
Hersey, John, *The Child Buyer*   CG
    White Lotus   CG
Hjortsberg, William, *Falling Angel*   H
Hoban, Russell, *Riddley Walker*   SF
Hoffman-Price, E., *The Devil Wives of Li Fong*   H
Hogan, James P., *Inherit the Stars*   SF
Holdstock, Robert, *Mythago Wood*   F
Holland, Cecelia, *Floating World*   SF
Hoppe, Stephanie T., *Windrider*   SF
Howard, Robert E., *Conan the Conqueror*   F
Hubbard, L. Ron, *Fear*   F
Huxley, Aldous, *Brave New World*   CG/SF

J

Jackson, Shirley, *The Haunting of Hill House*   H
   We Have Always Lived in the Castle   H
Jarrell, Randall, *The Animal Family*   SF
Jeter, K. W., *Dr. Adder*   SF

K

Kazantzakis, Nikos, *The Last Temptation of Christ*   CG
Kelly, James Patrick & John Kessel, *Freedom Beach*   CG
Kennedy, Leigh F., *The Journal of Nicholas the American*   F
Kersh, Gerald, *Prelude to a Certain Midnight*   H
King, Stephen, *Carrie*   H
   The Dead Zone   CG/F
   It   H
   Pet Sematary   H
   'Salem's Lot   H
   The Shining   H
   The Stand   CG
King, Stephen & Peter Straub, *The Talisman*   F
King, Tabitha, *Small World*   H/JNW
Kingsbury, Donald, *Courtship Rite*   SF
Kisner, James, *Nero's Vice*   CG
   Slice of Life   H/JNW
   Strands   H/JNW
Klein, T. E. D., *The Ceremonies*   H
Knight, Damon, *The Man in the Tree*   SF
Koontz, Dean R., *Darkfall*   H
   Phantoms   H
   Shattered   CG
   Strangers   CG/H
   Twilight Eyes   H
   Watchers   H/JNW
   Whispers   H
Kosinski, Jerzy, *The Painted Bird*   CG
Kotzwinkle, William, *Dr. Rat*   F
Kube-McDowell, Michael P., *Enigma*   SF
   The Trigon Disunity   F
Kurtz, Catherine, *Camber of Culdi* (one of the Deryni series)   F
Kuttner, Henry (as "Lester Padgett"), *Robots Have No Tails*   SF

L

Lafferty, R. A., *The Devil is Dead*   SF
   Fourth Mansions   SF
   Past Master   SF
Lansdale, Joe R., *Act of Love*   H
Laubenthal, Sanders Anne, *Excalibur*   F
Laumer, Keith, *Plague of Demons*   SF
   A Trace of Memory   SF
Le Guin, Ursula K., *The Dispossessed*   SF
   The Earthsea Trilogy   F

The Lathe of Heaven   SF
The Left Hand of Darkness   SF
The Word for World is Forest   SF
Lee, Tanith, *Anackfire*   F
   Birthgrave   F
   Death's Master   F
   Kill the Dead   CG/F
   Lycanthia   CG
   Night's Master   F
   The Silver Metal Lover   SF
   Sung in Shadow   CG
Leiber, Fritz, *The Big Time*   SF
   Conjure Wife   F
   Our Lady of Darkness   H
   Swords and Deviltry (collection of short stories)   F
   Swords of Lankhmar (collection of short stories)   F
   You're All Alone   H
Leiberman, Herbert, *Crawlspace*   H/JNW
Lem, Stanislaw, *Solaris*   SF
Lessing, Doris, *Canopus in Argos*   CG
Levi, Edward, *The Beast Within*   H
Levin, Ira, *The Boys from Brazil*   CG
   Rosemary's Baby   H
   The Stepford Wives   CG/H/JNW
Levinson, Richard & William Link, *The Playhouse*   H/JNW
Lewis, C. S., The Chronicles of Narnia (series title)   F
   Out of the Silent Planet (one of the Space trilogy)   SF
   Till We Have Faces   F
Lindsay, David, *A Voyage to Arcturus*   F
Lindholm, Megan, *Wizard of the Pigeons*   F
Lovecraft, H. P., *The Case of Charles Dexter Ward* (published posthumously in 1941)   H
Lumley, Brian, *Ka of Ancient Khem*   F
Lupoff, Richard, *Circumpolar!*   SF
   Countersolar!   SF
Lymington, John, *Froomb!*   SF
Lynn, Elizabeth, *Sardonyx Net*   SF

M

MacAvoy, R. A., *Tea with the Black Dragon*   SF
MacDonald, George, *At the Back of the North Wind*   F
MacLeish, Roderick, *Prince Ombra*   F
Mailer, Norman, *Ancient Evenings*   CG
Malzberg, Barry N., *Beyond Apollo*   SF
Marasco, Robert, *Burnt Offerings*   H
Marquez, Gabriel G., *One Hundred Years of Solitude*   CG/F
Martin, George R. R., *Armageddon Rag*   H
Masterson, Graham, *The Manitou*   H
Matheson, Richard, *Bid Time Return*   F
   Hell House   H

I Am Legend   CG/H
The Shrinking Man   CG/F
A Stir of Echoes   H
What Dreams May Come   CG/F
May, Julian, *The Many-Colored Land* (part of the Pliocene Saga)   F
Mayhar, Ardath, *Exile on Vlahil*   F/JNW
How the Gods Wove in Kyrannon   F/JNW
Khi to Freedom   F
Makra Choria   F/JNW
The Wall   H/JNW
The World Ends at Hickory Hollow   SF
Mayne, William, *Earthfasts*   SF
McCaffrey, Anne, *Dragonflight* (one of the Dragonriders of Pern series)   F
The Ship Who Sang   SF
McCammon, Robert R., *Baal*   H/JNW
Bethany's Sin   H
Mystery Walk   H
They Thirst   H
Usher's Passing   H
McDowell, Michael, *Cold Moon over Babylon*   H
The Elementals   H
Toplin   F
McIntyre, Vonda N., *Dreamsnake*   SF
The Entropy Effect   SF
McKillip, Patricia A., *The Forgotten Beasts of Eld*   F
The Riddlemaster of Hed (first of a trilogy)   F
The Throne of the Erril of Sherrill   F
McKinley, Robin, *The Blue Sword*   F
Merrill, Judith, *Daughters of Earth*   SF
Merrill, Judith & C. M. Kornbluth (as "Cyril Judd"), *Gunner Cade*   SF
Merritt, A., *The Face in the Abyss*   F
Meyers, Roy, *Dolphin Boy*   SF
Miller, Jr., Walter M., *A Canticle for Leibowitz*   SF
Millstead, Thomas E. *Cave of the Moving Shadows*   F
Miralee, Hope, *Lud in the Mist*   F
Michener, James, *Space*   CG
Moore, C. L., *Judgement Night*   SF
Moorcock, Michael, The Dancers at the End of Time trilogy   SF
Elric of Melnibone   F
Stormbringer   F
Warhound and the World's Pain   F
Morrell, David, *The Nesting*   H
Testament   H
The Totem   H
Myers, John Myers, *Silverlock*   F

N

Nathan, Robert, *Portrait of Jenny*   CG/F
Niven, Larry & Jerry Pournelle, *Footfall*   SF
Lucifer's Hammer   SF

The Mote in God's Eye   SF
Ringworld   SF
Nolan, William F. & George Clayton Johnson, *Logan's Run*   SF
Norton, Andre, *The Beast Master*   SF
    Catseye   SF
    Galactic Derelict   SF
    Starman's Son   SF
    the Witchworld series   F

O

Oliver, Chad, *Mists of the Dawn*   SF
Ooka, Shoie, *Fires on the Plain*   H
Orwell, George, *Animal Farm*   CG/F
    1984   CG/SF

P

Palmer, David R., *Emergence*   SF
Pangborn, Edgar, *A Mirror for Observers*   SF
Peake, Mervyn, the Gormenghast trilogy   F
Piercy, Marge, *The Woman on the Edge of Time*   SF
Piper, H. Beam, *Little Fuzzy*   SF
    Lord Kalvan of Otherwhen   SF
    Space Viking   SF
Pohl, Frederik, *Man Plus*   SF
Pohl, Frederik & C. M. Kornbluth, *The Space Merchants*   SF
Pournelle, Jerry, *King David's Spaceship*   SF
Powers, Tim, *The Anubis Gates*   SF
    The Drawing of the Dark   F
Pratt, Fletcher, *The Well of the Unicorn*   F
Priest, Christopher, *The Glamour*   SF
Pynchon, Thomas, *Gravity's Rainbow*   CG

Q

Queen, Ellery, *A Study in Terror*   CG

R

Rand, Ayn, *Atlas Shrugged*   CG
Reamy, Tom, *Blind Voices*   F
Resnick, Mike, *Santiago*   SF
Rice, Anne, *Interview with the Vampire*   H
    The Vampire Lestat   H
Roberts, John Maddox, *King of the Wood*   F
Roberts, Keith, *Pavane*   SF
Robinson, Kim Stanley, *The Wild Shore*   SF
Roth, Philip, *The Breast*   CG/F
Rucker, Rudy, *The Secret of Life*   SF
Russ, Joanna, *The Female Man*   SF
    Picnic on Paradise   F

Russell, Eric Frank, *Sinister Barrier*   CG/F
Russell, Ray, *The Case Against Satan*   H
    Incubus   H/JNW

S

Saberhagen, Fred, *Empire of the East*   F
    The Holmes-Dracula File   F
    An Old Friend of the Family   F
Sagan, Carl, *Contact*   CG/SF
Sampson, Joan, *The Auctioneer*   H
San Souci, Robert, *Blood Offerings*   H
Saunders, Charles R., the Imaro series   F
    The Trail of Bohy   F
Schenck, Gilbert, *A Rose for Armageddon*   SF
Schweitzer, Darrell, *The Shattered Goddess*   F
Scott, Jody, *I, Vampyre*   H
Selby, Curt, *I, Zombie*   H
Seltzer, David, *The Omen*   H
Shaffer, Anthony, *The Wicker Man*   H
Sheckley, Robert, *The Journey of Joenes*   SF
Shepard, Lucius, *Green Eyes*   SF
Shiras, Wilmar, *Children of the Atom*   SF
Shute, Nevil, *In the Wet*   F
    On the Beach   CG/SF
Siddons, Anne Rivers, *The House Next Door*   CG/H
Silverberg, Robert, *Downward to the Earth*   SF
    Dying Inside   SF
    Gilgamesh, the King   F
    Lord of Darkness   CG/SF
    Lord Valentine's Castle   SF
    Nightwings   SF
    Second Trip   SF
    Tower of Glass   SF
    Up the Line   SF
    The World Inside   SF
Simak, Clifford, *City*   SF
    Project Pope   SF
    Way Station   SF
Simmons, Dan, *Song of Kali*   H
Siodmak, Curt, *Donovan's Brain*   CG/SF
Sleator, William, *House of Stairs*   H
Sloane, William, *The Edge of Running Water*   H
    To Walk the Night   CG/F
Smith, Cordwainer, *Norstrilia*   SF
Smith, E. E., *Children of the Lens* (part of the Lensman series)   SF
Smith, Michael Cruz, *Nightwing*   H
St. Exupery, Antoine, *The Little Prince*   F
Stapleton, W. Olaf, *Last and First Men*   SF
    Last Men in London   SF
Stein, Sol, *The Resort*   H/JNW

Stewart, Fred Mustard, *Mephisto Waltz*   H
Stewart, George R., *Earth Abides*   SF
Stewart, Mary, *The Crystal Cave*   F
Straub, Peter, *Floating Dragon*   CG/H
    Ghost Story   CG/H
    If You Could See Me Now   H
    Shadowland   CG/F
Strieber, Whitley, *The Hunger*   H
    Night Church   CG/H
    The Wolfen   H
Sturgeon, Theodore, *The Dreaming Jewels*   SF
    More than Human   SF
    Some of Your Blood   CG
Sucharitkul, Somtow, *Vampire Junction*   H
Susann, Jacqueline, *Yargo*   CG/F
Sutcliff, Rosemary, *Sword at Sunset*   F

T

Taylor, Bernard, *The Godsend*   H/JNW
Temple, William F., *The Four-Sided Triangle*   SF
Tessier, Thomas, *Phantom*   H
Thayer, Tiffany, *One-Man Show*   F
Thomas, D. M., *White Hotel*   CG
Thurber, James, *The Thirteen Clocks*   CG/F
Tiptree Jr., James, *Up the Walls of the World*   SF
Tolkien, J. R. R. *The Hobbit*   F
    The Lord of the Rings trilogy   F
Topor, Roland, *The Tenement*   H
Trell, Max, *Small Gods and Mr. Barnum*   F
Tryon, Thomas, *The Other*   H
Tucker, Wilson, *The Long Loud Silence*   SF

V

Van Sickle, Dirck, *Montana Gothic*   H
Van Vogt, A. E., *Slan*   SF
    The Weapon Shops of Ishar   SF
    The World of Null-A   SF
Vance, Jack, *Big Planet*   SF
    Blue World   SF
    The Dying Earth   F
Varley, John, *The Ophiuchi Hotline*   SF
Vonnegut Jr., Kurt, *Breakfast of Champions*   CG/F
    Cat's Cradle   CG/F
    God Bless You, Mr. Rosewater   CG
    The Sirens of Titan   SF
    Slaughterhouse-Five   CG

W

Wagner, Karl Edward, *Dark Crusade*   F

Wall, Mervyn, *The Unfortunate Fursey*   F
Wallant, Edward Lewis, *The Pawnbroker*   CG/H
Waldrup, Howard, *Them Bones*   SF
Walton, Evangeline, *The Children of Llyr* (one of the Mabinogion series)   F
Watson, Ian, *Martian Inca*   SF
Waugh, Evelyn, *The Loved One*   CG
Waugh, Harriet, *Kate's House*   CG/H
Weinbaum, Stanley G., *The New Adam*   SF
Wellman, Manly Wade, *After Dark*   H
    Who Fears the Devil?   CG/H
White, E. B., *Charlotte's Web*   CG/F
White, T. H., *The Once and Future King*   CG/F
Whitten, Les, *Moon of the Wolf*   H
Wilhelm, Kate, *Where Late the Sweet Birds Sang*   SF
Williamson, J. N., *Babel's Children*   H/JNW
    The Banished   H
    Death Coach   H
    Ghost   H
    Horror House   H
    Horror Mansion   H
    The Houngan (a.k.a. *Profits*)   H
    Hour   CG/H/JNW
    The Longest Night   H
    Premonition   H
    The Ritual   H/JNW
    The Tulpa   H
Williamson, Jack, *Darker than You Think*   CG/F
    The Humanoids   SF
Willis, Connie, *Lincoln's Dream*   SF
Wilson, Colin, *God of the Labyrinth*   F
    The Philosopher's Stone   CG
    Space Vampires   CG/SF
Wilson, F. Paul, *The Keep*   H
Wolfe, Gene, the Book of the New Sun series   SF
    Fifth Head of Cerberus   SF
    Free Live Free   SF
Wood, Bari, *The Tribe*   H/JNW
Wright, T. M., *Strange Seed*   H
Wyndham, John, *Day of the Triffids*   CG/SF
    The Midwich Cuckoos   CG/SF
    Out of the Deeps   SF
    Re-Birth   SF

Y

Yarbro, Chelsea Quinn, *Hotel Transylvania*   H

Z

Zelazny, Roger, the Chronicles of Amber series   SF
    Creatures of Light and Darkness   SF
    The Dream Master   SF
    Jack of Shadows   SF

SHORT STORIES

A

Abartis, Cezarija, "The Rocking Horse"   H/JNW
Aickman, Robert, "Pages from a Young Girl's Diary"   H
  "The Swords"   H
Aiken, Conrad, "Silent Snow, Secret Snow"   CG/H
Alarcon, J., "Friend of Death"   H
Ammerman, Sioux, "Rita the Swallow-Woman"   F
Anderson, Kevin J., "Heroes Never Die"   H
  "Redmond's Private Screening"   H/JNW
Anderson, Poul, "The Man Who Came Early"   SF
  "The Pugilist"   SF
Aldiss, Brian W., "Let's Be Frank"   SF
  "The Saliva Tree"   F
  "Serpent Burning on an Altar"   F
Anthony, Piers, "The Barn"   F
Asimov, Isaac, "The Bicentennial Man"   SF
  "Eyes Do More than See"   SF
  "Liar!"   SF
  "Nightfall"   SF
  "Victory Unintentional"   SF
Attansio, A. A., "The Star Pools"   H

B

Ballard, J. G., "The Drowned Giant"
  "The Screen Game"   SF
  "Storm Bird, Storm Dreamer"   SF
  "The Subliminal Man"   SF
Barker, Clive, "Dread"   H
  "In the Hills, the Cities"   H
  "The Last Will and Testament of Jacqueline Ess"   H
  "Midnight Meat Train"   H
  "Pig Blood Blues"   H
  "Rawhead Rex"   H
  "Son of Celluloid"   H
  "The Yattering and Jack"   H
Bates, Harry, "Farewell to the Master"   SF
Beagle, Peter S., "Come, Lady Death"   F
  "Lila the Werewolf"   CG
Bear, Greg, "If I Die Before I Wake"   SF
Beaumont, Charles, "The Beautiful People"   H/JNW
  "The Crooked Man"   H
  "The Customers"   H/JNW
  "The Devil, You Say"   CG
  "Elegy"   SF/JNW
  "Fair Lady"   CG/JNW
  "Father, Dear Father"   SF/JNW
  "Free Dirt"   H
  "The Howling Man"   H
  "The Hunger"   H

"In His Image"   H
"Miss Gentilbelle"   H
"Mourning Song"   F
"The Music of the Yellow Brass"   H
"My Grandmother's Japonicas"   CG/F
"The Neighbors"   CG/JNW
"Night Ride"   CG/F
"Perchance to Dream"   H
Benford, Gregory, "Doing Lennon"   SF
Bertin, Eddy C., "My Beautiful Darling"   H
Bester, Alfred, "The Animal Fair"   H
  "5,271,009" (a.k.a. "The Starcomber")   SF
"Fondly Fahrenheit"   SF
Birkin, Charles, "The Hitch"   H
Bishop, Michael, "A Tapestry of Little Murders"   CG/H
  "Within the Walls of Tyre"   SF
Bixby, Jerome, "It's a *Good* Life!"   CG/H
Blish, James, "Black Easter"   SF
"Surface Tension"   SF
Bloch, Robert, "Beelzebub"   H/JNW
 "A Case of the Stubborns"   H
 "Catnip"   H
 "The Cure"   H
 "Daybroke"   H
 "Double-Cross"   H
 "Enoch"   H
 "Head Man"   H
 "The Man Who Collected Poe"   H
 "The Movie People"   F
 "Murder Castle"   H
 "The New Season"   H/JNW
 "The Old College Try"   SF/JNW
 "Picture"   H
 "Shadow from the Steeple"   H
 "Sweets to the Sweet"   H
 "That Hell-Bound Train"   H
 "Yours Truly, Jack the Ripper"   H
Borges, Jorge Luis, "The Approach to Al-Mutasim"   F
 "The Book of Sand"   F
 "The Circular Ruins"   F
Boucher, Anthony, "The Greatest Tertian"   F/JNW
 "Snulbug"   CG/F
Boyle, T. Cotaghessan, "We Are Norsemen"   SF
Bradbury, Ray, "The Drummer Boy of Shiloh"   F
 "The Crowd"   H
 "The Dragon"   F
 "The Foghorn"   CG/F
 "Forever and the Earth"   F
 "Heavy-Set"   H
 "The Homecoming"   H

"I Sing the Body Electric!"   CG/F
"The Illustrated Man"   CG
"The Invisible Boy"   F
"The Jar"   CG/H
"The Lake"   CG/H
"The Long Rain"   CG/F
"The Man Upstairs"   H
"Mars is Heaven"   CG/F
"A Medicine for Melancholy"   F
"The Million Year Picnic"   CG/F
"The Night"   H
"The October Game"   CG
"The Pedestrian"   H
"Pillar of Fire"   H
"The Playground"   H/JNW
"R is for Rocket"   SF
"Skeleton"   H
"The Small Assassin"   H
"The Smile"   F
"A Sound of Thunder"   CG/F
"There Will Come Soft Rains"   CG/SF
"The Town Where No One Got Off"   H/JNW
"Uncle Einar"   F
"The Veldt"   H
Brandner, Gary, "Julian's Hand"   H
Brennan, Joseph P., "Canavan's Back Yard"   H
  "Slime"   H
Brown, Fredric, "Abominable"   F/JNW
  "Arena"   SF
  "Armageddon"   H
  "Come and Go Mad"   H/JNW
  "Don't Look Behind You"   H
  "The Geezenstacks"   H
  "Imagine"   F
  "Knock"   SF/JNW
  "Letter to a Phoenix"   SF/JNW
  "Placet is a Crazy Place"   SF
  "Reconciliation"   H/JNW
  "Too Far"   F
Bruce, David, "Pillowman's Lover"   H
Bryant, Edward, "Dark Angel"   H
  "Strata"   H
  "Teeth Marks"   H
Burke, John, "Party Games"   H
Burns, Stephen, "Next!"   CG/F
Butler, Octavia, "Bloodchild"   H

C

Campbell, John W., "Who Goes There?"   H/JNW
Campbell, Ramsey, "Again"   H

"The Brood"   H
"Call First"   H
"The Chimney"   H
"The Companion"   H
"The Gap"   H
"Heading Home"   H
"MacKintosh Willie"   H
"Through the Walls"   H
"The Trick"   H
"The Words that Count"   H
Campton, David, "At the Bottom of the Garden"   H
Capote, Truman, "A Tree of Night"   CG/H
Card, Orson Scott, "Eumenides in the Fourth Floor Lavatory"   H/JNW
Carr, Terry, "They Live on Levels"   SF
Carr, Terry & Carol, "Some are Born Cats"   CG
Carrington, Leonara, "White Rabbits"   H
Carter, Angela, "The Courtship of McLyon"   F
Cartmill, Cleve, "The Shape of Desire"   H
Castle, Mort, "Altenmoor, Where the Dogs Danced"   CG/F
  "And of Gideon"   H
  "Love, Hate and the Beautiful Junkyard Sea"   H/JNW
Cave, Hugh B., "From the Lower Deep"   H
Chandler, A. Bertram, "Giant Killer"   SF
Cheever, John, "The Enormous Radio"   CG/SF
Cherryh, C. J., The Sunfall series   SF
Chetwin-Hayes, R., "The Ghost Who Limped"   H
Chin, M. Lucie, "Lan Lung"   F
Clarke, Arthur C., "Guardian Angel"   SF
  "The Nine Billion Names of God"   CG/SF
  "The Star"   SF
Clee, Mona B., "Dinosaurs"   H
  "Just Like Their Masters"   H/JNW
Cohen, Jan, "I Don't Know Why She Swallowed the Fly"   H
Collier, John, "Evening Primrose"   H
  "Thus I Refute Beelzey"   H
Counselman, Mary Elizabeth, "Seventh Sister"   H
  "The Three Marked Pennies"   H
Cross, John Keir, "Miss Thing and the Surrealist"   H

D

Dahl, Roald, "The Champion of the World"   F/JNW
  "Genesis and Catastrophe"   H/JNW
  "Lamb to the Slaughter"   H
  "Man from the South"   H
  "The Rat-Catcher"   H
  "Royal Jelly"   H
Dann, Jack, "Camps"   H
Davidson, Avram, "Naples"   CG/H
  "The Old Woman Who Lived with the Bear"   F

"Or All the Seas with Oysters"   SF
"The Tail-Tied Kings"   SF
del Rey, Lester, "For I Am a Jealous People!"   SF
"Helen O'Loy"   SF
Delany, Samuel R., "Driftglass"   SF
"The Star-Pit"   SF
"Time Considered as a Helix of Semi-Precious Stones"   SF
deLint, Charles, "The Fair at Emain Macha"   F
Derleth, August, "The Lonesome Place"   H
"Mr. George"   H
Disch, Thomas, "The Brave Little Toaster"   F
"Descending"   H
"The Roaches"   H
Doctorow, E. L., "Waterworks"   CG/H
Donaldson, Stephen R., "The Lady in White"   F
Dozois, Gardner, "Dinner Party"   SF
Dozois, Gardner & Jack Dann, "Touring"   CG
Drake, David, "Dancer in the Flames"   H
Drippé, Colleen, "The Women of Rattlesnake Hill"   H
du Maurier, Daphne, "The Pool"   F

E

Effinger, George Alec, "Target: Berlin!"   F
"The Thing from the Slush"   H
Elflandsson, Galad, "Drifting"   F/JNW
Ellin, Stanley, "The Specialty of the House"   CG/H
Ellison, Harlan, "All the Birds Come Home to Roost"   H
"All the Sounds of Fear"   F
"Basilisk"   H
"The City on the Edge of Forever"   SF
"Crotoan"   H
"The Deathbird"   SF
"I Have No Mouth, and I Must Scream"   CG/H
"Jefty is Five"   SF
"On the Downhill Side"   F
"Paingod"   SF
"Paladin of the Lost Hour"   F
"Pretty Maggie Moneyeyes"   SF
"The Prowler in the City at the Edge of the World"   CG/H
" 'Repent, Harlequin!' Said the Ticktockman"   SF
"Shatterday"   CG/F
"Shattered Like a Glass Goblin"   H
"The Whimper of Whipped Dogs"   CG/H
Ely, David, "The Academy"   H
Etchison, Dennis, "Daughters of the Golden West"   H
"It Only Comes Out at Night"   H
"Sitting in the Corner Whimpering Quietly"   H
"Talking in the Dark"   H
Eubank, Jerry & Parke Godwin, "Like an Unmarked Grave"   SF

F

Fancett, Elizabeth, "When Morning Comes"   H
Farmer, Philip José, "Riders of the Purple Wage"   SF
Faulkner, William, "A Rose for Emily"   CG
Fitzgerald, F. Scott, "News of Paris—Fifteen Years Ago"   CG/JNW
Fox, Janet, "The Babysitter"   H/JNW
  "The Bug Boy"   H/JNW
  "Garage Sale"   H
  "To a Crow, All Crows Are White"   H
  "Witches"   H
Frahm, Leanne, "High Tide"   H
Fritch, Charles E., "The One-Eyed Moth B-Longs to Sum Buddy Else"   H

G

Glass, Mignon, "River"   H/JNW
Gleisser, Benjamin, "The Dark"   H
Godwin, Tom, "The Cold Equations"   SF
Grant, Charles L., "Essence of Charlotte"   H
  "Garden of Blackred Roses"   H
  "If Damon Comes"   H
Gresham, Stephen, "The One Left Behind"   H
Grabowski, William J., "Squirrel"   H/JNW
Grubb, Davis, "The Horsehair Trunk"   H

H

Hague, Jo-Ann, "The Dreammaker"   F
Haining, Robert, "Montage of Death"   H
Hamilton, Dennis, "The Alteration"   H
Hammell, Dale, "Children of the Hurda"   H
Harding, Ralph, "The Song"   H
Heinlein, Robert A., "All You Zombies"   SF
  "And He Built a Crooked House"   SF
  "Common Sense"   SF
  "The Green Hills of Earth"   SF
  "The Roads Must Roll"   SF
  "They"   CG/F
  "The Unpleasant Profession of Jonathan Hoag" (as "John Riverside")   SF
Henderson, Zenna, "Something Bright"   SF
Hoch, Edward, "The Oblong Room"   H
Home, William Scott, "The Lamps are Lighted in the House of Hicks"   CG
Hopper, Jeannette M., "The Vigil"   H/JNW
Howard, Robert E., "Garden of Fear"   H
  "The Horror from the Mound"   H
  "Pigeons from Hell"   H
  "Valley of the Worm"   F

J

Jackson, Shirley, "The Beautiful Stranger"   H
  "The Lottery"   H

"One Ordinary Day, with Peanuts"   CG/H
"The Witch"   H
James, Adobe, "The Road to Mctantecutli"   H
Jarrell, Randall, "The Bat Poet"   F
Jones, Raymond F., "The Children's Hour"   SF

K

Keel, John A., "Follow the Bouncing Ball"   H/JNW
Keefauver, John, "Kill for Me"   H/JNW
Keller, David H., "The Thing in the Cellar"   H
Kennedy, Richard, "Come Again in the Spring"   F
Kersh, Gerald, "Men Without Bones"   H
Keyes, Daniel, "Flowers for Algernon"   CG/SF
King, Stephen, "Apt Pupil"   H
    "The Boogeyman"   H
    "The Breathing Method"   F
    "Children of the Corn"   H
    "Crouch End"   H
    "Do The Dead Sing?" (a.k.a "The Reach")   H
    "Gramma"   H
    "The Gunslinger"   F
    "I am the Doorway"   H
    "The Mist"   H
    "The Monkey"   H
    "Night Surf"   H
    "Nona"   H
    "Popsy"   CG/JNW
    "Quitters, Inc."   H
    "The Raft"   H
    "Sometimes They Come Back"   H
    "The Strawberry Spring"   CG/F
    "Survivor Type"   H
    "Word Processor of the Gods"   CG/F
Kiplinger, Christina, "Bookin"   H/JNW
Kirk, Russell, "There's a Long Trail a' Winding"   H
Kisner, James, "The Litter"   H
    "The Stoner"   H/JNW
    "The Willies"   H/JNW
Klein, T. E. D., "Black Man with a Horn"   H
    "Children of the Kingdom"   H
    "Petey"   H
Knight, Damon, "Country of the Kind"   SF
    "To Serve Man"   SF
Koontz, Dean R., "Down in the Darkness"   H
    "Snatchers"   H
Kornbluth, Cyril M., "The Little Black Bag"   SF
    "The Marching Morons"   SF
Kress, Nancy, "Green Thumb"   CG/H/JNW
    "Out of All Them Bright Stars"   SF
Kress, Nancy & Jeff Dunteman, "Borovsky's Hollow Woman"   SF

Kube-McDowell, Michael P., "Slippage"   CG/H
Kuttner, Henry, "Compliments of the Author" (as "Lester Padgett")   SF
  "Mimsy Were the Borogoves"   SF
  "The Proud Robot" (as "Lester Padgett")   SF

L

Lafferty, R. A., "Thou White Wall"   H
Laidlaw, Marc, "Tissue"   H
Lansdale, Joe. R., "Down by the Sea Near the Great Big Rock"   H
  "Fish Night"   F
  "The Pit"   H
  "Tight Little Stitches in a Dead Man's Back"   CG/SF
Langelaan, George, "The Fly"   H
Le Guin, Ursula K., "The Direction of the Road"   SF
  "The New Atlantis"   SF
  "Nine Lives"   SF
Lee, Tanith, "Elle Est Trois (La Mort)"   H
  "The Gorgon"   F
  "Kill the Dead"   F
  "Magritte's Secret Agent"   CG/H
  "Paid Piper"   F
  "Red as Blood"   F
Leiber, Fritz, "Adept's Gambit"   F
  "Bazaar of the Bizarre"   F
  "Black Glass"   SF
  "The Dreams of Albert Moreland"   H
  "Ghost Light"   H
  "The Girl with the Hungry Eyes"   H
  "Gonna Roll the Bones"   F
  "Ill Met in Lankhmar"   F
  "Smoke Ghost"   H
  "Space-Time for Springers"   CG
  "The Unholy Grail"   SF
Leinster, Murray, "First Contact"   SF
  "A Logic Named Joe"   SF
Leming, Ron, "Fox Goes Fission"   H
  "Through a Glass Darkly"   H/JNW
Leonard, Michael, "Ghosts of Christmas Past"   H/JNW
Ligotti, Thomas, "Dr. Voke and Mr. Veech"   H
Lonsdale, Joe R., "Fish Night"   F
Lovecraft, H. P., "Cool Air"   H
Lumley, Brian, "Dylath-Leen"   H
  "Snarker's Son"   H
Lupoff, Richard, "Sail the Tide of Mourning"   F
  "With the Bentfin Boomer Boys on Little Old New Alabama"   SF

M

Maclay, John, "Locking Up"   H/JNW
  "The Step Beyond"   H/JNW

"Who Walks the Night"   H
Marquez, Gabriel G., "A Very Old Man with Enormous Wings"   F
Martin, George R. R., "Nightflyers"   H
 "Remembering Melody"   H
 "SandKings"   CG/H
 "Song for Lya"   SF
 "Under Siege"   SF
Matheson, Richard, "Advance Notice"   F/JNW
 "Being"   H
 "Blood Son"   H
 "Born of Man and Woman"   H
 "The Children of Noah"   H/JNW
 "Dance of the Dead"   H
 "Deadline"   SF/JNW
 "The Distributor"   H
 "Duel"   H
 "Little Girl Lost"   CG
 "Long Distance Call"   H
 "Mute"   H
 "Nightmare at 20,000 Feet"   H
 "Prey"   H
 "Retch"   H
 "The Test"   CG/H
 "When Day is Dun"   SF/JNW
Matheson, Richard & Richard Christian, "Where There's a Will"   H/JNW
Matheson, Richard Christian, "The Dark Ones"   H
 "Deathbed"   F/JNW
 "Goosebumps"   H/JNW
 "Holiday"   H
 "The Last Day"   SF/JNW
 "Red"   H
 "Sentences"   H/JNW
 "Third Wind"   H
May, Julian, "Dune Roller"   SF
Mayhar, Ardath, "Crawfish"   H
 "A Meeting of Minds"   SF
 "A Night in Possum Holler"   H
 "The Tuck at the Foot of the Bed"   H/JNW
McCaffrey, Anne, "Decision at Doona"   SF
McCammon, Robert R., "The Deep End"   H/JNW
 "I Scream Man"   CG/H/JNW
 "Nightcrawlers"   H
McHardy, Vincent, "Angst for the Memory"   H
 "Take a Ticket"   H/JNW
McIntyre, Vonda N., "Aztecs"   H
 "Fireflood"   SF
McKillip, Patricia A., "The Harrowing of the Dragon of Hoarsbredth"   F
Merrill, Judith, "Daughters of the Earth"   SF
Merritt, A., "Through the Dragon Glass"   F
Miller, G. Wayne, "Wiping the Slate Clean"   H/JNW

Miller, J. J. & James Moore, "Incident at Smuggler's Gap"   H/JNW
Miller, P. Schuyler, "Spawn"   H
Mishima, Yukio, "Patriotism"   H
Moore, C. L., "No Woman Born"   SF
  "Scarlet Dream"   CG/F
  "Shambleau"   SF
Moorcock, Michael, "Behold the Man"   SF
  "The Dreaming City"   F
Morlan, A. R. "Does it Ploop?"   H/JNW

N

Nicoll, Gregory, "The Man Who Collected Lovecraft"   H
Niven, Larry, "Grammar Lesson"   SF
  "The Neutron Star"   SF
Nolan, William F., "Ceremony"   H
  "Dead Call"   H
  "The Halloween Man"   H/JNW
  "He Kilt It with a Stick"   H
  "Lap of the Primitive"   SF
  "The Pool"   H/JNW
  "Underdweller"   H
  "The Yard"   H/JNW
Norden, Eric, "Primary Solution"   H

O

O'Connor, Flannery, "A Good Man is Hard to Find"   H
  "River"   H
Oliver, Chad, "Transformer"   SF
Olson, Paul, "Valley of the Shadows"   H

P

Phillips, Peter, "Dreams are Sacred"   SF
Pickett, Stephen Charles, "Mirrors"   H/JNW
Piper, H. Beam, "Omnilingual"   SF
Plath, Sylvia, "Johnny Panic and the Bible of Dreams"   CG
Pohl, Frederik, "The Gold at Starbow's End"   SF
  "Man of the World"   SF
Priest, Christopher, "Palely Loitering"   SF
Prosser, Harold Lee, "Absalom, Do Not Go Gentle"   F/JNW

R

Reamy, Tom, "The Detwiler Boy"   SF
  "Twilla"   F
  "Under the Hollywood Sign"   H
Reed, Kit, "Chicken Soup"   H
Relling, Jr., William, "The King"   H
Reynolds, Mack, "Compounded Interest"   SF
Robinson, Spider & Jeanne, "Stardance"   SF

Rodgers, Alan, "The Boy Who Came Back from the Dead" F
Russ, Joanna, "When It Changed" SF
Russell, Eric Frank, "Dear Devil" SF
 "The Witness" SF
Russell, Ray, "The Cage" H/JNW
 "The Charm" F
 "Comet Wine" H
 "Czadek" H
 "The Devil's Mirror" H/JNW
 "Ghost of a Chance" H
 "I am Returning" H/JNW
 "Sanguinarius" CG/JNW
 "Sardonicus" H
 "The Secret of Rowena" CG/F
 "Skin Deep" CG/SF/JNW
 "Xong of Xuxan" CG/SF
Ryan, Alan, "Hear the Wind Blowing" H
Ryman, Geoff, "O Happy Day!" SF
 "The Unconquered Country" F

S

Salinger, J. D., "A Perfect Day for Bananafish" CG/F
Sallee, Wayne, "Rapid Transit" H
Salmonson, Jessica Amanda, "The View from Mt. Futaba" F
Sarrantonio, Al, "Corn Dolly" H
 "Two" H/JNW
Schmitz, James, "The Witches of Karres" SF
Schweitzer, Darrell, "The Clock" H/JNW
 "The Wrong Stop" F/JNW
Sellers, Sally A., "Perchance to Dream" F
Shaw, Bob, "Light of Other Days" SF
Shea, Michael, "The Autopsy" H
Sheckley, Robert, "Cost of Living" SF
 "The Monsters" SF
 "Pilgrimage to Earth" SF
Sheckley, Jay, "Bargain Cinema" H/JNW
Shepard, Lucius, "The Man Who Painted the Dragon Giraule" F
Shiras, Wilmar H., "In Hiding" SF
Silva, David B., "Ice Sculptures" H
 "The Turn of Time" H
Silverberg, Robert, "Born with the Dead" SF
 "Good News from the Vatican" SF
 "To See the Invisible Man" SF
 "When We Went to See the End of the World" SF
Simak, Clifford, "The Big Front Yard" SF
 "A Death in the House" SF
 "Grotto of the Dancing Deer" SF
 "Kindergarten" SF
Skipp, John & Craig Spector, "Shells" H
Slesar, Henry, "The Jam" CG/H

Smith, Cordwainer, "The Game of Rat and Dragon" SF
  "A Planet Named Shayol" SF
Steigler, Marc, "Petals of Rose" SF
Stephens, Lori, "Have You Seen the Garbage Man?" CG
Strete, Craig, "Time Deer" SF
Strieber, Whitley, "Perverts" H
Stuart, Kiel, "Chinese Lullaby" H/JNW
Sturgeon, Theodore, "And Now, the News" SF
  "Bianca's Hands" H
  "Bright Segment" CG/H
  "The Comedian's Children" SF
  "The Crate" SF
  "If All Men Were Brothers, Would You Let One Marry Your Sister?" SF
  "It" H
  "Microcosmic God" SF
  "One Foot and the Grave" F
  "The Professor's Teddy-Bear" SF
  "Saucer of Loneliness" SF
  "Shottle Bop" CG/H
  "The Silken-Swift" F
  "The Skills of Xanadu" SF
  "Slow Sculpture" SF
  "Thunder and Roses" SF
  "Vengeance *Is*" CG/H
  "Yesterday Was Monday" SF
Sullivan, Thomas, "The Man Who Drowned Puppies" H
Sykes, S. C., "Rockabye Baby" SF

T

Taylor, David W., "The Dew Drop Inn" H/JNW
Tem, Steve Rasnic, "Derelicts" H
  "Motherson" H/JNW
Timlett, Peter Valentine, "Without Rhyme or Reason" H
Tiptree Jr., James, "And I Awoke and Found Me Here on the Cold Hill's Side" SF
  "Beyond the Dead Reef" F
  "Houston, Houston, Do You Read?" SF
  "The Last Flight of Dr. Ain" SF
  "Things to Rats" CG/H
  "The Women Men Don't See" F
Tolkien, J. R. R., "Leaf by Niggle" F
  "Of Turin Tyrambar" F
Tuttle, Lisa, "The Bug House" H

V

Van Vogt, A. E., "Black Destroyer" SF
  "The Enchanted Village" SF
  "The Monster" SF
Vance, Jack, "The Dragon Masters" SF

"Guyal of Spere"   F
"The Last Castle"   SF
"Liane the Wayfarer"   CG
Varley, John, "Air Raid"   SF
"In the Barn"   SF
"In the Bowl"   SF
"The Persistence of Vision"   SF
Vinge, Joan, "To Bell the Cat"   SF
Vonnegut Jr., Kurt, "Harrison Bergeron"   SF

W

Wagner, Karl Edward, "Beyond Any Measure"   H
"River of Night's Dreaming"   H
"Sticks"   H
".220 Swift"   H
"Undertow"   F
Waldrop, Howard, "Flying Saucer Rock and Roll"   SF
Wellman, Manly Wade, "The Desrick on Yandro"   H
"One Other"   H
"Owls Hoot in the Daytime"   H
"Walk Like a Mountain"   F
Wilhelm, Kate, "The Gorgon Field"   F
"The Hounds"   F
"The Village"   SF
Williams, Tennessee, "Desire and the Black Masseur"   H
Williamson, J. N., "The Book of Webster's"   H
"Bopping It in Bohemia"   F
"The Bountiful Spirit"   H/JNW
"The Dotted Line"   H/JNW
"The Gap Nearly Closed Tonight"   H
"Hellter-Shelter"   H
"House Mothers"   H
"The House of Life"   H
"I'll Give You Magic if You'll Give Me Love"   H
"A Matter of Identification"   CG/F
"The Night Seasons"   H
"They Never Even See Me"   H
"Wordsong"   CG/F
Williamson, Jack, "With Folded Hands"   SF
Wilson, F. Paul, "Soft"   H
Wilson, Gahan, "The Substitute"   H
Wilson, Richard, "Mother to the World"   SF
Winter, Douglas E., "Office Hours"   H/JNW
Wolfe, Gene, "The Death of Doctor Island"   CG
"The Island of Dr. Death"   CG/H
"The Nebraskan and the Nereid"   CG
Wolfenbarger, Billy, "The Attic"   H
Wu, William F., "Wong's Lost and Found Emporium"   F

Y

Yarbro, Chelsea Quinn, "Disturb Not My Slumbering Fair"   H
  "Savoury, Sage, Rosemary and Thyme"   H
Yolen, Jane, "Evian Steel"   F
  "The Girl Who Loved the Wind"   F
  "The Lady and the Mermaid"   F
  "The Lady and the Merman"   F
  "The Pot Child"   F
  "Such Nice Neighbors"   F/JNW
  "The Tree's Wife"   F
  "The White Seal Maid"   F

Z

Zelazny, Roger, "Giant Killer"   SF
  "Home is the Hangman"   H
  "The Last Defender of Camelot"   F
  "A Rose for Ecclesiastes"   SF
  "The Stainless Steel Leech"   CG

Index

A-Team, The, 182
Aboriginal SF magazine, 167-168, 181
Action as suspense, 60; not suspense, 60
Action plot, 81
Adams, Robert, 8
Agents: choosing, 142, 152; need for and obtaining, 140-141, 153-154; what they do, 140-146; what they don't do, 141-146
Aldiss, Brian W., 3
Alfred Hitchcock (tv show), 54
Alfred Hitchcock's Mystery Magazine, 47
Alien, 132, 162
Alien: creating, 56-58; invasion, 110, 157
Alien Horizons, 50
Aliens, 60
Amazing, 50, 168, 180
Analog, 84, 168
"And Miles to Go Before I Sleep," 48
"And of Gideon," 33, 177
Anderson, Poul, 80
Anderson, Sherwood, 18
Andrews, V. C., 162
Anthologies, balancing by sex, 117
Anticipation, 60
Antihorror, 161-162
Archetypes and stereotypes, 112-119
Art, accidental, 25
Asimov, Isaac, 183
Astounding, 12
Astrology, 109
Atlantis, 110
Auctioneer, The, 69
Autobiographical materials, use of, 40
Author-agent relationship, 144-146
Authors as moralists, 111
Authors' representatives, 140-146
Azathoth, 43

Baal, 70, 180
Background, 84-85; 88
Bad taste, 159-160
Baen Books, 171
Baker, Sharon, 88-95
Baker Street Irregulars, The, 185

Ballard, J. G., 158
Balrog Awards, 185
Banks, Michael A., 82-87
Bantam Books, 50, 172
Barbarians, 78-80
Barker, Clive, 41, 52, 69, 161, 163
Baum, L. Frank, 43
Beaumont, Charles, 108
Beginner needs, 55
Behind You, 178
Belief, importance of, 108
Benny, Jack, 32
Beowulf, 79
Berberick, Nancy Varian, 3
Berger, Thomas, 122
Betancourt, John, 180
Bethany's Sin, 180
"Beyond Any Measure," 98
Beyond Belief, 72
Bible, The, 45, 110, 113
Bixby, Jerome, 2
Black Cat, The, 9
Black Wine, 184
Blatty, William Peter, 60, 103
"Bless Me, Father, For I Have Sinned," 17
Bloch, Robert, 2, 7-10, 12, 177, 183
Bloody Sun, The, 180
Bolton, Guy, 45
Books in Print, 85
Books of Blood, 52, 161
Book "writes itself," 137
Bowie, David, 162
Brackett, Leigh, 13, 17
Bradbury, Ray, 2, 11-19, 36, 55, 82, 108, 177
Bradley, Marion Zimmer, 8, 71-76, 115, 118, 180
Brady, Ian, 72
Brain, hemispheres of, 134-135, 138-139
Bridge Across Time, 178
Brown, Charles N., 1, 3, 5
Brunner, John, 53
Buddenbrooks, 133, 136
Bundy, Theodore, 72

Burning Tears of Sassurum, The, 181
Burnt Offerings, 178
Burroughs, Edgar Rice, 43, 68

Cain, James M., 102
Cameron, James, 60
Campbell, Ramsey, 38-39, 52, 96-100, 160, 163, 181
Capote, Truman, 71
Carpenter, John, 162
Carr, John Dickson, 73
Carrie, 163
Carroll, Lewis, 108
Castle, Mort, 5, 28-34, 177
Cave, Hugh B., 115
Cave of the Moving Shadows, 178
Ceremonies, The, 157
Chandler, Raymond, 78
Chaplin, J. P., 110
Characters, characterizations: 21, 24-25, 28-34, 35-41, 56-58, 65, 89, 102-105, 113-115, 117, 133, 158
Characters: and detail, 38-39, 73-74; as context, 36, 56-58, 65; do the work, 15, 32, 40; names, 42-44, 58
"Charly," 2
Charteris, Leslie, 178
Cherryh, C. J., 114, 118
"Christmas Carol, A," 67
City of Sorcery, 180
Clarke, Robert P., 110
Clemmie, 102
Cliches, 54, 98, 114, 115, 157
Close Encounters of the Third Kind, 162
Cocoon, 162
Collier, John, 17
Collins, Professor Robert A., 2
Comanche Stallion, 178
Comedy writing, 122
Conan, 78-81
Conrad, Joseph, 158
Contracts, 141, 144-145
Cooper, James Fenimore, 80
Copyright, 142
Cover letters, 141, 148-149
Craft of the Novel, The, 183
Crane, Stephen, 5
Craven, Wes, 159
Crime and Punishment, 136
Creating context, 36

Creating a new being, 56-57
Creation, joy of, 113
Creative imagination, 111, 138
Creative period, 99
Creativeness: feminine, 113-118; opposite of dissociation, 6
Credibility, 32-34, 35, 58, 108, 109, 111
Cronenberg, David, 162
Cthulu, 56
Cuckoo's Egg, 114
Cujo, 108, 158
Cultural research, 89-92, 108, 162
Curiosity, 25
Cutting Edge, 47

Dahl, Roald, 122
Damnation Game, The, 69
Dandelion Wine, 16
Dangerous Visions, 53
Danse Macabre, 53
Dark Carnival, 16
Dark fantasy, major ingredients, 64-66
Dark Forces, 182
Datlow, Ellen, 117
Day After Tomorrow, The, 86
Daydream fiction, 81
Day of the Dead, 163
"Day the Gorf Took Over, The," 49
DAW Books, 172
De Camp, L. Sprague, 77, 81, 118
"Dead Call," 49
Dead Zone, The, 44
Death Is a Lonely Business, 14, 177
Delany, Samuel, 38
Del Rey Books, 172
Dementia, 179
Deneuve, Catherine, 162
De Palma, Brian, 163
"Derelicts," 41
Detail, focus to solve character, 38, 89
Dick, Philip K., 53
Dickens, Charles, 5, 12, 50, 54, 67, 104
Dictionary of the Occult and Paranormal, 110
Different, what makes it, 54
Dime Detective, 14
Directory of Possibilities, The, 110
Doll Who Ate His Mother, The, 181
Donaldson, Stephen R., 8
Donning Company/Publishers, The, 173

Dostoevsky, Feodor, 136
Dot matrix, submissions in, 142, 153
Doubleday, 183
Double Indemnity, 102
"Down the Long Night," 48
Doyle, Sir Arthur Conan, 68, 73
Dracula, 43, 63, 73-74, 131, 162
Dracula's Children, 161
Dracula, Vlad, 44
Dragon magazine, 168
Dream characterization, 36-37
Dunsany, Lord, 78
"Dwarf, The," 17

E. C. Comics, 54
Eddison, E. R., 38
Editor, use of name, 152
Editors' methods, 148-150, 152, 165
Eldritch Tales, 176
Elements of horror, 67-70
Eliot, T. S., 89
Ellery Queen's Mystery Magazine, 178
"Emissary, The," 16, 17
Emotion, horror is, 158
Emotions: evoking, 102, 104, 129; lasting, 160; unmanly, 114, 126
Empathy, importance of evoking, 102
Encyclopedia of Occultism, 110
Encyclopedia of the Occult, the Esoteric, and the Supernatural, 110
"End with No Perhaps, The," 47
Environment, creating, 57-58
Erewhon, 44
Errors, five, new writers commit, 102-104
Erskine, John, 4
E. T., 59, 62
Etchison, Dennis, 41, 157, 183
Evil: controversy over, 106-108, 159; as force, 108; woman as, 113
Executioner's Song, The, 71
Existentialism, 126-127
Exorcist, The, 60, 75, 103, 107
Expiration Dates, 182
Explicitness, 160-161

Face That Must Die, The, 98
Faces of Fear, 184
Facts, 95
Faculty X, 131-139

Fafhrd, 78
"Fair Trade," 49
Fairies, 109
Faith, and fantasy, 3, 159
Famous Fantastic Mysteries, 14
Fantasy: characters, characterization, 56-58; hardest to write, 109; logic, 71-76, 109, 127; and magic, 80; masks, 161; pays, 1, 116; reason for writing, 51-52, 116, 127, 139, 147; sword and sorcery in, 77-81; umbrella term, 1
Fantasy Book, 174
Fantasy Macabre, 174
Fantasy Review, 2, 180, 184
Farmer, Philip José, 53
Farther Reaches of Human Nature, The, 2, 111, 112, 113
Fate magazine, 178
Faulkner, William, 158
Fear and anxiety, 41
Fear, horror elicits more than, 101-105, 128-129
Fiction and people, importance of, 104, 160
Fiction as credible lie, 29
Fiction as entertainment, 5, 21, 50
Fiction, magic of, 105
Fiction, must be engaging instantly, 50
Fiction, original, 51-55, 70
Fiction Writer's Market, 54, 142, 185
Fiend in You, The, 108
"Final Stone, The," 47
Finishing Touches, 160
Finney, Jack, 53
"Firebug," 177
Fitzgerald, F. Scott, 54
Flashback, narrative, 86
Fletch, 59
"Flowers for Algernon," 2
Flynn's Detective, 13
"Foghorn, The," 177
Ford, Harrison, 34
Formula fiction, 5
Fox, Janet, 165-176, 184
France, Anatole, 2
Frankenstein, 114, 134
Freelancing, 146, 151-153
Friday, 84
Friday the 13th, 68, 98, 128, 158, 161
Frights, 49

Fulci, Lucio, 161
Future Is Now, The, 47
Futuristic settings, opportunity for, 115

Gallery, 49, 184
Gamma, 46
Gardner, John, 20, 21, 23, 29, 53
Gateway, 86
Gazzaniga, Michael, 134
Gein, Edward, 120-121
Gender, artificial division of, 117
Genesis, 45
Genres: controversial, 106-108; idea of
   plot stronghold, 20, 52; writing, 8, 9,
   ·20, 26, 106-108
Ghost, 185
Ghost Mansion, 53
Ghosts in fiction, 30, 106-111
Ghost stories, 107-108, 125, 129, 134
Ghost Story, 53, 107
Gibson, William, 38
Gnaedinger, Mary, 14
God of the Labyrinth, 182
Good versus evil, 67, 69, 106, 122
Gordon, Cyrus, 91
Gothic novels, 72, 159, 161
"Grackel Question, The," 49
Grant, Charles L., 64-66, 68, 160-161,
   163
Grant, John, 110
*Great Tales of Terror and the Supernatu-
   ral*, 96
Greene, Graham, 97
"Gross-outs," 160
Grue magazine, 114, 175, 179

Hailey, Arthur, 82
Halloween, 161
"Halloween Man, The," 47
Hamilton, Dennis, 5
Hamilton, Edmond, 17
Hammett, Dashiell, 77
Hardcover houses, 143
Hard science, 82-87
Harper's Bazaar, 184
Harris, Thomas, 162
Haunting of Hill House, The, 98, 160
Heinlein, Robert A., 84, 86
Hell House, 53, 108
Hemingway, Ernest, 26

Herbert, James, 160
Heritage of Hastur, The, 180
Heroines, 81, 98
High fantasy, 8, 116
Hindley, Myra, 72
Hitching, Francis, 110
Holmes, Sherlock, 10, 73, 123
Hooking readers, 46, 148
Hooper, Tobe, 132
Hopkins, Bill, 131
Hopper, Jeannette M., 112-119, 181
Horae Sabbaticae, 55 (footnote)
Horror: beauty or enlightenment of, 6, 67;
   elements of best, 157-164; euphemisms for, 5, 9, 26, 67, 101, 106; expanding, 1, 6, 72, 130, 147, 158, 161,
   162, 163; fiction, 70; fun of, 68; humor of, 120-122; innocence and terror
   of, 67-70, 122; logic or reality of, 9,
   57, 59, 65, 71, 72, 121-122, 124, 127;
   morality of, 68-70, 106-107, 111,
   125, 130, 161; objects as character,
   37; popularity of, 5, 51-55, 124-125,
   163; psychology of 39, 124-130, 164;
   purges, 60; purposes of, 66, 67-69,
   76, 98-99, 101-105, 106-111; recalls
   primordial self, 127; subtlety of, 64,
   66, 160-161; subversive, 161; tradition of, 96-97; trends, 107, 116; where
   found, 6, 65, 67, 72, 120-122, 164
Horror films, 9, 10, 68, 163
Horror Show, The, magazine, 51, 53,
   117, 174, 175, 179, 180
Horror, source of healthy balance, 128-
   130
Horror story ending, 163
Horror Writers of America, 1, 179, 185
"Horseless Carriage," 84
Houngan, The, 111, 185
How to Write Best Selling Fiction, 20, 27
Howard, Robert E., 78
Human beings, subjective, 125
Hume, David, 125
Humor in fiction, 120-122
Hunger, The, 162
Huxley, Aldous, 8
Hypnagogic state, 131

I Am Legend, 158
Ideas, bloated, 96; getting, 11-19, 23,

110-111; importance of, 21; needless-
ly expanded, 8
Imagination, importance of training, 52,
111, 133-139; intimate act, 160; uses,
97, 157; untrapping, 135-139
Imaginative instincts, 52, 111, 128
Immortality, 109
Impact, 20, 47, 50
In Cold Blood, 71
Incredible Hulk, The, 182
Infinity SF, 48
Infinity Two, 49
Inheritor, The, 75
Innocence, 67-70
Insight, original, 53
Interaction of people, importance, 104
Interview With The Vampire, 69
"Into the Lion's Den," 47
Invincibility, 73, 74, 103
Involving readers, 46-50
Irving, Washington, 29
*Isaac Asimov's Science Fiction Maga-
zine*, 84, 169, 178, 180
Ishtar, 44
Island of Dr. Moreau, The, 161
"It's a *Good* Life," 2

Jack the Ripper, 133-134, 136
Jackson, Shirley, 98, 107, 160
Jagged Orbit, The, 53
James, Henry, 9
James, M. R., 9, 38, 41
Janet, Pierre, 139
"Jar, The," 16
Jeffries, Adi-Kent Thomas, 125
"Jefty Is Five," 2
"Jenny Among the Zeebs," 47
Johnson, George Clayton, 36, 178
Journey to Membliar, 88-95, 181
Joyce, James, 136
Jung, Carl, 108, 139

Kafka, Franz, 37, 41
Keyes, Daniel, 2
Khi to Freedom, 57
Kierkegaard, Soren, 182
King Kong, 132
"King of the Grey Spaces," 14
King, Stephen, 2, 9, 30, 39, 44-45, 53,
60, 68-69, 96, 97, 99, 102, 107, 108,

156, 157, 158, 161, 163
Kipling, Rudyard, 68
Kisner, James, 5, 51-55, 171
Klein, T. E. D., 157
Koontz, Dean R., 20, 27, 53-54, 59-63,
71, 101-105, 108, 179
Kosinski, Jerzy, 158
Kuttner, Henry, 12, 17

"Lake, The," 13
Landwall, Sam J., 4
Laughter, terror alike, 123
Lawrence, D. H., 161
"Legal Gothics," 184
LeGuin, Ursula K., 43, 74
Leiber, Fritz, 41, 78, 81
Leisure Books, 173
Levin, Ira, 44-45, 108
Lewis, C. S., 43
Lewis, Sinclair, 54
Library uses, 166
Lifeforce, 132-133
"Listen to the Music in My Hands," 66
Listings, market, 167-176
Literary agents, 140-146, 152-153
Literary Market Place, 142, 152
"Litter," 99
LoBrutto, Pat, 151-155
Locus, 1, 3, 5, 155
Logan's Run, 50, 178
Longest Night, The, 183
Lortz, Richard, 161
Lost Weekend, The, 17
Love, 104, 109, 158
Lovecraft, H. P., 9, 12, 43, 76, 96, 97

MacArdle, Dorothy, 75
MacDonald, John D., 53, 102
Machen, Arthur, 9, 157
Maclay, John, 20, 33
McCammon, Robert R., 30, 67-70, 108,
180
McDonald, Gregory, 59
*Magazine of Fantasy and Science Fiction,
The*, 47, 169
Magic, 110
Mailer, Norman, 71
Maltese Falcon, The, 79
Mancini, Henry, 132
Manhunt, 178

Manlove, Colin N., 2
Mann, Thomas, 133
Manuscript appearance and preparation, 141-144, 148-150, 152-155
Marketing with one's strengths, 166, 167
Marketplace, knowing it, 144, 165-176
Martian Chronicles, The, 2, 18, 177
Maslow, Abraham H., 2, 3, 6, 111, 112-113
Masques, 53, 177, 178, 182, 183, 185
Masques II, 48, 53, 108, 177, 178, 179, 181, 182, 183, 185
Matheson, Richard, 2, 36, 53, 55, 158-159, 182
Matheson, Richard Christian, 120-123, 182
"Mating of Thirdburt, The," 50
Mayhar, Ardath, 51-52, 56-58, 179
Meacham, Beth, 3
Mechanics of novel selling, 151-155
Medusa, 181
Melville, Herman, 5
Mental health, horror benefits, 130
"Message," 104
Metaphysics, 111, 159
Michaels, Barbara, 75
Michener, James, 82
Mike Shayne's Mystery Magazine, 48
Millstead, Thomas, 42-44, 178
Mind Parasites, The, 131, 182
Moby Dick, 5
"Monkey's Paw, The," 96
Monsters, 65, 106, 114, 162-163
Moorcock, Michael, 78
Moore, Catherine L., 81
Morris, William, 79
Mother-Goddess, 114
"My Name Is Dolly," 46
Mysteries, 110, 183
Mysterious World, The, 110
Mystery, 10, 150
Mystery of Udolpho, The, 159
Mystery Walk, 30, 69, 180
Mystery Writer's Handbook, The, 54
Mythology, 90-92, 109, 110-111

Nabokov, Vladimir, 97
Nadramia, Peggy, 114
"Name" writers, 116-117
Names: ambiguous, 118; inevitability and power, 93

Naming characters, 42-44
Narrative, must be clear, direct, 50
Nebula awards, 185
Necessary Doubt, 132
Nelson, Willie, 32
Nero's Vice, 179
"Networking," 166
Nevermore!, 5
Newman, Paul, 34
New Pathways in Psychology, 183
New Terrors, 181
Nichols, Leigh, 179. *See* Koontz, Dean R.
"Nightcrawlers," 108, 180
Night Cry magazine, 47, 141, 147, 149, 169, 179, 181, 183
Night's Black Agents, 41
Nightmare on Elm Street, 159
Nightmare Seasons, 180
Nightmares, creating waking, 28-34
Night of the Ripper, 177, 185
Night Seasons, 185
Night Visions, 178
Nightwalker, The, 162
Niven, Larry, 86
Nolan, William F., 46-50, 55, 178
Noonspell, 185
Northwest Review of Books, 181
Norton, Andre, 8
Notes, 12, 100
Nouns, use of, 13
Novel, conclusion, 163
Novel, partials, 142-143, 152
Novels: agenting, 142-146; plotting, 20; publishers of, 151-155; submitting, 142-146
Nuclear holocaust, 33, 69, 161, 177
Nukes: Four Horror Writers on the Ultimate Horror, 33, 177

Obsession, 96
Occult fiction, 106-111
Occult, The, 110, 133
O'Connell, Dr. Walter E., 121
O'Connor, Flannery, 60
October Country, 177
Odysseus Solution, The, 181
"Of Time and Kathy Benedict," 49
"Old College Try," 177
Omni, 17, 117, 160
On Becoming a Novelist, 20, 23

"On Thud and Blunder," 80
"One of Those Days," 47
Opar, City of Gold, 43
Opening paragraphs, 46-50
Order of Assassins, 11, 183
Originality, 10, 51-55, 96-99, 110-111, 157-158
Origins of the Sexual Impulse, 183
Orwell, George, 8, 68
Outer Limits, The, 54
Outlines, 22, 23, 99
Outsider, The, 11, 182
Outsider, The and Others, 76
Oz, 43, 71

Pandora, 175
Paperback houses, 143
Parapsychology, 75, 109
Parasite, The, 38, 181
Parente, Audrey, 115
Partials, 142-143, 152
Perception of events necessary, 158
Perelandra, 43
Personal contact helpful, 153-154
Pet, The, 66, 68
Pet Sematary, 96, 108
Phantoms, 101, 179
Philosopher's Stone, The, 131
"Pickman's Model," 76
Picture of Dorian Gray, The, 161
"Pit and the Pendulum, The," 9
Playboy, 166
Plot: crisis, 24-25; defining the, 20
Plotting: 20-27; importance of, 21, 63, 99; unpredictably, 20, 21
Poe, Edgar Allan, 5, 9, 12, 161
Pohl, Frederik, 86
Poltergeist (book), 110, 183
Poltergeist (film), 103
Poltergeists, 73
"Poor, The," 41
Popularity, 27
Porter, Katherine Anne, 17
Postman Always Rings Twice, The, 102
Primitive romantic, 78
Profits, 111
Protagonist, identifying with, 102, 117
Proust, Marcel, 135
Pseudonyms, 118, 148
Psycho, 60, 177
Ptacek, Katherine, 180

"Public Loves of Johnny, The," 50
Publishing, sexism in, 113-119
Pursuit, 185

Quarreling, They Met the Dragon, 88-95, 181
Query letter, 1; 43
Quincy, 182

"R Is for Rocket," 14
Radcliffe, Ann, 159
Rage, The, 181
"Rain in the Doorway," 17
Ramsland, Katherine, 124-130, 182
Rasputin, Grigori, 183
Reader's Guide to Periodical Literature, The, 85
Reading, necessary, 52-53, 85, 96-97; outside genre, 97, 158
"Real Nice Guy," 48
Reality as background, 30-31, 65, 72, 74, 135-139, 158-159
Reality in fiction, 28, 75, 84, 89, 136
"Reality Function," the, 139
Red Dragon, 162
Regional magazines, 166
Reich, Wilhelm, 182
Reincarnation, 109, 110
Religion and the Rebel, 183
Research, cultural, 89-92; into feminine creativeness, 113; methods, 84-85, 88-89; mythology, 90-93
Revision, 24, 99
Revulsion, 64
Rice, Anne, 69
Riley, James Whitcomb, 111
Ringworld, 86
Rip Van Winkle, 29
Ritual in the Dark, 133, 136, 137
Rodgers, Alan, 247-250
Romero, George, 163
Rosemary's Baby, 44-45, 75, 107
Ryan, Alan, 178

"Sacred genre, the," 77
" 'Salem's Lot," 45, 161
Salmonson, Jessica Amanda, 114, 116-117
Samson, Joan, 69
Saturday Review, 184
Scariest scene, 61

Scavenger's Newsletter, 3, 184
Schoolgirl Murder Case, The, 182
Schwarzenegger, Arnold, 63
Schweitzer, Darrell, 77-81, 180
Science: needed in science fiction, 83, 116; overreliance on, 126; a put-off, 82; research methods, 84-85
Science fantasy, 88-95; researching, 88-95
Science fiction: conventions, 154-155; films, 9; formula, 87; hackwork in, 7; hard, and hard conflict, 82-87; maturity, 53; percentage of novels sold, 1; reality in, 3; setting, 28-34; substantiation for, 4; writers, few, 82
Science Fiction and Fantasy Workshop, 1, 181
Science Fiction Chronicle, 155
Science Fiction Review, 180
Science Fiction: What's It All About, 4
Science Fiction Writers of America, 1, 180, 184
Scientific American, 92, 134
Scientific approach to horror, 107
Scientific knowledge, how to acquire it, 84-85; how to use it, 85-87
Seaman, Donald, 137
"Season of Disbelief," 16
Serling, Rod, 149. *See Twilight Zone*
Sexism, 112-119
Shadowland, 68
Shadow-pieces, 64-66
Shadows, 170, 177, 180
Shattered, 179
Shattered Chain, The, 160, 177
Shelley, Mary, 114, 134
Sherbourne Press, 49
Shining, The, 44, 60, 61, 102, 108, 158
Shock in writing, 60, 64
Short story submissions, 141-142, 147-150
Shrinking Man, The, 158
Silva, David B., 117, 174
Simultaneous submissions, 153
Slice of Life, 179, 183
"Slushpile" editing, 46, 148, 153
"Small Assassin, The," 17, 177
Small press strengths, 174
Small Press Writers and Artists Organization, 1, 115, 117, 184

Smith, Clark Ashton, 12
Something Wicked This Way Comes, 14, 177
Song of Roland, The, 79
"Southern Indiana" tales, 179
Space operas, 53, 116
Spence, Lewis, 110
Sperry, Roger, 134
Spider World, 137, 138
Spielberg, Steven, 59, 162, 182
Spillane, Mickey, 53
Split brain research, 134-135
Spontaneous human combustion, 109
"Stairs, The," 19
Standards of excellence, 156-164
Starman, 162
Star Wars, 132
Steinbeck, John, 54
Stephen, J. F., 55 (footnote)
Stephen King: The Art of Darkness, 184
Stereotypes, 98, 112-119
Stevenson, Robert Louis, 136, 162
Stewart, Justice Potter, 156
Stoker, Bram, 42, 44-45, 162
Stories of Ray Bradbury, The, 177
Story submissions, first paragraph, 46
Strands, 179
Strange Case of Dr. Jekyll and Mr. Hyde, 162
Strangers, 102, 179
Strangers, The, 30-31
Straub, Peter, 53, 68, 107, 119, 157
Strieber, Whitley, 162
Sturgeon, Theodore, 2
Style, worth seeking, 12, 61-62
Subtext, 161
Subtlety in horror, 64-66, 160-161
Subversion, 161
Sullivan, Eleanor, 54
Supernatural, as fantasy, 107
Supernatural, The, 110
Supernatural fiction, 67-70, 73, 75, 106-111, 159
Supernatural Horror in Literature, 76
Suspense, 25, 59-63, 103, 121-123
Suspense, examples of, 59
Suspense, not action, 60
Swan Song, 69
Swann's Way, 135
Sword and Sorceress, 171

Sword and sorcery: 77-81; based on pre-fabricated images, 77; depends on, 78; and magic, 80
Synergy, 171

Tafoya, Terry, 118
Tale of Two Cities, A, 104
Talisman, The, 68
Taylor, David W., 6
Technical orientation needed, 83
Techniques, backgrounding, 86; suspense, 60-63
Tem, Steve Rasnic, 35-41
Tension, 60-61, 65, 121-123
Terminator, The, 63
Terror and innocence, 67-70
Terror Detective, 48, 115
Tessier, Thomas, 41, 160, 162
Tevis, Walter, 183
Theme, 21, 96
"There Was an Old Woman," 16
"There Will Come Soft Rains," 177
Thesaurus, use of, 25
Thing, The, 162
Things After Midnight, 178
Three Coffins, The, 73
Thriller, 54
"Tie That Binds, The," 84
Time and Again, 53
Time travel, 53, 116, 165
Tolkien, J. R. R., 80
Tolstoy, Leo, 136
Tom O'Bedlam's Night Out, 180
Tomoe Gozen, 114
Tor Books, 173
Toynbee, Arnold, 135
Tradition, not excuse for repetition, 98, 113-115, 158-159
Traitor to the Living, 53
Transmogrification, 109
Tulpas, 128
Turn of the Screw, The, 9
Twain, Mark, 5, 54, 68, 80
2001, 132
Twilight Eyes, 179
Twilight Zone Magazine, Rod Serling's, 36, 141, 147, 149, 157, 170, 178, 180, 183, 184
Twilight Zone: The Motion Picture, 177
Twilight Zone (tv), 54, 106, 108, 158, 180

UBIK, 53
UFO, 109, 110, 111, 116
Ulysses, 136
Umbral Anthology of Science Fiction Poetry, 178
Unagented problems, 152-153
Uninvited, The, 75
Unknown, the, 66, 72, 108, 129
Unobstructed Universe, The, 75
Urras, 43
Usher's Passing, 69, 180

Vampires, 9, 21, 40, 43, 53, 63, 69, 73, 74, 109, 110, 124, 131, 132, 159, 161, 162
Vignette, 20
Villains and suspense, 63, 104
Vision, The, 61, 179
Visualization, 133-135
Voice of the Night, 61
Vonnegut, Kurt, 122
Voodoo, 109, 110

Wagner, Karl Edward, 98
Walker, Benjamin, 110
War and Peace, 134, 136
War of the Worlds, 163
Wards of Armageddon, 20
Wasp Factory, The, 160
Watchers, 103, 179
Weirdbook, 176, 179
Weird Tales, 12, 13
Well at the World's End, The, 79
Wells, H. G., 8, 68, 136, 161, 163
Welty, Eudora, 17
Werewolves, 30, 40, 41, 63, 73, 74, 162
Western fiction, 77
Westheimer, Dr. Ruth, 162
Wharton, Edith, 68
"What Horrid People!," 51
Whispers (anthology), 49
Whispers (novel), 63, 71, 101, 178
Whispers V (anthology), 49
Whispers VI (anthology), 46
"White Cad Cross-Up, The," 49
White, Stuart Edward, 75
Wilde, Oscar, 161
Williams, Emlyn, 72
Williamson, Jack, 4
Williamson, J. N., 1, 5, 20-27, 30, 44, 53, 106-111, 117, 118, 184, 185

Williamson, Mary T., 140-146, 183
Wilson, Colin, 110, 131-139, 182
Winesburg, Ohio, 18
Winter, Douglas E., 156-164, 184
Witches, witchcraft, 109, 124
Wizard of Earthsea, A, 74
Wodehouse, Pelham Grenville, 45
Wolfe, Gene, 38
Wolfen, The, 152
Women characters, 113-115
Word derivation, 89
World building, creating, 57-58, 71-76
World Fantasy Awards, 180, 183, 184, 185
World Science Fiction Convention, 147
"Worlds of Monty Wilson, The," 50
Wray, Fay, 132
Writer's block, 99; goal, 52
Writer's Digest School, 24, 177, 179, 181, 182, 185
Writer's Handbook, 185
Writer's Market, 54, 119, 142, 149, 152-153

Writers conferences, conventions, 147, 154, 166; coping with tiredness, 24; horror, 129-130, 157-164; income, 145-146, 147; new, common errors, 102-104, 158; women, 112-119
Writers' persistence, 149-150, 164; "Rule One," 133; work habits, 99, 100, 137-139
Writing freedom, 51-55; hardest to create, 22, 109; imitating others, 97-98; influenced by, 12, 97; production, 145; starting new kind, 12, 97, 98; timeless, 8; what you know, 32, 34, 158
Writing Popular Fiction, 53

Yarbro, Chelsea Quinn, 9, 74
"Yard, The," 48
Year's Best Horror, 117
Yoda, 44
"Yours Truly, Jack the Ripper," 177

Zombie films, 161
Zoroastrianism, 110